Postcolonial Europe
in the Crucible of Cultures

CURRENTS OF ENCOUNTER

STUDIES ON THE CONTACT BETWEEN CHRISTIANITY AND OTHER RELIGIONS, BELIEFS, AND CULTURES

GENERAL EDITORS

JERALD D. GORT
HENRY JANSEN
LOURENS MINNEMA
HENDRIK M. VROOM
ANTON WESSELS

VOL. 34

Postcolonial Europe in the Crucible of Cultures

Reckoning with God in a World of Conflicts

Edited by

Jacques Haers SJ, Norbert Hintersteiner and Georges De Schrijver SJ

Amsterdam - New York, NY 2007

This publication is sponsored by the European Commission (Erasmus Socrates Programme), Missio Vlaanderen, the VLIR, and the Flemish Jesuits in Heverlee.

Copy and Manuscript Editors: Henry Jansen

Cover illustration and design:
Rita Dick & Thomas Stadler
A-5011 Oberndorf
Austria

The paper on which this book is printed meets the requirements of "ISO 9706:1994, Information and documentation - Paper for documents - Requirements for permanence".

ISBN set volume 1-3: 978-90-420-2204-1
ISBN: 978-90-420-2238-6
©Editions Rodopi B.V., Amsterdam - New York, NY 2007
Printed in the Netherlands

Contents

Introduction   1
Jacques Haers SJ, Leuven

Part I - Globalization   19

"Back to the Rough Ground":   21
Locating Resistance in Times of Globalization
Daniel Franklin Pilario, CM, Quezon City

Economic Globalization and the Ethical Debate   53
Georges De Schrijver SJ, Leuven

The Postcolonial Claim for Culture: 79
Inculturation and Africanism
Norbert Hintersteiner, Washington DC

"The Future of the Church is in our Hands":   99
Christian Migrants in the Netherlands
Frans Wijsen, Nijmegen

Part II - Wars and Violent Conflicts   111

Towards a Theological Hermeneutics of Violence   113
Siegfried Wiedenhofer, Frankfurt

"You Love Life and We Love Death":   125
A Crucible Difference Concerning God's Power
in the Aftermath of Terror
Hans-Joachim Sander, Salzburg

Recognizing God in Nonviolence: 133
A Reflection on Mark 15:39
François Bousquet, Paris

Opportunities and Threats for Religions
in Conflict and Violence: 141
How (Not) to Use the Name of God
Jamal Khader, Bethlehem

Why Are We So Inclined to Evil? 163
Religious Views on the Sources of Evil
Hendrik M. Vroom, Amsterdam

Part III - Environmental and Ecological Challenges 177

Globalization, Ecology and Sustainability: 179
How Sustainable is Sustainable Development?
Peter Tom Jones and Roger Jacobs, Leuven and Hasselt

Whose Universality? Which Interdependence? 193
Human Rights, Social Responsibility and Ecological Integrity
John D'Arcy May, Dublin

Part IV - Gender 213

Latin-American Theologies Developed by Women 215
Gabriela Di Renzo, Rosario

Human Dignity Violated by Increasing Aggression: 225
A Gender Analysis
Veerle Draulans, Tilburg / Leuven

List of Authors 249

Jacques Haers SJ

Introduction: Europe's Global Context as a Theological Challenge

The European September 2004 Intensive Program Meeting *Postcolonial Europe in the Crucible of Cultures: Reckoning with God in a World of Conflicts* (the IP Program is a part of the European Commission's Socrates Program) involved the participation of 23 European universities. Around 100 students and professors from these universities gathered in Leuven, together with several guests from the so-called Two-Thirds World, to reflect on how the understanding of God is constructed in Europe amid the tensions and conflicts of a global world. This meeting was the second in a set of three, intended to reflect on God in Europe. The first, held in Vienna in 2003, provided a general overview of the issues of religion in Europe, while the third meeting, held in Paris in 2005, focused on interreligious aspects. The Leuven meeting, chaired by the Centre of Liberation Theologies at the Faculty of Theology at the Catholic University of Leuven, aimed at exploring the consequences of Europe's place and role in today's global world for religious and theological endeavors. The dynamics of the 10-day meeting included specialized conferences, discussion groups to further explore the ideas that had been presented, and broader debates in the evening. This publication presents a selection of some of the most challenging contributions to the meeting. The underlying mood was to explore, but also to construct new ideas and approaches, and some of the most interesting insights surfaced amid heated controversies, in which strong prejudices had to be recognized, admitted, and overcome.

The point of departure for the Leuven meeting was the awareness that theology as a discourse about God cannot be dissociated from its real – political, social, economic, material, cultural, etc. – context. This is particularly true in the case of Christian theology, with its strong emphasis on the incarnation. So, those who want to reflect on God in Europe will have to take into account Europe as a context, as well as the broader global context in which Europe plays an important role. Moreover, in this context precisely those who suffer the burden of reality – the poor, the excluded, the downtrodden, those who have no voices, the crucified, those living on the "rough grounds" of reality as Danny Pilario points out in his contribution[1] – should be paid special attention, in their cry as well as in their creative potential. The preferential option for the poor, therefore, was always present in our exchanges.

Professors Georges De Schrijver, François Bousquet, and Norbert Hintersteiner, as well as myself, prepared the 10 day meeting, and decided to highlight four main concerns that represent major and interconnected[2] challenges for European theology today in its global context: the process of globalization itself, ecological and environmental issues, violence and conflicts, and gender. We decided not to emphasize interreligious relations, as they were to be the core focus of the Paris Meeting in 2005. I will briefly explore these four issues in the first part of my contribution. In the second part, I will focus on some

---

[1] Danny Pilario's concept challenges the traditional understandings of the notion of the "preferential option for the poor," in the line of Aloysius' Pieris understanding of the role of the two types of poor in the perspective of God's Reign (see his *God's Reign for God's Poor: A Return to the Jesus Formula*, second revised edition, Tulana Research Centre, 1998). Dietrich Bonhoeffer, a theologian crucial for understanding theological developments in post Second World War II Europe, in a similar way stressed the "Perspektive von unten" that should not turn into a "Parteinahme für die ewig Unzufriedenen" (see his 1942 "Nach Zehn Jahren," in *Widerstand und Erge-bung: Briefe und Aufzeichnungen aus der Haft*, edited by C. Gremmels, E. Bethge and R. Bethge in collaboration with I. Tödt, Dietrich Bonhoeffer Werke, vol. 8 [Gütersloh: Chr. Kaiser, 1998], 19-39, 38).

[2] Although I will not develop this interconnectedness in more detail here, it is important at least to perceive that these four issues are profoundly interrelated. Globalization is perceived increasingly as a violent conflict, while many of the so-called "local" violent conflicts prove to have global dimensions. The environmental challenges and the ecological crises clearly have a global character, while the search for just global life together requires taking into account issues of environmental sustainability. Gender issues reflect profound methodological debates and increasingly shape our models and approaches for understanding the world in which we live. Moreover, the power relations and abuses of globalization are clearly gendered, and it is through gender sensibility that we may gain access to cultural differences and complementarities.

of the theological perspectives at stake that constitute stimuli for further theological development and thought in Europe. Many of these theological perspectives surfaced during the Leuven encounter. I am convinced that we are living in a time of deep and threatening crises – particularly the environmental crisis shows many characteristics of a Damocles' sword – but I also think that these crises represent opportunities and challenges, and that, therefore, in all the four issues chosen we are called to discover opportunities for a more dignified and full human life.

Europe in its Global Context

Increasingly, Europe has become a crucial actor in its own right on the scene of international affairs. Through a complex, multifacetted and difficult historical process of mutual interactions between countries and regions, sparked off by the brutal experience of two destructive world wars and inspired by visionary politicians like Jean Monet and Jacques Delors, "Europe" came about as an effort at reconciliation between former antagonists. In 2006, at the time this contribution is written, the European Union[3] boasted a membership of 25 countries, a more or less common European currency, embryonic common defense and foreign policies, common institutions and legal frameworks, etc. It is also in the process of writing a European constitution that will clearly define its identity and vision. Although Europe's place in the global world is still in the making, and not everyone agrees on its precise identity, it has already acquired the status of an important worldwide actor. There are tensions within Europe – as, for example, the question to what extent the Christian history of Europe should be acknowledged in its constitution – as there are also differences of mind as to how Europe defines itself or is perceived in its relationships towards the USA, towards strongly developing world scale actors such as China or India, and towards the so-called Two Thirds World. During the Leuven meeting strong differences of opinion on these issues were expressed. Such debates will undoubtedly prove crucial to Europe's self-definition. It is obvious, however, that Europe is a

---

[3] See the website of the European Union: http://europe.eu/.

global player – this means that Europeans, and their theologians, will increasingly have to address global issues, such as: globalization, violence, conflict transformation, sustainable peacebuilding, environmental crises, and gender.

Globalization

It is very difficult to provide a generally accepted definition of the term globalization,[4] as it refers to a multifacetted and complex fact of life for people, who experience and perceive this fact very differently all over the world, whether as an opportunity or as a threat. To some it means increased facilities to communicate – e.g. through the worldwide web – and to travel; to others it takes the shape of new forms of economic exploitation and cultural hegemony. Some consider it to be a new phenomenon in world history, while others perceive it as a worse repetition of colonialism. Some want to promote globalization, others prefer to resist, and still others claim that it is a fact we have to live with and make the best of. Europeans, for example, still have to decide how they will consider globalization: as a huge and risky competitive market or as a place where the challenge is to maintain value standards to support worldwide life together. But whatever the differences of opinions and interpretations, most people will agree that we are facing increasing, sometimes even risky, interdependencies at various levels (economic, political, cultural, etc.), and that our life conditions increasingly depend on the decisions and ways of life of people who live geographically and culturally at a distance. Problems and challenges that are confronting us appear ever more complex and we feel the need to approach them "holistically," taking into account worldwide networks, webs, factors and conditions. Globalization also means that issues that would have previously been considered local, now appear to have worldwide implications – the interconnectedness

---

[4] For an introduction to the issue of globalization one should read: D. Held *et al.*, *Global Transformations: Politics, Economics and Culture* (Cambridge: Polity 1999); D. Held and A. McGrew (eds.), *The Global Transformations Reader: An Introduction to the Globalization Debate* (Cambridge: Polity 2000); Z. Bauman, *Wasted Lives: Modernity and its Outcasts* (Cambridge: Polity 2004).

of markets and banking systems is a clear example, as are refugee crises, violent conflicts, and gross violations of human rights or genocides. We can no longer live in some kind of "splendid isolation": the problems of other world citizens have become ours, as ours have become theirs. Therefore, in my understanding, the core issue with regard to globalization is how a worldwide sustainable and dignified life together can be organized in such a way that the real and tangible evils and injustices that arise in the context of and because of processes of globalization may be fought with the resources of solidarity and interconnectedness present in these very processes of globalization. Of course, global challenges also surface in religions and theology, e.g. in the field of interreligious dialogue and encounter, that is acquiring increasing political importance, as was recently admitted by Madeleine Albright in her 2006 book, *The Mighty and the Almighty*.[5] Moreover, religions, churches and religious organizations constitute important global and international networks, profoundly influencing the minds and deep convictions of millions of people.

Wars and Violent Conflicts

The European Union plays an increasing role in the transformation and resolution of conflicts worldwide, both on a military and political level, and it has been working to develop its own peace building and conflict resolution strategies. Since September 11th 2001, the understanding of and ways of dealing with violent conflicts have profoundly changed: terrorism and its worldwide political, social and military causes and consequences dominate our perceptions and actions. Many conflict scientists, however, point out that too narrow a focus on terrorism may well lead us to turn a blind eye with regard to other forms of violence, such as bad governance or global economic and social imbalances. These represent much greater killing fields and generate high levels of frustration, anger, hatred and physical violence. In this context, conflict studies as a science that develops models to understand the complexities of violent conflicts, suggesting preventive poli-

---

[5] *The Mighty and the Almighty: Reflections on America, God, and World Affairs* (New York: Harper Collins, 2006).

cies, and unfolding sustainable peace architecture[6] have become important areas of research and policy development. Many authors, such as R. Scott Appleby and J.P. Lederach, have further explored the role of religion in the sustaining of conflicts as well as in peacebuilding. Obviously, theologians have a role to play here, not only on the level of exploring theological concepts and ideas and their possible use or abuse in concrete political contexts, but also in the effort to interact with conflict scientists and decision makers. Religious leaders and those responsible for the church, moreover, will also be able to offer help in concrete conflict situations because of their close contacts in the field (among the opposing parties) and the influence they can exert on the parties at war. It is crucial for conflict studies to stress the fact that conflict transformation and sustainable peacebuilding are relational processes, in which not only the positions of opposing parties are sorted out, but also the concern for sustainable life together is heeded. The work that has been done on restorative justice by authors such as Howard Zehr and Luc Huyse has to a large extent been influenced and inspired by religious perspectives and frames of thought and illustrates this well.[7]

Environmental and Ecological Challenges

Today's most crucial and urgent global threat is without a doubt the environmental challenge. The recent discussions on whether and to what extent existing and real ecological crises and catastrophes – e.g. global warming and its consequences, the extinction of species, the depletion of natural resources and more specifically fossil fuel – are

---

[6] For good introductions to contemporary conflict studies, see L. Reychler and T. Paffenholz (eds.), *Peacebuilding: A Field Guide* (Boulder / London: Lynne Rienner 2001); the *Berghof Handbook for Conflict Transformation* can be found at the following website: http://www.berghof-handbook.net/.

[7] Another example is given in Hannah Arendt's emphasis on the political importance of forgiveness. I am grateful to Elias Lopez for clarifying to me these issues at the boundary between politics and religion.

caused by humans, illustrate the urgency of an issue[8] that is not yet fully understood because of its complexity and the inadequacy of some of our scientific models. The environmental issues, that today require political action and scientific investigation, are also clearly challenges in which the European Union has an important role to play, in its stance over against the US refusal to commit itself to international agreements, in its relationship to China and India who are in need of resources to sustain their further development, and in its advocacy for Two-Thirds World countries that will suffer greatly from worldwide environmental degradation but that, because of their precarious and vulnerable situation, do not have the means to develop much needed environmental policies. Some theologians, such as Leonardo Boff, Marcelo Barros and Yvonne Gebara, have taken on the ecological challenges but it still seems very difficult to make people realize the seriousness of these threats and to move them towards acting politically in the direction of globally sustainable lifestyles. In my opinion, however, we will be facing catastrophe type ecological crises very soon, in which global church resources will be called for. Are religions, and more particularly the Christian churches, prepared for this? Some of the more important challenges to theological research are: to articulate the environmental challenges within our theological frameworks of protology, ecclesiology and eschatology, while at the same time allowing for a profound reframing of these theological frameworks; to rethink our existentialist and person-oriented theological patterns of thought so as to also incorporate cosmological and holistic perspectives; to explore with more precision the relationships between injustice and environmental degradation; to emphasize the de-

---

[8] For up to date scientific information, see the website of the Intergovernmental Panel on Climate Change: http://www.ipcc.ch/. A good introduction to the issues at hand is: W. Burroughs (ed.), *Climate Into the 21st Century* (Cambridge: Cambridge University Press, 2003) (published by the World Meteorological Organization). J. Diamond, *Collapse: How Societies Choose to Fail or Survive* (London: Allan Lane, 2005), offers an interesting historical perspective. The BBC World website offers interesting environmental news. Lord May's very challenging Royal Society Anniversary Address 2005, "Threats to Tomorrow's World," can be found via the Royal Society's website: http://www.royalsoc.ac.uk/.

velopment of new lifestyles and spiritual approaches. Theologians have to keep in mind here that ethical or moral theological reflection will not be enough but that there is also a need for systematic and fundamental theological approaches.

Gender

It took liberation theologians too long to discover that in their theological struggle with (structural) injustice they had forgotten to take the plight of women and of the power games within gender relations into account. Feminist theologians reminded liberation theologians that even they themselves could harbor structures of oppression and blindness. Today gender issues have become global and very complex challenges,[9] as we have come to discover how worldwide injustices and exploitation are "gendered" and how closely linked they are to the construction of sociocultural identities and human self-understanding. Apart from articulating structural injustices, women's studies also touch on two of the most challenging research fields in contemporary theology. From a hermeneutical point of view, not only the hermeneutics of the biblical texts, but also the fact that the biblical texts themselves represent a hermeneutical endeavor, stimulate gender debate. From an ecological perspective on the other hand, eco-feminist theologians such as Y. Gebara, have emphasized more holistic and community-oriented approaches and praxes, enjoining theologians to emphasize new hermeneutical models. While gender issues have come to play an important role in the Western world, at the same time first world feminist movements are being criticized for their insufficient awareness of gender-related poverty and injustice on a worldwide scale. The understanding of what is meant by gender injustice has, in itself, become a global and intercultural issue.

These four challenges were offered as a framework for the Leuven meeting. They correspond to elements that are important for today's European context, while also representing issues that disturb classical theological thought and require fresh theological thinking. In this minimal sense, the process of European unification is theologi-

---

[9] They are, for example, clearly represented in the Millennium Goals.

cally relevant. In the second part of this contribution, I want to highlight some of these theological challenges. Several of them also surfaced during the Leuven meeting, as is evident from the various contributions in this book.

Theologians Learn

Theology is a hermeneutical endeavor in many senses of the word. It interprets a tradition in its many faces and multiple perspectives, referring to its foundational texts or classics, to its long history, and to its liturgical and ritual practices, so as to clarify it and bring it into the space of intelligible articulation, clear discourse, and fruitful conversation. This means that theologians will, inevitably, proceed contextually; not only will they take into account past historical contexts – as for example the context in which Jesus of Nazareth lived or the contexts in which the creedal and dogmatic formulations originated – they will also relate theological claims and formulations to the context in which they themselves live. The latter entails a doubly critical attitude: first, out of their understanding of tradition they may come to view or evaluate their own life context very critically, as they may also, by tapping the resources of the tradition, open new perspectives and visions for their own contexts; secondly, theologians may also come to critically question so-called classic or common interpretations of tradition as they confront them with their own contextual experiences. In fact, this may even lead to a renewed and better understanding of the tradition itself. These are very delicate and subtle processes of communal discernment, in which the faith community plays an important leading role while at the same time constituting and reshaping itself. In view of the contemporary context of Europe, I think theologians should heed the following so as to be faithful to their hermeneutical calling.

(1) Global issues and the attitude of the European Union within the global world are *life and death issues* for many people and, therefore, of great concern to theologians. European consumption patterns and use of natural resources are unsustainable from a global point of view and, therefore, also the cause of injustice and oppression – will European citizens be capable to take into account global sustainability concerns when determining their lifestyles? The very process of Euro-

pean unification offers a political model for global governance – but is this model, in which the reference to values is often replaced by economic productivity, administrative efficiency and legal rulings, really the great example it pretends to be, and will Europe not succumb to the temptation of fortress Europe, a kind of well-protected safe haven amid a world in chaos, facing the threats of massive immigration? Europe is a commanding economic power that exercises a strong influence in global development – but will its economic power be driven by competitive urges and fears or by the concern for the worldwide common good? Europe's history, both in the positive (e.g. some of its values and cultural developments) and in the negative sense (e.g. the crusades and the colonial past), continues to profoundly influence today's world – will Europeans be capable of understanding why some perceive them as arrogant when they attempt to impose their insights which they claim have a universal reach? Europe's efforts at developing a coherent foreign policy and at committing military resources for peace keeping and peace building operations are already an important factor in world politics – will these efforts and resources be hijacked by the narrow perspective of a war on terrorism? These are but a few examples, yet they illustrate how developments in Europe have consequences for many people other than Europeans themselves, and that European attitudes, policies, actions and interventions may well mean life or death for those living outside of Europe. The challenges of globalization, violence, the environment and gender concern the possibility of future life, they touch the very survival not only of Europeans but of human beings in general and of the very world in which we live.

Life and death issues, as well as the deep human desire for a dignified life together, are primary concerns for theologians, as they are a primary concern for God. Therefore, both prophetic and saptiential tasks rest with the faithful and their theologians. On the one side, they will denounce the threats to dignified human lives when Europeans forget their privileged positions and egoistically attempt to defend their unsustainable lifestyles. On the other hand, they will develop and point to visions at the service of the construction of a better world. It may be of help to European theologians to remain aware that the process of European unification itself has roots in the Christian perspectives of some visionary politicians such as Jean Monet and Jacques Delors, who responded to the wounds and suffering caused by the violent histories of two world wars and aimed at sustainable peace and life together, using growing economic, social and political interdependencies to foster their goals. At the core of Europe's endeavors lies a set of values and convictions on reconciliation and dignified life together, as well as very practical methods and tools to put these values into practice. These values and convictions are very close to the Christian heart and represent attitudes that many would call religious in the broad sense of the word. European theologians are aware that these values and convictions can be egoistically perverted and that they represent a challenge also for life together with the non-European world. During the Leuven meeting, it became clear that Western Europeans and to a much lesser extent Eastern Europeans and their theologians are not always aware of the very privileged position and circumstances they enjoy. In their own painful history, however, they can find the resources for a compassionate awareness of the suffering of non-Europeans and for acting upon that awareness. The so-called "European values" are meant not only for Europeans – they go beyond Europe. It is the task of theologians to make space for God's universal vision for the world and not to focus solely on one's own private relationship with God or the safe haven that Europe could represent for its own citizens even at the cost of massive suffering elsewhere in the world. Rather, the emphasis is on the vision of the world one acquires when taking into account the fact that God considers the world as a whole. Therefore, the dream Europe fosters is a lie, if it is not also a dream for the non-European world. At this moment of the construction of Europe, these issues are crucial: are Europeans going to emphasize a value perspective – that aims at a dignified life together not only for Europeans but for all world inhabitants – or will they merely constitute a new powerful specific identity that maintains itself competitively and at the cost of great suffering to others?

(2) All the issues mentioned concern a dignified life together and as such sustainable community building and fundamental interconnectedness.[10] Globalization is about relationships in a world of inequalities; violence and wars challenge our capacities to tackle conflicts that are inevitable when people live together and in interdependence; environmental issues touch the holistic perspectives of life together as

---

[10] For an introduction to these ideas, see J. Haers and P. De Mey (eds.), *Theology and Conversation: Towards a Relational Theology*, BETL, 172 (Leuven: Peeters, 2003).

well as the challenge to long term sustainability; and gender issues help us to focus on that lies in differences. In the Western and European context, life together is primarily thought of as how to bring and maintain distinct and well defined identities and subjects together – this ties in well with the traditional patterns of European philosophy and theology. The challenges we are confronting today invite us to take our point of departure not in separate and well-defined identities or subjects that we attempt to connect in a second move, but rather in the already living together, belonging together, and interdependencies of such subjects, whose identities are shaped and reshaped precisely in and through the networks of relations to which they belong. This move to the primacy of interconnectedness over subjectivity is quite radical for a European mind, while it may be more congenial to non-European cultures.

There are many theological challenges and opportunities here. In the first place, it is good to realize that religion always concerns life together, not only as the relationship with God, but also as life together of human beings and with the environment in which they live. In the case of Christianity, it is striking how strong the emphasis on fundamental interconnectedness and co-belonging is: it is reflected in the theological ideas of the Trinity, of creation, of the Reign of God, and of the church. This is so powerful, that it is possible to answer the question as to the meaning of salvation, by referring to the faith in the capacity to build a sustainable life together, against all odds, in the concreteness of our broken lives. The vision of the Kingdom or Reign of God is not just about ultimate personal bliss in the presence of God, it is foremost about sharing life together in a renewed creation. The church, as an effort to build sustainable communities, reflects the faith to pursue this vision and dream of life together in collaboration with a God, who is described as Tri-Une, as community. Creation is an expression through which Christians articulate total dependence upon God, but precisely through total interdependence in the cosmos, in the world as a whole. In Christian ontology the belonging to God and the belonging to one another and to the creation as a whole, are crucial.

The concrete real world seems very different, however. It requires a more than human effort to build sustainable togetherness ... i.e., this vision, out of which Christians draw their strength, reflects a reality that will always also remains a gift from God. Yet precisely because they trust in this gift, Christians can commit themselves wholeheartedly to community building, to reconciliation, to holistic perspectives of co-belonging and to lifestyles that respect longterm environmental sustainability, and to creative human relationships.

Some theological models can help in the reflection on fundamental co-belonging and togetherness. In Leuven, at the Centre for Liberation Theologies (CLT)[11] and the Advanced Master's Program for Conflict and Sustainable Peace (MaCSP),[12] we refer to the concept of *mestizaje* as developed by Virgilio Elizondo[13] and to the metaphor of frontier spaces for encounter, as opposed to dividing and excluding borderlines. So, for example, globalization comes to be understood as the creation of frontier spaces of encounter where new patterns emerge that will structure life together; the transformation of violent conflicts is at its most creative in the frontier spaces created by the conflict, where the victims of violence cry out for new ways of living together; environmental challenges are met when people realize the conditions of possibility for sustainable life together precisely in the frontier spaces where they encounter the limits of growth and the constraints of life together and in the world; and gender encounters are frontiers where human closeness and distance, difference and sameness, coincide to generate new patterns of life.

(3) As soon as theologians begin to focus on the new global challenges, as well as on the rearticulation of the major theological concepts from the perspective of fundamental togetherness and belonging, they become aware of the necessity of a profound *methodological reflection* that will seem threatening to some. I want to highlight some of the methodological accents that we have come to see as crucial for theologians today.

Firstly, there is a great need for *transdisciplinarity*. Not only should theologians be able to transcend the limits and borders of their own disciplines and subdisciplines (intradisciplinarity), not only should they be aware of the existence of other disciplines (multidisciplinarity) and of the creative interactions between various disciplines (interdisciplinarity), they are also called to allow new ways of

---

[11] See http://www.theo.kuleuven.be/clt/.

[12] See http://www.kuleuven.be/macsp/.

[13] See, for example, his *The Future is Mestizo: Life Where Cultures Meet* (Boulder: University Press of Colorado, 2000).

thinking and altogether new fields of research to *emerge*[14] from the interdisciplinary interactions in close contact with reality itself and the concreteness of the objects under study (transdisciplinarity). A new body of knowledge and understanding will arise or emerge, which will require new research criteria and views on reality. This means that theologians will have to work in teams with other scholars and researchers, who are willing to see their teamwork as the bringing about of totally new perspectives and approaches. This also means that research today requires conversations and interactions between people, and that team building has become a core activity of scientific research, as the latter is not possible without the former. This idea – i.e. that "knowledge is to be found between noses and not only between ears," that tackling problems and challenges also requires simultaneously the building of the community of problem solvers – lies at the heart of *social constructionism* as René Bouwen explores it. Knowledge and research are socially constructed through *learning communities of practice*.[15]

Learning communities and teams, in which specialists, practitioners – people in the field – and decision makers at various levels participate, are crucial if we want to address the *complex* issues and networks that determine today's global challenges. Such learning communities arise as *transitional spaces* where people meet and interact to tackle problems and challenges. Such research needs to be *action research*, where close encounters with the suffering reality and sociopolitical praxes and advocacy are both a source for multifaceted reflection as well as its result.[16]

Theologians and church leaders have another important role to play. Apart from the fact that they are internationally and globally

---

[14] The idea of emergence is very popular today, but theologians will remember that it was used already by Pierre Teilhard de Chardin, as well as by Karl Rahner who analysed the notion of *Selbstüberbietung*.

[15] See for example: R. Bouwen, "Relational Organizing: The Social Construction of Communities of Practice and Shared Meaning," in D. Resch *et al.* (eds.), *Organisationspsychologie als Dialog: Inquiring Social Constructionist Possibilities in Organizational Life* (Lengerich: Berlin Pabst Science Publishers, 2005), 55-70.

[16] Cf methods of praxis and mediations in liberation theologies as well as the focus on the preferential option for the poor.

connected, that they have contacts in the field, that they can rely on research centres and educational institutions, and that they reach out to the circles of decision-makers at different levels, they also find themselves in the privileged position of being able to *convene meetings and teams of people* from various backgrounds so as to build the necessary transitional spaces to address global challenges. In addition to this role of convenor, religions also possess the capacity to address people's spiritual energies, to empower and motivate, and to develop visions (e.g., the Kingdom of God) and liturgical and ritual practices that embody those visions amid the broken reality so as to empower people in their commitments towards sustainable global life. Above all, religious leaders can greatly affect the human experience in various ways: people's fears and anxieties can be heightened and politically abused just as they can be made fruitful by converting and releasing the creative energies enclosed in them; prejudices can be sustained or removed – this will be particularly important with regard to the prejudices and frustrations that are the result of colonial experiences and histories; and, they can lead to a collision course by promoting religious intolerance and fundamentalism just as they can stimulate inter-religious dialogue and openness to the world.

This Collection

Many of these life and death issues that concern the quality of a sustainable life together and require novel scientific methodological approaches, appear in the articles in this collection.

We begin with four articles from the field of globalization. In his analysis of globalization, Daniel Franklin Pilario refers to the "rough grounds," to those people who suffer the consequences of globalization and who attempt, in various praxes, to resist the global powers that oppress them. These people are the real source of our theological endeavors. In his contribution, Georges De Schrijver emphasizes post second world war economic globalization in which the financial world and global markets determine the structures of life on earth. Europeans are also victims here, although in the return to a well-understood Enlightenment, they find the resources to resist and to commit themselves to an alternative globalization from below. Norbert Hintersteiner analyses patterns of thought, mainly in Africa, that resist colonial worldviews, but at the same time become entangled in complex postcolonial dependencies. Finally, Frans Wijsen reflects on the results of migrant studies in the Netherlands, to plead in favor of intercultural encounter and intercultural theology, i.e. for "theological reflection on the dialogue between people who share the same faith but come from different cultural backgrounds."

The following four articles concern violent conflicts. Siegfried Wiedenhofer analyses the tension between peace and violence in religious traditions, particularly in Christianity. He explores hermeneutical approaches and steps to construct a Christian understanding of violence that unmasks the ambiguities present in all religions. Hans-Joachim Sander turns to the question of a Christian European identity in times of war against terrorism. The Christian identity of Europe is not a question of naming God in the European constitution, but rather of discovering a God who allows for the strength of identities without dominating them as weak others, and so to resist the logic of resentment and to love life in a way that does not fear death. François Bousquet explores the nonviolence of God as it surfaces in Jesus' death on the cross (Mark 15:39). Jamal Khader looks at the role of fundamentalism in the Middle Eastern crisis as the expression of the very human spiral of violence and hatred. Over against these violent attitudes, religious leaders should emphasize that God is the Creator of all persons and of all peoples, and that out of this being of God flow the claims for justice and peace. In an article concluding this section, Hendrik M. Vroom poses questions about the meaning of evil and the sources of evil from the perspectives of various religions.

In their article on globalization, ecology and sustainability, Peter Tom Jones and Roger Jacobs explore various approaches towards today's ecological crisis. They attempt to redefine the concept of "sustainability" and mercilessly unmask the myth of a society that depends on the idea of economic growth, while pleading for a radical redistribution of the existing economic pie. At the same time, they point out the need for global eco-management and for the proper use of the precautionary principle. In his reflection on human rights, social responsibility and ecological integrity, John D'Arcy May comes to recognize that in our world "universal values and principles" can only refer to continuously constructed interdependent reality.

With regard to gender, while Gabriela Di Renzo analyses Latin American feminist theologies of liberation (e.g. Maria Pilar Aquino) and theologies from the perspective of women (e.g. Maria Teresa Porcile), Veerle Draulans provides a gender analysis of human dignity violations and in doing so offers a critical overview of the developments of gender thought in relation to the violence exercised against women.

I want to end this introduction by expressing the gratitude of the organizers of the 2004 Leuven IP meeting. The European Commission and its Socrates Program, Missio Vlaanderen, the VLIR, and the Flemish Jesuits in Heverlee were among our generous benefactors, who not only gave financially but shared advice and provided facilities for our meetings. The Centre for Liberation Theologies of Faculty of Theology of the Catholic University of Leuven provided support for the organization of the project. A special word of thanks goes to Ms. Anya Diedrich Topolski for her organizational skills and unwavering energies in preparing the meeting, the reports and this book.

PART I

GLOBALIZATION

> *We have got on to slippery ice where there is no friction and so in a certain sense the conditions are ideal, but also, just because of that, we are unable to walk: so we need friction. Back to the rough ground!*
>
> L. Wittgenstein, *Philosophical Investigations,* §107

Daniel Franklin Pilario, CM

"Back to the Rough Ground": Locating Resistance in Times of Globalization

"Borderless World": Ambivalent Views from the Margins

On May 14, 2004, a young student from the Philippines – Patricia Evangelista – won first prize in the 2004 International Public Speaking Competition sponsored by the English Speaking Union (ESU) in London. Her speech suggests a way of understanding one of our themes in this conference: postcolonialism and globalization. "When I was little," she starts, "I wanted what many Filipino children all over the country wanted. I wanted to be blond, blue-eyed, white. I thought if I just wished hard enough and was good enough, I'd wake up on Christmas morning with snow outside my window and freckles across my nose! More than four centuries under Western domination does that to you."[1] A sense of nationalist sentiment, a disdain of anything foreign or "colonial" – characteristic of the late 60s and 70s – is still prevalent among many Filipino youth today. But the new global consciousness has tempered this nationalism with some sense of open optimism. The so-called Filipino "diaspora" has become a trend. Eight million of us are scattered around the globe thanks to this "borderless world." She continues:

> A borderless world presents a bigger opportunity, yet one that is not so much abandonment but an extension of identity. Even as we take, we give back. We are 40,000 skilled nurses who support the

---

[1] P. Evangelista, "Borderless World," in http://premara.com/archives/300/.

UK National Health Service. We are a quarter-of-a-million seafarers manning most of the world's commercial ships. We are your software engineers in Ireland, your construction workers in the Middle East, your doctors and caregivers in North America, and your musical artists in London's West End.[2]

This is quite a rosy picture of Filipinos freely serving humanity! What Patricia forgot in her list, however, is the equally numerous Filipinos who clean other people's homes, wash their dishes, do their laundry, cook their food or take care of their children while they are at work.[3] Scattered all over Asia, the Middle East, United States and the European continent, most of them do not even have permits to work or reside, thus, also living clandestinely. This has become so widespread that one edition of the Websters Dictionary equated the word "Filipina" with "housemaid." Many of these are mothers themselves who left their own children to their neighbors in the Philippines whom they would also pay in return with the wages earned abroad. Some are fathers who need to learn new skills like housekeeping or babysitting after spending the whole of their lives farming or fishing. Knowing the great social cost of family separation, why have they chosen to come? Or do they have any choice at all in the first place? In Zygmunt Bauman's apt metaphors, the "tourist" and the "vagabond" (or the economic migrant, the asylum seeker, the refugee) are two images of the global and postmodern life.

> The tourists stay or move at their hearts' desire. They abandon the site when new untried opportunities beckon elsewhere. The vagabonds, however, know they won't stay for long, however strongly they wish to, since nowhere they stop are they welcome: if the tourists move because they find the world irresistibly *attractive*,

---

[2] E. San Juan, "Filipino Diaspora," in *Philippine Studies* 49 (2001): 255-64.

[3] Cf. Eric Hobsbawm: "[T]o me it seems inevitable that, one way or another, the countries that don't reproduce their populations... will import cheap labor or people who will do these jobs that the indigenous population no longer wants to do .... We have already seen migratory exchanges of this kind: the most common of which is the use of Filipinos as domestic servants." E. Hobsbawm, *The New Century* (London: Abacus 2000), 144.

the vagabonds move because they find the world unbearably *in-hospitable* .... The tourists travel because they *want to*; the vagabonds – because they have *no other choice*.[4]

In reality, the "vagabond" represents the waste of a global world configured to serve the pleasures of the "tourist." These already "wasted lives"[5] – themselves the refuse of capital as they were laid off from their local jobs due to liberalization policies – now try to service the waste of the same capital in their Western abodes. The type of job they land are those which the First World population does not actually like doing. Not much choice though. The "vagabond" still scrambles and is always grateful for the "crumbs that fell off the master's table." For the real garbage of the infernal global machine is back home – a country whose social, cultural and economic fibers are wrecked by 350 of Spanish oppression, 50 years of American rule, two decades of dictatorship, successive corrupt governments and the unbearable imposition of the present global economy. The Philippines once grabbed international headlines when one Filipino truck driver in Iraq, Angelo de la Cruz, was taken hostage by some militant groups. Their demand was that the Philippines withdraw its troops from Iraq – a small peacekeeping force which the Philippine government sent in support of the US campaign. While negotiations were underway, thousands were still lining up in Manila overseas employment agencies applying for jobs in Iraq and never intending to back out. When asked if they were not afraid, they replied: "We are more afraid that our children will die of hunger here than for us to be beheaded elsewhere in the world."

To talk of opportunity in this "borderless world" is at best ambivalent. Globalization means one thing for Patricia; another thing for Angelo and for millions like him. Globalization could mean the erasure of borders for greater mobility, a celebration of opportunity, a respect for diversity and "difference." But it can also signify the absorption into a consumerist culture, the imprisonment into one's socioeconomic boundaries and the rule of sameness and "identity" under the

---

[4] Z. Bauman, *Postmodernity and Its Discontents* (Cambridge: Polity, 1997), 92-93.

[5] Z. Bauman, *Wasted Lives: Modernity and Its Outcasts* (Cambridge: Polity, 2004).

banner of the ever-powerful global capital. Whichever way one views it, the "vagabonds" – these wasted lives – are compelled to resist in order to survive.

This paper intends to do three things: (1) to explicate this complex discourse on globalization and its repercussions to those from the margins; (2) to locate the locus of resistance in this deeply ambiguous reality; and, from there, (3) discern where God-talk can commence in these new contexts.

Globalization: Identity or Difference?

Globalization: A Complex Discourse. Though globalization is a difficult phenomenon to pin down, there are two contrasting yet complementary perspectives which can help illuminate this complex reality. Frederic Jameson suggests viewing it from its cultural and economic dimensions.[6] Heightened by the development of information technology, globalization makes its impact on all cultures as they are also given a hearing on the world's stage to join the joyous dance of diversity. Yet this cultural phenomenon also slides into the economic realm since what goes into circulation are not only the niceties of culture but hard cash in its "soft" electronic forms. This development leaves two distinct philosophical imprints. On the one hand, an emphasis on the "cultural" leads to the postmodern celebration of *difference*, the empowerment of the subalterns and the recognition of the once-forgotten genders and ethnicities; while, on the other hand, an emphasis on the "economic" ushers in sameness and *identity* since national productive zones now need to adopt their production to the demands of the global market. But these dual perspectives, Jameson continues to analyze, are also dialectically related as each of their discourses are displaced into the other. Thus, when the discourse of economic *identity* is shifted to the cultural sphere, what we see is an analysis, reminiscent of the early Frankfurt School, on the alarming vision of the "McDonaldization of the world" and the "Disneyfication of cultures." Conversely, transferring the talk of cultural *difference* to the economic realm bears out the

---

[6] F. Jameson, "Notes on Globalization as a Philosophical Issue," in F. Jameson and M. Miyoshi (eds.), *The Cultures of Globalization* (Durham and London: Duke University Press, 1998), 54-77, here 55.

optimistic language of the apologists of free market, i.e., the rich variety of local productivity and the mushrooming of new economic initiatives. These tensions only warn us that globalization is a slippery image which, if it has to be understood, needs to be taken in its utmost complexity.

A Postcolonial Celebration of "Difference." If there is any postcolonial theorist who hinges his analysis of globalization on the notion of "difference," it is Arjun Appadurai in his seminal work entitled *Modernity at Large* (1996). He thinks that culture should no longer be thought of as substance but as a dimension of phenomena that attends to "situated and embodied difference." When we say "cultural," we in fact mean "situated difference," that is, "difference in relation to something local, embodied and significant."[7] This can be better understood within Appadurai's analysis of contemporary developments. For Appadurai, "the globe has begun to spin in new ways."[8] The revolutions in *electronic media* and *mass migrations* are "two major and interconnected diacritics" that make possible such a rupture ushering us into a "postnational" and postcolonial world characterized by diasporas, transnationalism and deterritorialization. It is in this work that he introduces the now famous dimensions of global cultural flows – *ethno-scapes*, *mediascapes*, *technoscapes*, *financescapes* and *ideoscapes*[9] – these "deeply perspectival constructs" that shape our imaginary worlds. Thus, identities both personal and communal can no longer be taken as given but should be constantly constructed. Appadurai alerts us to "moving images that meet deterritorialized viewers" whose imagination of their own personal identities also shift as fast as the mobile images around them. Yet even if some agents do not actually move locally, "few persons in the world today do not have a friend, relative, or coworker who is not on the road to somewhere else or already coming back home bearing stories and possibilities."[10] Beyond the issue of personal identities, communal experience of mass media can also create "communities of sentiment," "sodalities of wor-

---

[7] A. Appadurai, *Modernity at Large: Cultural Dimensions of Globalization* (Minneapolis: University of Minnesota, 1996), 12-13.

[8] Appadurai, *Modernity at Large*, 58.

[9] Appadurai, *Modernity at Large*, 33-37.

[10] Appadurai, *Modernity at Large*, 4.

ship and charisma," groups that "think and feel things together" like fans clubs or political and religious followings.[11] This explains why the notion of "community" or "neighborhood" – both substantive social forms of communal identity – had to shed their ontological moorings as they can only be constituted in relation to global cultural flows. These terms should give way to the production of what Appadurai calls "localities" that emphasizes relationality, contextuality and agency.[12] As a postcolonial thinker, Appadurai wants to bring about heightened agency among ordinary peoples. Their experience of these global flows is said to engender "resistance, irony, selectivity" within the daily "imaginary" of these agents which when collectivized creates convergences for translocal collective action otherwise difficult to imagine.[13]

While Appadurai's emphasis on cultural "difference" being made possible by mass media and worldwide migration is quite perceptive as it reinforces a host of other categories that flood the contemporary postmodern/postcolonial market (e.g., mestizaje, creolization, glocalization, hybridity, etc.)[14] I think it is too "soft" a theory to be able to

---

[11] Appadurai, *Modernity at Large*, 8. See also A. Appadurai, "Topographies of the Self: Praise and Emotion in Hindu India," in C. A. Lutz and L. Abu-Lughod (eds.), *Language and the Politics of Emotion* (Cambridge: Cambridge University Press, 1990).

[12] Appadurai, *Modernity at Large*, 178-99.

[13] Appadurai, *Modernity at Large*, 7: "Terrorists modeling themselves on Rambo-like figures (who have themselves generated a host of non-Western counterparts); housewives reading romances and soap operas as part of their efforts to construct their own lives; Muslim family gatherings listening to speeches by Islamic leaders on cassette tapes; domestic servants in South India taking packaged tours to Kashmir: these are all examples of the active way in which media are appropriated by people throughout the world. T-shirts, billboards, and grafitti as well as rap music, street dancing, and slum housing all show that the images of the media are quickly moved into local repertoires of irony, anger, humor and resistance."

[14] See N. Garcîa Canclini, *Culturas Hibridas: Strategias para entrar y salir de la modernidad* México: Editorial Grijaldo, 1990; U. Hannerz, *Transnational Connections: Cultures, Peoples and Places* London: Routledge, 1996; R. Robertson, "Glocalization: Time-Space and Homogeneity-Heterogeniety," in Lash and Robertson (eds.), *Global Moderni-*

take account of the unevenness of global reality. First, the so-called revolution in media technology is fundamentally asymmetric, a dimension that does not feature significantly in Appadurai's analysis. It is true that there are 429 million people in the world today who are online.[15] This is not much though: it is just 6% of the world population (the remaining 94% of whom barely have access to telephone or television). Forty-one percent (41%) of 429 million are in the US and Canada, 25% in Europe, 20% in Asia-Pacific and a mere 4% in Latin America. The UNDP Director, Mark Malloch Brown, admits that "Tokyo has more telephones than the whole of Africa and Finland has more internet hosts than the whole of Latin America."[16] The so-called "digital divide" is very much real and the gap is increasing.[17] Thus, to posit the emergence of collective translocal resistance based on exposure to media and its consequent transformative effect on the imagination, as Appadurai does, is overly presumptuous. What resistance and whose imagination is he talking about? It is quite telling that, in his framework, human agency is not so much founded on increased freedom of choice in peoples as on the pleasure of consumption of media images.[18] But to base resistance on asymmetric media consumption capabilities due to unequal access to communication services leads to a lopsided social theory.

Second, the notion of fluid and flexible identities caused by deterritorialization, dislocation and disjunction is questionable. Appadurai argues that cultural identities no longer possess stable points of refer-

---

ties London: SAGE, 1995; V. Elizondo, *The Future is Mestizo: Life Where Cultures Meet* (Boulder: University Press of Colorado, 2000).

[15] See http://www.digitaldividenetwork.org/content/stories/index. cfm?key =168.

[16] See http://www.sdnp.undp.org/it4dev/.

[17] For a comprehensive research on this widening "digital divide" even in the US context, see National Telecomunications and Information Administration (NTIA), *Falling Through the Net: Toward Digital Inclusion* in http://www.ntia.doc.gov/ntiahome/ fttn 99/contents.html.

[18] Appadurai, *Modernity at Large,* 7: "Where there is consumption, there is pleasure, and where there is pleasure, there is agency. Freedom, on the other hand, is a rather more elusive category."

ence; they have become utterly dynamic as they are more a product of conscious choice, deliberation and justification, thanks to the media and migration.[19] Though it is true that economic migrants and refugees creatively adopt to the changing circumstances of their new situations in order to survive, it is also an observed fact that the consciousness of their original ethnic identities is heightened in an act of self-defense as they feel threatened by the encroachment of new cultures – a stance which has also become the breeding ground for fundamentalist tendencies. For those who live far away, the thought of home and the security it provides serve as a fundamental resource in difficult moments – something which one does not easily let go of.[20] Even in the so-called diasporic public spheres, Imre Szeman asks, "why is it that Turkish guest workers continue to watch Turkish films, and the Pakistani cabdrivers, in their solitary journeys through the modernist monuments of Chicago's city center, listen to prayers recorded in another time, another world?" "Conscious choices" and "free deliberation" towards utterly mobile cultural identities are more of an option of agents in privileged locations. Those in the lower strata just make do with whatever comes their way for reasons of survival. We can thus ask if Appadurai's theory does not reveal his own social location. Raymond Williams, for instance, argues that the discourse on "mobility" in fact betrays the social location of intellectuals:

> One reason is that many minority liberals and socialists, and especially those who by the nature of their work or formation are themselves nationally and internationally mobile, have little experience of those rooted settlements from which, though now under severe

---

[19] Appadurai, *Modernity at Large*, 44: "As group pasts become increasingly parts of museums, exhibits and collection, both in national and transnational spectacles, culture becomes less and less what Pierre Bourdieu would have called *habitus* (a tacit realm of reproductive practices and dispositions) and more an arena for conscious choice, justification, and representation, the latter often to multiple and spacially dislocated audiences."

[20] I. Szeman, "Review of *Modernity at Large*," in http://eserver.org/clogic/1-1/szeman.html.

complications and pressures, most people still derive their communal identities.[21]

What I intend to bring out in the above critique of the postcolonial celebration of difference is its often forgotten dimension: personal and communal identities do not just move as freely in the social space just as most people could not be jetsetters. Their movement is in fact largely dictated by their social and economic locations. To apply for a Schengen visa alone actually costs a fortune which many cannot even dream of affording. As Jameson reminds us, when the cultural discourse on difference displaces itself into the economic, what is concealed behind this diversity is the asymmetry brought about by the march of global capital.

The Triumph of Capitalist "Identity." Globalization can also be understood as a triumphant march, to the tune of capitalist production, at its most advanced stage. Malcolm Waters offers us a colorful metaphor: all polities and cultures are engaged in one big economic race towards "Mount Progress."[22] The stronger mountain climbers are ahead; the weaker ones lag behind, most often held back by poor training, second-class equipments ("hand-me-downs" from those on top) and unfavorable climatic conditions. Sometimes, the ones ahead throw down ropes to hurl up those behind but most often they are selective as to who receives them. Also, the ropes given are not the best ones there are. All climbers are also made to believe that there is no other way to the top. Only by following their lead can one reach the summit. When everyone is there, it will be one big party, that is only for those who make it. So, good luck to the only game in town!

The metaphor both sounds like a project of modernization and a dependency theory (e.g., the positive assessment and critical view of Western capitalism), respectively. Yet it is also from this same perspective that globalization is read both by its apologists and its critics. Many globalization discourses present the world in two parts: "developed" and "underdeveloped" (1960s); "first world" and "third world" (1970s), with the "second world" as concession to the unclassifiable socialist economies; the "more developed countries" (MDCs) and "less devoloped" ones (LDCs), with "developing" as a condescending

---

[21] R. Williams, *Towards 2000* (Harmondsworth: Penguin, 1985), 195-96.

[22] M. Waters, *Globalization* (London: Routledge, 1995), 19-20.

description for those strugglers-in-between in the 1980s; "industrialized countries" and "newly industrialized" ones (NICs) in the 1990s. In this scheme, we seem to get the picture of a bipolar world expressed in geo-political terms – the "North" and the "South" – a positioning understandable only *vis-à-vis* the one global economic game. The others are ahead; the rest are behind – all marching to the resolute tune of global economic capital. While one group of theorists herald its coming and try so hard to make it real (IMF-WB, GATT, WTO, TNCs, etc.), others renounce the evil of its regime and try as much as possible to mitigate its consequences (anti-globalization theorists).[23] Two players, one game, one uniform – the "golden straightjacket" (to use a term from Thomas Friedman) – a "one size fits all" vest which all have to don:

> It leaves people behind quicker than ever if they shuck it off, and it helps them catch up quicker than ever if they wear it right [or so it seems]. It is not always pretty or gentle or comfortable. But it's here and it's the only model on the rack this historical season.[24]

Naked economic interest and brute capital, however, will never be as affective as when they are misrecognized and concealed.[25] The discourse of "difference" and diversity is therefore summoned by the market apologists to mask the violence of global economic "identity." Francis Fukuyama, for instance, argues that centralized economies are no longer viable. The "end of his history," thus, is to give free reign to the market as this ushers in "incredible diversity of products and ser-

---

[23] For a comprehensive survey of these positions on globalization, see D. Held *et al.*, *Global Transformations: Politics, Economics and Culture* (Stanford: Stanford University Press, 1999).

[24] T. Friedman, *The Lexus and the Olive Tree* (New York: Anchor Books, 2000), 105. Or (106): "Once your country puts it on [the golden straightjacket], its political choices gets reduced to Pepsi or Coke – to slight nuances of taste, slight nuances of policy, slight alterations in design to account for local traditions, some loosening here or there, but never any major deviation from the core golden rules."

[25] For the politics of misrecognition (*méconnaissance*) in economic and cultural universes, see P. Bourdieu, *Language and Symbolic Power* (Cambridge: Harvard University Press, 1991).

vices" for the benefit of all participants: "It is capable of linking different societies around the globe to one another physically through the creation of global markets, and of creating parallel economic aspirations and practices in a host of diverse societies."[26] The only condition of success, however, is participation in the game. And the best way to receive the blessings of the global game is also to subscribe to *liberal democracy* as its accompanying political system since this guarantees individual freedoms, a sense of pluralism, conducive to the free play of the market.[27] For instance, the student revolt in Tiananmen Square and the collapse of the Soviet system are marshaled to support such a contention: it is capitalism that brings about clamors for democracy; it is only democracy that makes possible capitalist progress.

But is there really diversity (in economy, politics and culture) within the global economic world? One only needs to go to an assembly line in any Export Processing Zone in the South in order to experience what "uniformity" is all about: large box type buildings without air conditioning, tedious work in a monotonous rhythm, a hazardous environment and workers in identical vests with IDs, being watched in surveillance by bosses from the management office (also called the "aquarium," reminiscent of Bentham's panopticon) in the center and above the production floor.[28] Aldous Huxley's *Brave New World* has

---

[26] F. Fukuyama, *The End of History and the Last Man* (New York: Perennial, 1992), 108.

[27] Fukuyama, *The End of History*, 45: "What is emerging victorious ... is not so much liberal practice, as the liberal *idea*. That is to say, for a very large part of the world, there is now no ideology with pretensions to universality that is in a position to challenge liberal democracy, and no universal principle of legitimacy other than the sovereignty of the people .... Even non-democrats will have to speak the language of democracy in order to justify their deviation from the single universal standard."

[28] A.M.C. Patungal, *Nimble Fingers, Clenched Fists: Dynamics of Structure, Agency and Women's Spaces in a Manufacturing Company* (Diliman: UP University Center for Women Studies, 2000), 46-51 "From the outside the factory looks decent, even worker friendly, complete with basketball court, purporting a concern for the welfare of its workers. Upon closer inspection, the factory becomes imposing with its large gates surrounded by barbed wire and with three or four security guards who greeted me when I peeked in. A sense of order is exuded with the

finally become reality.²⁹ Fukuyama's "diversity of products and services" is in fact a repetition of the same throughout the globe (or is it mainly in the South?). For even the once diverse local production has given way to export crops for the global market. The indigenous people's rich resources of traditional knowledge (medicinal plants, food varieties, indigenous arts) have also been patented by multinational entrepreneurs to be traded as one standard product in the international markets.³⁰

On the political level, the promise of a healthy democracy is also a farce. John Gray argues that democracy and the free market are not partners but competitors.³¹ Globalization is in fact seen as the New

---

uniformed workers queuing for work, identification cards pinned on their chests. All workers are required to don company shirts, which are color-coded according to their departments .... Looming above the production section is the 'aquarium,' a term used by workers to refer to window at the management office, where the owner would do his surveillance. Ironically, I believe the workers below are likewise seen from a 'capitalist gaze' as fishes in an aquarium."

²⁹ A. Huxley, *Brave New World* (New York: Perennial, 1998 [1932]), 7: "Standard men and women; in uniform batches. The whole of a small factory staffed with products of a single bokanovskified egg. 'Ninety-six identical twins working ninety-six identical machines!' The voice was almost tremulous with enthusiasm .... Solved by standard Gammas, unvarying Deltas, uniform Epsilons. Millions of identical twins. The principle of mass production at last applied to biology."

³⁰ Around 7000 patents have been granted for the "unauthorized use of traditional knowledge or the misappropriation of medicinal plants, states a survey made in March 2000. See UNDP, *Human Development Report 2004: Cultural Liberty in Today's Diverse World* (New York, 2004), 86.

³¹ J. Gray, *False Dawn: The Delusions of Global Capitalism* (New York: New Press, 1998), 213: "Democratic capitalism – the vacuous rallying cry of neoconservatives everywhere – designates (or conceals) a deeply problematic relationship."

Hellenism.³² Alexander the Great's project was a plan to export Hellenistic democratic institutions from the *polis* to the whole cosmopolis in an effort to crush oligarchic rules and local tyrannies. In reality, it led to the accumulation of wealth and power among monarchies and oligarchies, increased slave-driven production, disempowered peoples and entrenched economic exploitation – factors which ultimately led to its own destruction. The process of concealment was quite effective: "The rich could pose as democrats while being indirectly responsible for the growing power of the rich."³³ The present liberal political economy runs in a parallel manner: the proclamation of individual freedom *vis-à-vis* the concentration of wealth among the neo-oligarchs and their cohorts. In such contexts, "freedom" becomes mere lip service since, in order to survive, economies and polities need to comply with the demands of the market and the powerful dictates of its policing institutions. When a country like the Philippines has a debt of $58.6 billion and has to allocate 32% of its annual budget to service its interest alone (an amount higher that what it spends for its social services [29%])³⁴ how can one speak of freedom? Amartya Sen, the 1998 Nobel Prize winner for economics, has rightly established a direct correlation between poverty and social incapability, between development and freedom.³⁵ Mired in poverty, all we can have is a sham democracy.

When the discourse of capital encroachment spreads to all corners of contemporary society (e.g., McDonaldization, Coca-Colonization, Disneyfication, etc.), what we get is a very pessimistic forecast leading to some form of a global doomsday. It feels like Althusser's "ideological apparatus" or Goffman's "total institution" have success-

---

[32] Barry Gills, "Whither Democracy?: Globalization and the New Hellenism," in C. Thomas and P. Wilkin (eds.), *Globalization and the South* (London: Macmillan Press, 1997), 60-75.

[33] S. Price, "The History of Hellenistic Period," in J. Boardman *et al.* (eds.), *The Oxford History of Classical Art* (Oxford / New York: Oxford University Press), 316.

[34] R.B. Guzman, "The Philippine Crisis: Will a New Presidency Still Make a Difference," *Birdtalk: Economic and Political Briefing* (Quezon City: IBON Foundation, 15 July 2004): 3-22.

[35] A. Sen, *Development as Freedom* (Oxford: Oxford University Press, 1999).

fully eaten up every social fabric leading to a seeming deadend. It is such a view that I would like to put into question. For I am coming from the experience of resilient peoples who have resisted and outlived centuries of colonial oppression, dictatorships, political corruption and indescribable poverty. When I go home to the small village where I come from, the people whom I know from childhood really find life so difficult and they often express it with tears: they are anxious about their next meal; they have no jobs, experience poor harvest, have no medicine even for basic illnesses, etc. But even as these problems are very real, it is also these peoples who can laugh to their hearts' content during their lighter moments with others in the community. In the Manila dumpsite where I spend my weekend ministry, people literally get their meals by sorting through the city garbage as they also pitch their makeshift "houses" (if you can call it that) made of the same junk beside the smoking heap of unbearably stinking waste. Yet they also ironically call their place *"Lupang Pangako"* – a "Promised Land" which for them is not only a promise but also a task. Through grassroots saving schemes, some have already acquired a decent home in a housing project nearby which they themselves also helped design and build.[36] Life moves on with such a resilience founded on the people's utter will to survive, their skills of "making do," their personal social networks (family, friends, immediate relations) and on the living faith in a God who promised "life" despite the palpable death around them.

Locating Resistance in the Context of Globalization

"Back to the Rough Ground." This sense of hope is either exaggerated or forgotten by grand theories of progress or doom, respectively. This resilient resistance is blown up via the notion of celebratory difference in "soft" globalization theories or obliterated in the discourse of the march of monologic capital. I argue that these untenable positions are in fact products of what Pierre Bourdieu calls the "scholastic point of

---

[36] See Vincentian Missionaries Social Development Foundation Incorporated, "Meet the Philippines Homeless People's Federation," *Environment and Urbanization* 13/2 (2001): 73-84. For parallel experiences in other countries of the south, see other articles in the same volume.

view."[37] *Skholè* – the Greek term for "leisure" (from which the term "scholastic" proceeds and of which the "school" and the "academe" are present progenies) engenders a social location and *habitus* that detaches it from the actual movement of historical human practice. The "intellectual gaze" – by the mere fact of being a "gaze" – turns the world into a *spectacle,* "a set of significations to be interpreted rather than as concrete problems to be solved."[38] It thus needs to locate itself in some vantage point where it can have an overview, as it were, thus, also retreating from the "play of time" which characterizes human practice together with all its roughness, uncertainties and ambiguities. Intellectual activity appears to be a serious enterprise yet, in fact, it is also a game – a "playworld" where people can tune in to the "as if" or "let's pretend" mode without real life-and-death stakes that beset the rough grounds of praxis – as epitomized by the ancient philosopher Thales who fell into a pit because he was always looking up, engrossed with the stars. It is here that a quote from Wittgenstein alluded to in our title comes in handy: "We have got on to slippery ice where there is no friction and so in a certain sense the conditions are ideal, but also, just because of that, we are unable to walk: so we need friction. Back to the rough ground."[39] Wittgenstein was reacting to the

---

[37] See P. Bourdieu, "The Scholastic Point of View," in P. Bourdieu, *Practical Reason: On the Theory of Action* (Cambridge: Polity Press, 1998 [1994]), 127-40; P. Bourdieu, *Pascalian Meditations* (London: Polity Press, 2000).

[38] P. Bourdieu and L. Wacquant, *Introduction to Reflexive Sociology* (Chicago: Chicago University Press, 1992), 39: "As soon as we observe (*theorein*) the social world, we introduce in our perception of it a bias due to the fact that, to study it, to describe it, to talk about it, we must retire from it more or less completely. This *theoreticist* or *intellectualist bias* consists in forgetting to inscribe into the theory we build of the social world the fact that it is the product of a theoretical gaze, a 'contemplative eye.' A genuinely reflexive sociology must constantly guard itself against this epistemocentrism, or this 'ethnocentrism of the scientist,' which consists in ignoring everything that the analyst injects into his perception of the object by virtue of the fact that he is placed outside the object, that he observes it from afar and from above" (Bourdieu and Wacquant, *Reflexive Sociology,* 69-70).

[39] L. Wittgenstein, *Philosophical Investigations* (Oxford: Basil Blackwell, 1958), §107.

"crystalline purity of logic" as the required lens to view the world. On pure crystal ice, the promise of unhindered motion actually renders us motionless unless we risk breaking our limbs. It is my contention that globalization discourses which exclusively heralds either "difference" or "identity" are products of *skholè* as I have shown earlier. The daily talk of revolution in people's imaginations brought about by the media and migration leading to collective action is at best unrealistic if not altogether impossible. The view of the world as becoming a "total capitalist institution" renders "walking" impossible. But we want to walk; we need to survive, not to be rendered totally helpless in front of a totalizing power. So back to the rough ground!

If we want to locate resistance in times of globalization, we need to bring analysis back to the rough grounds or to what Raymond Williams calls "placeable social identities" – "places where we have lived and want to go on living, where generations not only of economic but also of social effort and human care have been invested, and which new generations will inherit."[40] For all the talk of global mobility, Williams observes that "in societies as different as Wales and Italy, people say where they come from, where they were formed or belong, in these insistently local ways."[41] No matter how postmodern, people chatting on the Internet still ask for one's "location." In global times, these "placeable bondings" might have been disrupted or could have even moved elsewhere beyond regional confines. But wherever this may be, durable cultural dispositions (or what Bourdieu calls *habitus*) in agents – engendered by knowable and locatable interactions – endure even as their interaction with new circumstance makes them capable of "regulated improvisations."[42] This insistence on the "local" does not signal a nostalgia for the static and organic *Gemeinschaft*. It eschews the romantic consensual view as it is also aware that these social identities were products of fierce social historical conflicts as they molded their destinies against new forces, new ethnicities, and new challenges. For whatever disruption the global capital has caused

---

[40] R. Williams, "Mining the Meaning: Keywords in the Miners' Strike," in R. Gable (ed.), *Resources of Hope* (London: Verso, 1989), 124.

[41] Williams, *Towards 2000*, 180-81.

[42] P. Bourdieu, *The Logic of Practice* (Stanford: Stanford University Press, 1990), 52-79; Bouridieu *Pascalian Meditations*, 128-63.

these communities, they continue to "adjust, because they must, to altered, even radically altered conditions."[43] Thus, beyond grand theories of bust and boom, it is these placeable "rough grounds" in their "actual material historical process" that need to be faced, to be analyzed and worked out.[44] For it is here – and only here – that people have actually resisted and survived.[45]

"Poaching on the Dominant." Is resistance really possible in response to a hegemonic power such as "global capitalism"? Where, on the rough ground, in these "placeable bondings," can it be found/discovered/uncovered? For most people, hegemony – a notion made popular by Gramsci – constitutes their sense of reality, their ordinary or common sense experience. It is another world for "culture"; in our case, a global capitalist culture. Yet a lived hegemony is never a totalizing, singular abstract system. It is a complex of relationships, experiences and activities. The dominant position must constantly renew, recreate, defend and modify itself as it is also continually being resisted and subverted by forces from within its margins. According to Williams, "there is no mode of production and therefore no dominant

---

[43] Williams, *Towards 2000,* 187.

[44] Against the postmodern aversion to "roots" and the capitalist penchant for mobility, "it is legitimate and indeed imperative that we seek a form of rootedness which is sheltered from overthrow by technologies and market processes which in achieving a global reach that is disembedded from any community or culture, cannot avoid desolating the earth's human settlements and its human environments" (John Gray, *Enlightenment's Wake* [London: Routledge, 1995], 181).

[45] "Placeable social identities" is equivalent to Stuart Hall's insistence on "ethnicity" in global times – that "face-to-face communities that are knowable, that are locatable, one can give them a place. One knows what the voices are. One knows what the faces are …. Ethnicity is the necessary place or space from which people speak… Modern theories of enunciation [like the emancipative discourse of the margins] always oblige us to recognize that enunciation comes from somewhere. It cannot be unplaced, it cannot be unpositioned, it is always positioned in a discourse. It is when a discourse forgets that it is placed that it tries to speak everybody else." Cf. S. Hall, "The Local and the Global: Globalization and Ethnicity," in A King (ed.,), *Culture, Globalization and the World-System: Contemporary Conditions for the Representation of Identity* (London: Macmillan, 1991), 35-36.

social order and therefore no dominant culture ever in reality includes or exhausts all human practice, human energy and human intention."[46] Thus, resistance can be located within what Williams calls the "residual" and the "emergent" which, together with the "dominant" hegemonic force constitutes the entire cultural process. In other words, there is more to culture than the "dominant" hegemonic force since actual human practice in the rough grounds can never be totally exhausted by its control, despite its universalizing intentions.

> For there is always, though in varying degrees, practical consciousness, in specific relationships, specific skills, specific perceptions, that is unquestionably social and that a specifically dominant social order neglects, excludes, represses, or simply fails to recognize.[47]

It is from these areas that "emergent voices" – both alternative and oppositional – emerge in order to exert pressure on the hegemonic.

Michel de Certeau provides us with a very colorful military metaphor: the notion of *tactic* as "poaching on the dominant." While *strategy* refers to the calculated actions of powerful institutions whose possession of a "territory" is needed to regroup or recharge for the next moves thus placing it in an advantageous position, *tactic* is the scheme of resistance available to the weak. Bereft of a place, the "weak" can only play within the terrain of the "strong." They have no time to strategize and thus, their attacks depend on the possibilities afforded by cracks and fissures within the structure of their powerful adversary. "It poaches on them; it creates surprises for them. It can be where it is least expected. It is a guileful ruse."[48] The weak thus turns

---

[46] R. Williams, *Marxism and Literature* (London: Oxford University Press, 1977), 125.

[47] Williams, *Marxism and Literature*, 125.

[48] De Certeau continues to explain in *The Practice of Everyday Life* (Berkeley: University of California Press, 1984), 307: "A *tactic* is a calculated action determined by the absence of proper locus. No delimitation of an exteriority, then, provides it with the condition necessary for autonomy. The space of the tactic is the space of the other. Thus it must play on and with a terrain imposed on it and organized by the law of the foreign power. It does not have the means *to keep to itself*, at a distance,

its own smallness into a gain and cunningly transforms the enemy's size and visibility into an utter disadvantage. This reminds us of the Greek *metis* – the sense of cunning intelligence valuable to the Pre-Socratics that came to be suppressed by the dominant Greek narrative from Plato onwards.[49] In certain activities like navigation, medicine or hunting, the Greeks value a type of intelligence that combines "flair, wisdom, forethought, subtlety of mind, deception, resourcefulness, vigilance, opportunism, various skills and experiences acquired over the years" as they are made to bear upon the "transient, shifting, disconcerting and ambiguous situations."[50] *Metis* does not so much use force as "cunning trickery" through its ability to play the game to the limit in order to subvert its rules. It plays with the time at its disposal. It can strike swiftly or wait patiently for the right moment. It is pliable, flexible and polymorphous as it does not intend to fight but play with the winds so as to reach the harbour, i.e., to achieve its ends. It can appear weak and foolish in order to mislead only to take advantage of the game by surprise. In the face of such overwhelming power, this type of oblique resistance is the only way to survive.

---

in a position of withdrawal, foresight, and self-collection: it is a maneuver 'within the enemy's field of vision,' as von Büllow put it, and within the enemy territory. It does not, therefore have the options of planning general strategy and viewing the adversary as a whole within a district, visible, and objectionable space. It operates in isolated actions, blow by blow ...."

[49] "Cunning intelligence" has been subsumed under the one and only *Truth of Philosophy* just as Metis was swallowed by her husband Zeus. In Greek mythology, Zeus lured Metis, the Titaness of Wisdom, unto a couch and swallowed her for fear that if she gave birth to his child, the child would depose of him just as he himself earlier dislodged his father Chronus from his throne. By doing so, Athene (the figure of Greece) is thus born of Zeus, not of Metis. Metis and her ingenious wisdom (e.g., she can transform herself into many shapes to escape capture by Zeus) have been banished from existence. But there is one interesting footnote to the story: Zeus later claimed that Metis still continues to give him counsel from inside his belly. See R. Graves, *The Greek Myths,* vol. 1 (Harmondsworth: Penguin, 1960), 45-47.

[50] M. Detienne and J.-P. Vernant, *Cunning Intelligence in Greek Culture and Society* (Sussex: Harvester Press, 1978), 3-4.

Oblique Resistance in (Post)Colonial and Global Contexts. Let us provide some concrete examples of this type of resistance among grassroots communities in colonial, postcolonial and global contexts:

(1) The first case is the role of sacramental confession in the Spanish colonial project in the Philippines. It must be remembered that the Philippines had fewer missionaries in the field and far less military force than the Americas had from the Spanish. Yet in the mid-1600s, less than a century after Christianity's arrival to the islands, more than half a million Filipinos had already converted to the faith. A Filipino historian, Vicente Rafael, attributes the rapid spread of Christianity to a double "reduction" – that of "language" and of "bodies," both of which are related to "conversion."[51] Just as the local native scripts were reduced to Latin-Castillian grammatical structures of declensions and conjugations, people were also relocated to administrative centers (i.e., *pueblos, cabeceras y poblaciones*) so that these "native bodies" would live *bajo de la campana* ("under the bell"), that is, within the range of evangelization but also of political control. One of the more effective ways to pursue conversion was through *sacramental confession*. That the practice of confession was crucial to the evangelization-colonization project is attested to by the numerous vernacular translations of confession manuals during this time. Early missionary accounts also attest to the eagerness with which the natives rushed to the confessional, sometimes to the point of begging the priest on their knees. Yet these same missionaries also found the native practice confusing since, instead of following the confessional rules laid down in the manuals, the penitents turned this event into opportunities for justification of one's deeds or for "showing off" since they would not tell the priest their own sins but those of "their wives, mothers-in-laws and the people they do not like." Does this mean that the natives did not have the intellectual capacity to comprehend the intricacy of this foreign religious practice, as some missionaries believed? Or was it a different dynamics that was at play altogether? Rafael's conclusion is quite insightful. The *Tagalog* word (the language of Central Philippines) for asking for forgiveness in confession is *tawad*, which also means "to bargain, to haggle or to use evasions

---

[51] V. Rafael, *Contracting Colonialism: Translation and Christian Conversion in Tagalog Society under Early Spanish Rule* (Quezon City: Ateneo de Manila University Press, 1988).

(or in Spanish *regatear*)." In other words, the practice of confession which was used as a machinery of the colonial powers to control the bodies and minds of the Filipinos, was in fact also employed by the natives as a way of bargaining with authority – a sort of oblique resistance against the totalizing grip of a dominant power.[52]

(2) The second set of examples refers to research in rural agricultural contexts – the sector most affected by both colonialism and globalization. In the *Weapons of the Weak,* James Scott distinguishes between two forms of resistance: formal revolutionary politics and everyday resistance. "Where institutionalized politics is formal, overt, concerned with systematic, de jure change, everyday resistance is informal, often covert, and concerned largely with the immediate, de facto gains."[53] Most often, the more formal revolutionary activity is an

---

[52] The fiesta phenomenon prevalent in the Philippines does a parallel act. In order to attract the natives to the town centers or *reducciones* where the missionaries can indoctrinate them into the rudiments of the faith (and of the empire), the colonizers organized fiestas – a colorful mixture of Spanish Christian practices and local cultures, of fireworks, processions, High Masses, theater, gambling, banquets, etc. But the indigenous populations later transformed the occasion to oppose foreign rule. Plays became critical of the Spanish abuses so much so that the friars needed to exercise censorship on which show to ban or permit. Itinerant preachers also use this occasion not only to preach the imminent end of this unjust order but also to forward some subversive political programs. R. Wendt, "Philippine Fiesta and Colonial Culture," *Philippine Studies* 46 (1998): 3-23. Even pacifism and nonviolence can also be a form of resistance. This is the case of a still existing indigenous people's community called the *Hanunuo* (in Mindoro, Philippines). They are known to be a very passive and gentle people who prefer to run than to fight the aggressor. But each family has spears or arrows in the corner posts of their huts. One author remarks: "One can only wonder what series of defeats and futile resistance led to their passive gentleness. Should we judge it as a sign of broken spirits? Or should we understand it as a tactic imposed by unfavourable circumstances?" See E. de la Torre, *Touching Ground, Taking Root: Theological and Political Reflections on the Philippine Struggle* (Manila: Socio-Pastoral Institute and Catholic Institute for International Relations, 1986), 13.

[53] J. Scott, *Weapons of the Weak: Everyday Forms of Peasant Resistance* (New Haven: Yale University Press, 1985), 33.

obsession of the *élite* and the intelligentsia. Ordinary subordinate classes do not so much opt for dramatic changes in sociopolitical structures even as their rhetoric is often radical. In the precarious state of life they are in, such a goal is either too far-fetched or too risky and dangerous. This subaltern option for anonymous and oblique resistance betrays their sense of cunning and "feel for the game" since an overt and open defiance would be suicidal on their part. A parent of plantation workers has this advice:

> [R]emember, you're selling your labor and the one who buys it wants to *see* that he gets something for it, so work when he's around, then you can relax when he goes away, but make sure you always *look like* you're working when the inspectors are there.[54]

This type of resistance among agricultural subaltern groups takes on different forms: foot dragging, dissimulation, false compliance, pilfering, feigned ignorance, slander, sabotage, cultural defiance, etc. – activities that require no coordination and planning. But since this form of resistance is widespread among the dominated classes, it can be called a "social movement" in itself – one "with no formal organization, no formal leaders, no manifestoes, no dues, no name and no banner."[55]

(3) A third example comes from research on female workers in multinational companies (also called "free trade zones") in the South. The harsh working conditions, low wages, contractual hiring, sexual and verbal abuse, compulsory overtime hours, control of female bodies and complete surveillance make these factories into total capitalist "apparatuses." Not quite so. A range of oblique resistance strategies is

---

[54] A. Stouler, *Capitalism and Confrontation in Sumatra's Plantation Belt 1870-1979* (New Haven: Yale University Press, 1985), 184.

[55] Scott, *Weapons of the Weak,* 35. Many studies have already been done on these practices among subaltern groups: foot dragging in American slavery, feigned illness or ignorance among the Dalits in India, evasive labor practices in a Sumatra plantation or everyday resistance among peasants in a Malay village. See J. Silverberg (ed.), *Social Mobility in the Caste System in India: An Interdisciplinary Symposium.* (The Hague: Mouton, 1968).

in fact practiced in the everyday life of the workers.[56] Since the open contestation of rules might not be viable (as it would lead to termination), indirect defiance of authority through derogatory remarks towards their rude supervisors, gossip so as to destroy their names, going around prohibitions, etc. are resorted to. Pilferage is also justified due to low wages. Machine wrecking, work stoppage or slackening to sabotage production quota: all these are forms of "anonymous protests," neither collective nor organized, done independently of each other, behind the scene and almost in silence. Retreating to the locker rooms to eat; withdrawing to the toilets on the pretext of "woman's needs"; or extending time in the "prayer rooms" (which some Islam factories have) are employed as a way to reclaim human autonomy in the midst of the capitalist gaze and masculine control. Recurring "mass hysteria" (simultaneous "possession of the spirits" in the shop floors) is also seen as the women's idiom of protest, a sort of "ritualized rebellion" which calls public attention to their distressed conditions.[57]

It can be asked whether these forms of resistance are really effective to transform the whole social order. Can they not be easily contained by global capital? Beyond the subversive dimension of these everyday practices, should resistance to hegemonic power be not more deliberate, systematic and organized? Our emphasis on oblique resistance is not meant to deny the need for more organized action. Comprehensive and wide-ranging alternatives like rejection of Structural Adjustment Programs, moratorium on foreign debt servicing, Tobin tax, developmental aid, consumer revolt, anti-globalization protests, etc. are as urgent and necessary.[58] But many of these alternatives to

---

[56] See, among others, A. Ong, *Spirits of Resistance and Capitalist Discipline: Factory Women in Malaysia,* Alban: State University of New York Press 1987; Paguntalan, *Nimble Fingers, Clenched Fists.*

[57] See A. Ong, "The Production of Possession: Spirits and the Multinational Corporation in Malaysia," *American Ethnologist* 15 (1988) 28-42.

[58] See, among others, A. Aziz Choudry (ed.), *Effective Strategies in Confronting Transnational Corporations,* Manila: Asia-Pacific Research Networks, 2003; K. Singh, *Taming Global Financial Flows,* London: ZED Books 2001; J. Madeley, *A People's World,* London: ZED Books 2003; J. Mandle, *Globalization and the Poor,* Cambridge: Cambridge University Press 2003; H. Shutt, *A New Democracy: Alternatives to a*

globalization are beyond the reach of those at the grassroots.[59] For instance, it might be laudable to boycott products of multinational companies that employ child labor or neglect the environment but there is not much choice as to the brand of shoes, milk or rice in these communities. Any brand that is available is a real "grace," certainly better than nothing. Even as we know the evils of the contractualization of labour, workers would prefer a temporary job contract without any long-term benefits (e.g., retirement, social security, etc) than no work at all. Anti-globalization demonstrations like in Seattle or Genoa are praiseworthy and need to be replicated as much elsewhere. But the really poor do not have the leisure to spend a whole day protesting in the streets and going home later without food on the family table. What is at issue is the more basic day to day survival. Given the power of the hegemon, the subalterns do not have a wide territory to maneuver; they can only poach on the dominant in order to survive.

The revolutionary potentials of these everyday practices of survival should not be easily dismissed. First, most of these practices of resistance are not ill-intentioned or consciously planned to topple the dominant power. They are to the result of, in all honesty, the only available means to survive. Bourdieu also says that the most effective strategies are "usually those produced, without any calculation, and in the illusion of the most absolute 'sincerity'."[60] For instance, a Marian

---

Bankrupt World Order, London: ZED Books 2001; IBON Databank and Research Center, *Privatization: Corporate Takeover of Government,* Manila: IBON Foundation 2003.

[59] There are also more positive small-scale initiatives available to the grassroots: cooperative building, micro-financial schemes, organic farming and sustainable agriculture, grassroots networking, etc. For a range of examples, see U. Duchrow, *Alternative to Global Capitalism* (The Netherlands: International Books, 1995), 240-77; J. Feffer, *Living in Hope: People Challenging Globalization* (London: ZED Books, 2002). But even these micro-alternatives are not accessible to the grassroots without the needed financial and human resources assistance (e.g., grants, loans, subsidies, training, networking) from well-established support institution. However, it is also these fields of resistance that need to be strengthened as a way of positively empowering the subaltern classes.

[60] Bourdieu, *The Logic of Practice,* 292.

pilgrimage or a funeral procession can organically turn out to be protest march against Martial law (e.g., the funeral of Ninoy Aquino during Marcos rule). An ancient practice of communal meditation (e.g., Falun Gong) can serve as an indictment of the status quo and drive its leaders to panic. Or, the practice of community-based daily savings (e.g., Grameen banking) can challenge the dominant view held by the mainstream banking system of the poor as "non-bankable."[61]

Second, even as these regular practices of daily life are in constant danger of being co-opted by capitalism, they can also serve as foundations to structural transformation. According to Marc Bloch, great rebellions are mere "flashes in the pan" compared to the stubborn persistence and regularity of everyday resistance. "Almost invariably doomed to defeat and eventual massacre, the great insurrections were altogether too disorganized to achieve any lasting results. The patient, silent struggles, stubbornly carried on by the rural communities over the years would accomplish more than these flashes in the pan."[62] James Scott also argues that everyday resistance in the rough grounds is "the stubborn bedrock upon which other forms of resistance may grow and they are likely to persist after such other forms failed or produced, in turn, a new pattern of inequality."[63]

Theologizing from the Rough Grounds

Let us summarize what has been done so far. Firstly, I have engaged Appadurai's postcolonial discourse of "difference" which, though concerned with resistance in people's consumption of media images and migratory dislocations, does not take into account the asymmetric power present in these global disruptions. Second, even as I concur with the anti-globalization theorists on the unstoppable march of capi-

---

[61] See S. Boonyanbancha, "Savings and Loans: Drawing Lessons from Some Experiences in Asia," *Environment and Urbanization* 13, 2 (2001) 9-21; T. Bauman, "Shack / Slum Dwellers International and Banks," *Environment and Urbanization* 13/2 (2001): 139-43.

[62] M. Bloch, *French Rural History* (Berkeley: University of California Press, 1970), 170.

[63] Scott, *Weapons of the Weak*, 273.

talist "identity," I have also shown that most of these discourses do not provide a space of hope for dominated people to be able to resist the clutches of the new hegemon. Third, I have tried to locate resistance not so much in those grand theories of exaggerated optimism and cynical gloom, most of which are products of leisurely social locations, but in the daily practices of survival among the subalterns themselves.

My next question is how does this analysis relate to theology? I do not intend to explicate a concrete theological method in times of globalization. I will only engage two theologians who attempted to do theology from this new context – John Milbank and Robert Schreiter – hoping that my positions *vis-à-vis* these thinkers will yield some concrete directions in the future.

A Theology of Harmonious Difference: John Milbank. One theologian who consciously responds to the postmodern discourse of "difference" in a global world is John Milbank. For him, the task of theology hinges on a "repetition" of the Christ event – each time made different, "made strange." The theological task, thus, is "to articulate Christian difference in such a fashion as to make it strange."[64] In his first methodological work, *Theology and Social Theory,* Milbank registers his antagonism to narratives of secular modern reason and postmodern nihilism; he opposes these narratives to that of a different story, that of Christianity. In his latest book, *Being Reconciled,* he is more specific with regard to his adversary: "In the face of globalization and the new American Empire, we need to counterpose Augustine's counter-empire, the City of God."[65] As I have elsewhere

---

[64] J. Milbank, *Theology and Social Theory,* 381. Cf. also J. Milbank, "Postmodern Critical Augustinianism: A Short Summa in Forty-Two Responses to Unasked Questions," *Modern Theology* 7 (1991): 268 "Explication of Christian practice, the task of theology, tries to pinpoint the peculiarity, the difference, of this practice 'by making it strange,' finding a new language for this difference less tainted with the overfamiliarity of too many Christian words which tend to obscure Christian singularity." See also J. Milbank, *The Word Made Strange: Theology, Language and Culture* (Oxford: Blackwell, 1996).

[65] J. Milbank, *Being Reconciled: Ontology and Pardon* (London: Routledge, 2003), 210.

extensively engaged Milbank's framework,⁶⁶ in this context, I would like to mention two objections to his theological project related to the topic at hand: (1) the danger of a new Christian imperialism and (2) the problem of a Christian social theory far from the rough grounds.

First, for all his discourse on "difference" in the context of a pluralist globalized world, Milbank actually wants to impose a new hegemony, that of Christian "identity." In one of his lectures which I attended while still a student, I asked how his very assertive Christian theological framework can be applicable, say, to the Christian-Muslim dialogue in Southern Philippines. He started his reply by comparing the openness of medieval Islam to the fundamentalist trends of their contemporary counterparts. I pursued the questioning: "But don't you think your proposal is not as fundamentalist?" Milbank of course irritatingly denied my charge, and the subject was quickly changed. But this has really left me wondering what would my Muslim friend feel if I keep on insisting that my Christian narrative is much better than his – and it is all "a matter of taste" – a Milbankian postmodern strategy intended to show respect for personal preferences but which in reality adds insult to injury. As many of his commentators point out, in Milbank's hands, we see the "Christian story become a Christian imperialism that polices the sublime."⁶⁷ Even as he acknowledges that in the postmodern context, the Christian tradition is but one narrative among others, it in fact is viewed as *the* narrative, the only meta-narrative capable of "out-narrating" the others. In Milbank, we again observe Jameson's keen comment on many globalization theories – a discourse of plural "difference" which can subtly shift, often for ideological reasons, into imperialist "identity," not very different from the jubilation of cultural diversities in all corners of the world which also conceals an imperialist meta-narrative of global capital.

The second comment concerns Milbank's preferred social theory – "socialism by grace" or "socialism of the gift."⁶⁸ In his theological

---

⁶⁶ D.F. Pilario, *Back to the Rough Grounds of Praxis: Exploring Theological Method with Pierre Bourdieu*, BETL Series (Leuven: Peeters, 2005).

⁶⁷ G. Ward, "John Milbank's Divina Commedia," *New Blackfriars* 73 (1992): 317.

⁶⁸ J. Milbank, *Being Reconciled*, 162-86. Originally published as "Socialism of the Gift, Socialism by Grace," *New Blackfriars* 77 (1996): 532-48.

program, Milbank is against any social theory. He asserts that the "City of God" is itself a viable blueprint for society. Politically, however, Milbank has always been "left of center" (as he hails from a "generation of non-conformists," by his own account).[69] His preference thus is for *Christian socialism* which, against Marxist dialectical materialism, exhibits a nonviolent alternative as it also provides a moral critique to consumerist capitalism gone global. For the Christian socialist, the ecclesiological vision of the "mystical body of Christ" is presented as the paradigm of a just society as it is consistent with Milbank's non-agonistic paradigm modeled on the Augustinian ontology of peace. Despite widespread social differences and global asymmetrical relations, it decidedly eschews the violence of the dialectical game. "Instead it is what arises "by grace" as a thousand different specific models of social harmony, a thousand different gifts of specific social bonding, a thousand kinds of community."[70] Milbank consistently shows preference for pacifist alternatives detesting any trace of conflict and violence. His only preoccupation is for "harmonious difference." What concerns me here is this idealist direction of Milbank's theologizing. To pose abstract categories as the ineffable "City of God," "socialism by grace" or "ontological peace" (at the same time condemning Marxism as dialectically violent) without immersing one's analysis in the actual circumstance is also to succumb to the danger of "scholastic illusion" where the intellectual (in this case, the theologian) arrogates unto him/ herself the role of the solitary interpreter of the Christian message from one's theological ivory towers. Such a stance is not only oblivious but also disrespectful to the personal and structural violence grassroots communities suffer everyday in their waking lives and the often "violent" struggle that these people have to undergo to bring about the so-called "peace" of the Kingdom. What I wish to forward here is the desire not to condemn any social theory before considering the concrete analysis of the actual material historical process. Only from there can one judge its viability, relevance or incongruence with the Christian praxis.

---

[69] See J. Milbank, "Theology and Social Theory and its Significance for Community Building," (December 16, 2000) on: http://livedtheology.org/pdfs/Milbank.pdf.

[70] Milbank, *Being Reconciled,* 167.

Theology and "New Catholicity": Robert Schreiter

More open than Milbank's project is the theological method of Robert Schreiter in his work, *The New Catholicity* (1997).[71] Schreiter's objective is to engage the theories of globalization in the search for a viable theological method for our times. If space is compressed and the world has become one, he asks, what repercussions does this have for theology? Beyond Milbank's imperialist direction, Schreiter intends to give place to local resistance as he also acknowledges that no local culture today is unaffected by global flows. Against Milbank's total condemnation of the global and the postmodern, Schreiter acknowledges both the significant improvements as well as the havoc this new phenomenon has brought. In Jameson's categories, Schreiter aims to negotiate between difference and identity as any theological method needs to locate itself between the local and the global. Let me then put forward two issues for discussion within Schreiter's project: (1) his use of intercultural hermeneutics, and (2) the notion of "universal theology" and "catholicity."

First, Schreiter posits intercultural hermeneutics as the framework of theological method in our multicultural global context. In intercultural interaction, there are three crucial factors which need to be taken into account for communication to be effective: the interlocutors (speakers and listeners), the context and the message. For instance, the attitude or behavioral qualities of the speakers or listeners (e.g., openness, knowledge of other cultures, ability to empathize or to tolerate ambiguity) are as crucial to enhancing communication of the message across cultural boundaries as they are between persons. The familiarity both speaker and listener have with each other's cultural contexts and the different ways in which the message is expressed (e.g., ideas, acts and signs) are all decisive in the communicative exchange. The aim, therefore, is *intercultural communication competence*, that is, how to effectively transmit the message in a way that does not violate the cultural codes of the other. In the theological context, Schreiter demonstrates that a viable theological method should foster the skills of acquiring such competence to be able to proclaim the Gospel more effectively in times when cultures rapidly blend and merge. In our discussion of the unevenness of globalization, this seems too "ideal,"

---

[71] R. Schreiter, *The New Catholicity* (Maryknoll: Orbis Books 1997).

thus, also an unrealistic framework. For all his talk of "disruptive experience" and "asymmetry" as the foundation of theological reflection,[72] Schreiter ends up glossing over these with his adoption of intercultural communication theory – a paradigm which is also derived from *interpersonal* communication research.[73] What is neglected in interpersonal communication models, asserts Bourdieu (in his polemics with speech-act theorists), is the effect asymmetric power produces on the whole interaction.[74] To communicate effectively, one does not only have to ascertain the clarity of the message, its content and meaning, and its transmission between the interlocutors in their differing contexts, one also has to include the power relations between them into the intercultural equation, such as for example, between a doctor and a nurse, manager and labourer, or United States and the Philippines. What impedes the communication of the gospel, for instance, is not only the cultural differences that separate the missionary from the so-called "native" but also the unequal positions of power that show themselves in their discourses. Unless this asymmetry is addressed, intercultural communication will never be successful regardless of the competence both speakers and listeners possess. As Schreiter appropriates into theology Appadurai's category of "global flows," he also imbibes it with the same framework of "soft" theory of cultural diasporic mobility in the vain hope that this disruption transforms the imagination and engenders resistance. Yet without a theory that accounts integrally for asymmetrical power, Schreiter will not have the theoretical resources to resolve the dilemmas he finds himself in – e.g., between the violence unleashed by globalization and his longing for an "ontology of peace"; between the phenomenon of "two Churches" divided by economic injustice and his insistence on "reconciliation" as its solution[75]; between the recognition that liberation theology is a positive development as a "theological global flow" and his contrary assertion that developing liberation theology in Europe seems "to miss the mark."[76]

---

[72] Schreiter, *The New Catholicity*, 59, 93.

[73] Schreiter, *The New Catholicity*, 28, 235.

[74] Bourdieu, *Language and Symbolic Power*.

[75] Schreiter, *The New Catholicity*, 78, 60.

[76] Schreiter, *The New Catholicity*, 20, 86 n3.

The second theme which I see as problematic in Schreiter's theological method is his notion of "catholicity" and the need for a "universal theology." He started his analysis of contemporary global culture with the discourse of fragmentation, change and plural diversity. One finds references to "glocalization," "creolization," "hybridization" and "tiempos mixtos" all of which give the impression that globalization is not a homogenization of the world. Even in theology, "global theological flows" – contemporary theological movements with quite diverse concerns as liberation, gender, ecology and human rights – are anti-systemic processes which call into question the universalizing hegemony of Western rationality. Thus in the globalized view of the world, theological reflection is "a study in surprise, in turning up the unexpected, in celebrating the small victories, for the experience of a globalized world lies in its peripheries, in the moments of risk and change, in the celebration of survival of yet another day."[77] This is only at the start. In the end of his work, however, Schreiter's discourse shifts to terms like "new universalism," "catholicity," and a "new type of universalizing theology" necessary in a "World Church."[78] "Faced with the diversity of cultures and the implications of taking them seriously, and the challenge of maintaining the *unity and integrity of the Church worldwide*, the eschatological sense of catholicity ... takes on new salience at the interface of the global and the local."[79] We may ask why this concern for unity and integrity when the context is one of diversity and asymmetry? From whose perspective has this need arisen? Who has an interest in universalism? To ask again as Bourdieu and Williams do, does not the search for global "universal forms" betray the social location of the intellectual who can only see universals because s/he oversees the reality from some objectivist perspectives, him/herself more mobile than most people? Aloysius Pieris's comments on the book's back cover are unwittingly quite revealing: "Robert Schreiter, as in his previous works, looks

---

[77] Schreiter, *The New Catholicity*, 59.

[78] Schreiter, *The New Catholicity*, 116-1\33. This universalist discourse could also be found in other parts of the work. For instance, he alludes to Pannikar's and Krieger's proposal for a "new universalism," (45, 58). Or, in the context of the ontology of violence, he asks (60), "Can a non-dominative form of universalism be found?"

[79] Schreiter, *The New Catholicity*, 128.

from his observation tower and monitors all the main movements of humankind ...."[80]

Conclusion: Towards Theological Reflexivity

The argument of this paper is simple: if we want to understand what globalization is and, in this new context, seek to explore a viable theological method, let us bring our analysis back to the rough ground where people struggle to survive. This direction in effect calls for greater reflexivity on behalf of intellectuals (in our case, theologians) who, because of their specific sociocultural, economic and professional locations, are not really there with them where the action is. To think and "theorize" about historical praxis also means to retreat from it and to abdicate its urgency, threats, surprises and uncertainty. In other words, intellectuals (of which all of us are or still intending or pretending to be) by the mere fact of being intellectuals, have ceased playing the game, turned themselves into observers, frozen the action, as it were, in order to recount it. Such a social location bears an impact on theoretical frameworks, as my earlier analysis of globalization theories and theologies shows. I do not, however, disavow the need for theorizing and reflection. These theoretical representations of the people's praxis should be accompanied by the realization that they are mere representation; that they can never fully account for what happens on the rough grounds. As liberation theologians love to assert: "Theology (as reflection) is only a second act; the first act of which is *praxis*." That is why theological theory needs "reflexivity," to use a term from Bourdieu. Or in more pious parlance, "theology needs much modesty,"[81] to quote Felix Wilfred. For theological *theoria*, even as it is indispensable, has to recognize that it always falls short of the surprises of *praxis* – those often muted voices of resistance in peoples and the silence of an emaciated God revealing Himself or Herself in the concrete faces of today's "wasted lives."

---

[80] See Schreiter, *The New Catholicity*, back cover.

[81] F. Wilfred, "Response to Questionnaire," in R. Fornet-Betancourt (ed.), *Theologie im III. Millenium – Quo Vadis?* (Frankfurt: IKO-Verlag für Interkulturelle Kommu-nikation, 2000), 298-301.

Georges De Schrijver SJ

Economic Globalization and the Ethical Debate

Globalization can be defined by the flow of capital which makes inroads everywhere. "The increasing volume and rapidity of the flows of money, goods, people, information, technology, and images"[1] draw the various parts of the world together to form "the global village." Trade and financial transactions are now freed from the constraints once imposed by the nation state. This is expressed in the names by which the corporations of the "postmodern" era are identified – "transnational corporations" and "multinational corporations" – which, besides the stock markets and the banking world, are the main private actors of economic globalization. At the same time one ought to keep in mind the geopolitical constellation. For the moment we are living in an American cycle in which the US, the strongest military force today, is acting as the policeman of the world. There are already indications, however, that the next cycle will be an Asian one. Think of Japan and the four East Asian Tigers –South Korea, Taiwan, Hong Kong and Singapore – and more recently of the rise of China and India. Yet, even this geographic data alone does not yet give us a complete picture. In addition, one ought to mention the activities of the International Monetary Fund (IMF), the World Bank (WB), and the World Trade Organization (WTO), for these organizations are instrumental in shaping the economic world order. This new world order is shaped by the "dogma" of the free market.

This article will examine the phenomenon of the neo-liberal free market, as it is endorsed by the WTO, the IMF (and to a lesser extent by the WB). First I will sketch the geopolitical context in which these institutions must be understood. It is my conviction that what we call "economic globalization" has, to a large extent, been the project of the US government after the Second World War, much more so than that it has been the result of European colonization. Following this, I will

---

[1] M. Featherstone, *Undoing Culture: Globalization, Postmodernity and Identity* (London / Thousand Oaks / New Delhi: Sage Publications 1995), 81.

present the workings of these institutions. This is followed by a critical assessment of them by Joseph Stiglitz, the author of *Globalization and its Discontents*. Part four presents the view of the Belgian economist Riccardo Petrella who issued a warning against the "pitfalls of globalization." Part five, finally, reviews some philosophical questions posed to globalization by the Cuban-German thinker Raúl Fornet-Betancourt.

Geopolitical Context: The Immediate Antecedents of Globalization

In his work *The Long Twentieth Century*[2] Arrighi pays close attention to the Marshall plan (1947) which was meant to bring Europe and Japan firmly into the American sphere of influence after the Second World War. This incorporation was planned by the US government with the aim of making its own financial and military powers grow with the help of two geopolitically important allies who were to be remade in the "image of the US." Crucial in this respect was the creation of the Bretton Woods Institutions: the World Bank and the IMF. Here, too, the US government, with the support of the British government, took the initiative: "At Bretton Woods bankers and financiers were conspicuous by their absence. Washington rather than New York was confirmed as the primary seat of "production" of world money."[3] A major objective of these institutions was to link the exchange rates of the local markets to the parity of the dollar, and to keep the dollar stable through its linkage to the gold standard. Too many fluctuations in the financial markets would have impeded the rebuilding of Europe and Japan. I will treat this respective rebuilding separately.

As far as the reconstruction of Europe is concerned, it was accompanied by an invasion of US corporations. The US economy at that time followed the Fordist-Keynesian model which entails a highly centralized and standardized production system. The US government

---

[2] G. Arrighi, *The Long Twentieth Century* (London / New York: Verso, 1994).

[3] Arrighi, *The Long Twentieth Century*, 279.

could count on the loyalty of its domestic entrepreneurs and businessmen. For, unlike the European countries, the federal states in the US were not caught up in mutual competition. Moreover, the American economy was rather "autocentric,"[4] not excessively dependent on the import of products from abroad. This "autocentric" character served the interests of the US well, for the model was solid enough to be exported – in the form of transnational corporations (American enterprises often act as Trojan horses, able to destabilize other systems).

At the same time the US banks sought to exert control over the European banks which struggled to emancipate themselves. Indeed, very soon Europe developed a flourishing Eurodollar market, where dollars earned in Western Europe were traded. These "Eurodollars" found their way to the Bank of England at the expense of the banks of New York, thus escaping the control of the US. Let us note in passing that in order for the communist countries to keep up their "dollar balances" in trade with the West, they deposited these funds in European banks out of fear that they might be confiscated by the US. So, a rescue operation had to be undertaken. The largest New York bank entered the Eurodollar market, and, by 1961, had acquired a 50 percent share of the Eurodollar business. In this light one ought also to see the creation of the European Community (EC) in 1965 (rendered effective in 1967): the aim was to establish a completely integrated common market and an eventual federation of Europe (European Union).

It was during this period that US banks entered the "offshore" world financial market. This set the tone for US corporate capital – soon to be followed by Eurodollar capital – to engage in foreign direct investment on a global scale. This led, on the emerging scene of globalization, to a competetion between Europe and America. In their commerce with their former colonies the European corporations were even to outcompete US-based transnationals. So, the US government felt the need to intervene, the more so because "control over world liquidity had begun to shift back from public to private hands."[5] In 1973, President Nixon decided to uncouple the dollar from the gold

---

[4] "Autocratic" means that all the "constituent elements – branches of production, pro-ducers and consumers, capital and labor etc – are integrated organically into one national reality." Cf. Arrighi, *The Long Twentieth Century*, 281.

[5] Arrighi, *The Long Twentieth Century*, 308.

standard. This resulted in a pure dollar standard that could fluctuate in relation to the values of other currencies. It allowed the US to release an overabundant supply of dollars, "thus providing the means for the self-expansion of US capital not just at home but abroad as well."[6]

This measure boosted American business, and made the US competitive again in the market against Europe and Japan between 1974 and 1979. If necessary the government – in connivance with the United States Federal Reserve – could depreciate the exchange rate of the dollar. This would make the export of American products – included those of the US multinationals – cheaper abroad. The direct victims of this depreciation of the dollar were the Third World countries, since most of their transactions were done in dollars. In order to hedge against the financial losses flowing from the devalued US dollar, these countries had to borrow money from European banks, the World Bank and the IMF, and to pay high interest rates for the money borrowed.[7]

The year 1973 was also the year of the first oil crisis. This crisis affected the whole world, although by 1979 the average cost of oil in the US was still a good 40 % below market levels. This crisis prompted the US to orient their geopolitical interest to the Middle East – to Iran, Kuwait, Saudi Arabia – and – as the two Iraq wars have proven – also to Iraq. But other measures also had to be taken. By the end of the Carter administration (1977-81) the US had tightened its financial policies. There was a plea for more state intervention instead of loose money policies, whereas means had to be sought to divert the worldwide circulation of liquidity again to the US. Ronald Reagan (1981-89) brought this program to full realization. He, first of all, raised the interest rates well above the level of current inflation. Second, he decided to give pecuniary incentives to recentralize mobile capital in the US. This gave "US and non-US corporations and financial institutions a virtually unrestricted freedom for action in the

---

[6] Arrighi, *The Long Twentieth Century*, 310.

[7] As to the US-based transnationals, they had to diversify their production to arm themselves against possible risks in the market. This coincided with the replacement, within the US, of Fordism with more flexible and diversified modes of production: See D. Harvey, *The Conditions of Postmodernity* (Cambridge and Oxford: Blackwell 1990), 147.

United States."[8] Third, he initiated one of the most spectacular expansions of state debt in history. During his administration the federal budget deficit quadrupled.[9] Fourth, he used the money earned from the debt to escalate the cold war with the USSR, and engaged in punitive actions against unfriendly regimes of the Third World – Granada, Nicaragua, Libya and Panama.[10]

Ten years after the Vietnam War, which it lost in 1973, the US under the Reagan administration, was again able to show America's clout, resulting in the disintegration of the East Bloc in 1989. From this point forward, it has become commonplace to hear the US referred to as "the policeman of the world." The trauma of September 11, 2001 only had the effect of intensifying this role with George W. Bush's crusade against "the axis of evil." This culminated in the Afghan war (which was also about oil) and the toppling of Sadam Hussein without the consent of the UN. These events are still fresh in our memories.

I now turn to Japan and its hinterland. Japan's rebuilding must also be seen in the context of the cold war, namely its strategic position with respect to communist China. The eastern aspect of the Marshall plan consisted of the reconstruction of Japan and its former colonies, Korea and Taiwan (Manchuria had gone back to China). It aimed at an integration of these regions into the US sphere of influence – regions that had been making significant advances down the path of industrialization since the 1930s.[11] Moreover, Japan and its former colonies did not have to spend money on a standing army, since they were denied the right to have one. Instead, the US military was in place to

---

[8] Arrighi, *The Long Twentieth Century*, 316.

[9] Arrighi, *The Long Twentieth Century*, 316: "When Reagan entered the White House in 1981 the federal budget deficit stood at $ 74 billion and the total national debt at $ 1 trillion. By 1991 the budget deficit had quadrupled to more than $ 300 billion a year and the national debt had quadrupled to nearly $ 4 trillion."

[10] Arrighi, *The Long Twentieth Century*, 317.

[11] Already in the 1930s Japan had started to industrialize its "colonies": steel, chemicals, hydroelectric facilities in Korea, and Manchuria, automobile production in Manchuria and factory employment and mining in Taiwan. So the US aid to Japan, Korea and Taiwan did not start from scratch.

defend the US national security, as can be seen in the Korean War (1950-53), which led to the division of North and South Korea.

In the 1950s, the US promoted the separate integration of Japan and its former colonies into its network of trade and patronage. Also starting in the 1960s, the US worked out a plan for integrating South Korea and Taiwan into the Japanese economy.[12] These countries opened up their frontiers to trade with Japan. The US government sought to strengthen Japan for strategic reasons. It saw to it that Japan became a member of the GATT, and had privileged access to the US market.[13] The more the US engaged in warfare (and the tremendous expenditures this entailed), the more Japanese firms were invited to procure, at lower costs than were possible within the US economy, the means of war and livelihood for their "hegemonic patron." Japan served the interests of the US by helping it in its pursuit of world domination.

The docile relationship with the US cooled down in 1971 when the Japanese government was asked to revaluate the yen, and to open up the Japanese economy to foreign capital and trade. Japan reacted in its own way. The imposed revaluation of the yen led to tremendous losses. To make up for it, however, Japanese economic planners decided to apply their system of subcontracting networks to select East Asian locations – Singapore, Hong Kong, Taiwan, and South Korea (the countries that would later be called the "four Tigers"). This transborder operation incorporated the surrounding region within Japan's own network.

The Japanese subcontracting system is multilayered.[14] It consists

---

[12] Arrighi, *The Long Twentieth Century*, 340.

[13] The US protection of Japan went so far that it closed the Japanese economy to foreign private enterprise.

[14] In the 1970s the US economy replaced the centralized system of Fordism in favor of a more flexible, diversified mode of production. This more flexible system can also be called a system of subcontracting networks, in that e.g. the electronic components of a sports car are produced in one sub-company, whereas the coach work is made in another sub-company. In this flexible system, however, there is an built-in limit to the proliferation of sub-companies because of strong subordination to the top managers.

of primary subcontractors (who subcontract directly from the top layer), secondary subcontractors (who directly subcontract from secondary subcontractors), tertiary subcontractors, and so on, until the chain reaches the bottom layer which is formed by a large mass of households that subcontract simple operations. Without the assistance of all these subordinate layers or formally independent subcontractors ... Japanese big business would flounder and sink.[15]

This system is very efficient because it creates, so to speak, a family relationship between the "parents companies" and the "child subcontractors" which allows for cooperation, mutual loyalties, and long term planning.[16] It is this flexible system that Japan transplanted to its hinterland. In the beginning South Korea, Taiwan, Singapore and Hong Kong organized their labor force so as to serve as secondary and tertiary subcontractors to Japan-based companies. By the mid 1980s, however, as rising wages undermined the comparative advantages of the four Tigers in industrial production, "enterprises from these states joined Japanese business in tapping the still abundant and cheap labor resources of a poorer and more populous group of neighboring, mostly ASEAN, countries."[17] The four Tigers began to set up their own subcontracting system stretching to regions with still cheaper labor forces in Thailand, Vietnam, and parts of China.

During the Reagan era Japan continued to comply with US requests. It oriented its capital to the US to alleviate the latter's internal fiscal imbalance. It also let its policy of bilateral aid programs be dictated by the US, pumping money into states the US deemed of strategic importance, such as Turkey, Pakistan, Egypt, and Sudan. Furthermore, Japan did nothing to upset US dominance in high finance. Although it knew of the mechanisms by which the US enticed a great many Latin American countries into external debt and bankruptcy, Japan continued to follow the US guidelines: the US government had

---

[15] Arrighi, *The Long Twentieth Century*, 342.

[16] One ought also to mention the working of powerful trade companies, the *sogo shosha*, who provide raw material, and if necessary also financial and marketing assistance to their own networks of medium and small firms.

[17] Arrighi, *The Long Twentieth Century*, 347.

decided to bolster the IMF and the World Bank to handle the financial crisis, "and Japan readily agreed to increase its contributions to these organizations in ways that did not significantly alter their voting structure."[18]

This benevolent attitude began to change in 1987, when the US devalued the dollar and forced Japan to revalue the yen. At that time, the world of Japanese banking and high finance suffered tremendous losses because of money invested in the US. So, Japan stopped its money flow to the US, and redirected it to the Asian hinterland: "Having lost enormous amounts of money in the United States, Japanese capital finally discovered that the largest profits were not to be made in a futile attempt to take over US technology and culture or in financing the US's increasingly irresponsible military expenses. Rather, these profits were to be made in pursuing more thoroughly and extensively the exploitation of Asian labor resources."[19] Betting on the Asian miracle, rather than continuing to co-finance the US's military crusades, became Japan's decisive option from the 1990s onward. Japan was no longer willing to serve its "hegemon." As early as 1988, it had stood up against US regulations for handling Third World debt. In 1989 the Bank of Japan raised interest rates, which led to a massive withdrawal of Japanese-owned money from the US. In 1990, in spite of US opposition, Japan succeeded in raising to second place its voting share in the IMF. All these are indications that the next economic cycle will be Asian. Japan and the East Asian Tigers can boast of a tremendous financial expansion. Yet, since they had no significant military power, they still had to act "with the consent of the organizations that control the legitimate use of violence on a world scale"[20].

IMF, World Bank, and GATT (WTO)

The above sketch – in which I have not examined the recent rise of two new giants, China, and India – allows us to situate the workings of the IMF, the World Bank and the WTO. The Washington based

---

[18] Arrighi, *The Long Twentieth Century*, 349.

[19] Arrighi, *The Long Twentieth Century*, 351.

[20] Arrighi, *The Long Twentieth Century*, 353.

IMF and World Bank, as well as the GATT (now called WTO) originated in the period of the Marshall plan (1947). The World Bank and its sister organization, the International Monetary Fund, were created before the end of the Second World War by the US and Great Britain at Bretton Woods, New Hampshire in 1944. Together they are referred to as the Bretton Woods Institutions or BWIs. They were geared towards bolstering the postwar world economy. The General Agreement on Tariffs and Trade (GATT) was first signed in 1947. The agreement was designed to provide an international forum that encouraged free trade between member states by regulating and reducing tariffs on traded goods and by elaborating mechanisms for settling trade disputes. GATT served as a vehicle for dismantling protectionism and for initiating a global free market system. It "left in the hands of governments in general, and of the US government in particular, control over the pace and direction of trade liberalization."[21]

From the outset the Bretton Woods sister institutions had different functions. Whereas the IMF acts as an international institution of surveillance in fiscal matters – overseeing the safety of the fiscal policies of the states so that economic growth and full employment can be guaranteed, the World Bank set for itself the task of facilitating postwar (and later also postcolonial) reconstruction – by lending money for financing the development of infrastructures, such as railways, roads, canals, ports, dams, etc. In fact, the sister institutions work together, for the IMF also acts as a bank. Via the quotas of its member states, and transactions with various banks, the IMF also possesses a pool of money that can be used to help these member countries in case of balance of payments deficits. These countries receive loans to relaunch their domestic economies and to eliminate their deficits. A fine example is South Korea. In December 1997 this country got a loan of $21 billion from the IMF and with this money it was able to "restore financial stability by early 1998 and strong growth the following year. And Korea repaid the IMF ahead of schedule."[22]

However, serious strings are attached to the IMF loans. The receiving countries are obliged to implement reform programs – the so

---

[21] Arrighi, *The Long Twentieth Century*, 72.

[22] R. de Rato y Figarede, "The IMF at 60 – Evolving Challenges, Evolving Role, IMF External Relation Department, June 14, 2004," http://www.imf.org/external/np/ speeches/2004/ 061404.htm.

called Structural Adjustment Programs (SAPs) to restore financial stability, and it is for these programs that the IMF has earned a lot of criticism, especially from developing countries. The core of the criticism relates to the free market ideology which the IMF shares with the WTO (World Trade Organization, the new name for GATT). And, some critical voices remark, this free market option is beneficial to the economic expansion of the US, and of the G7 countries (US, Canada, Japan, France, Germany, Italy and the United Kingdom). It comprises: liberalization of commerce and trade, encouraging the production of export-oriented goods, clearing the ground for direct foreign investment, privatization of state-owned or state-controlled services (such as the railways, the telephone system, and the water supply) and state-owned industries (petrochemical industries and others) in order to ease the way for new flows of capital and for the generation of more wealth. Moreover, free market ideology seeks to reduce the role of the state, especially in less rich and developing countries, so that these countries will "open up" to the influx of foreign capital. This explains why the WTO wagers a battle against protectionism – protectionism through the levying of high tariffs or by granting government subsidies to agriculture – as this is the case of the European Union. It also explains why the IMF insists that the state should stop spending huge amounts of money on hospitals, schools and social services.

To restore the balance of payment disorder, the IMF imposes two sorts of conditionalities. First, fiscal austerity: the state must refrain from "unnecessary" spending, including spending on social services, health care, and schooling. This spending should be kept within limits (for to the extent that the state acts as the great benefactor, laziness is propagated, which erodes the spirit of free initiative among the citizens). And, second, to boost the economy fresh flows of capital and foreign direct investment should be ushered in. Enhanced circulation of money is believed to flow from free trade, privatization of state-owned services, and liberalization of hitherto closed economies and financial markets.

Joseph Stiglitz's Critical Assessment

A considerable number of action groups have protested against this state of affairs. One of them is "Global Exchange," which published a letter "How the International Monetary Fund and the World Bank Undermine Democracy and Erode Human Rights" (Sept 2001).[23] In it one finds the accusation that the SAPs often serve the interests of international investors – and the economic interests of the US – more than the needs of the local communities.[24] This accusation is substantiated in an article written by Joseph Stiglitz. Stiglitz is a senior fellow in economic studies, and was from 1996 until 1999 the chief economist at the World Bank. He takes a retrospectively critical look at what the IMF, in tandem with the US Treasury Department, did to counter the Asian crisis at the end of the 1990s, and says "I was appalled." Below is a short review of his text.[25]

---

[23] One might object that this letter more reflects moral indignation than real expertise in what the Bretton Woods Institutions stand for. As a matter of fact, it puts the IMF and the World Bank on the same footing, which is strictly speaking not correct. The fact however remains that in order to be eligible for becoming a member of the World Bank, the country in question must first become a member of the IMF. This means that in any case IMF imposed conditions to its loans.

[24] In this letter one reads the following: "The institutions have forced debtor countries to cut social spending on health, education, and other public services. They have pressured poor nations to charge their own citizens for the use of public schools and public hospitals. And they have demanded that countries keep their wage levels low, a policy which harms ordinary citizens but benefits multinational corporations. In compelling countries to adopt such policies, the IMF and the World Bank have not only threatened communities' right to social security; they have also undermined the countries' democratic systems .... As soon as government officials begin worrying more about what Wall Street will think than what their own people think, democracy has been perverted." Cf. http://www.globalexchange.org/campaigns/wbimf/imfwbReport 2001. html.

[25] J. Stiglitz, "The Insider: What I learned at the World Economic Crisis," in *The New Republic* (April 17, 2000), http://www.globalexchange.org/campaigns/wbimf/stiglitz 041700.html. Stiglitz is also the author of *Globalization and its Discontents* (New York: Norton & Co, 2002).

What comes out in his assessment is that the personnel of the IMF think in macroeconomic terms; they work out universal devices that must apply to each and every country, wherever situated and in whichever circumstances. Their approach is primarily theoretical, and – Stiglitz adds – relies on outdated economic theories and methods of mathematical calculation. The World Bank, on the contrary, is more pragmatic and attaches much more importance to expertise than to theories. It studies the social stratification of a country, its microeconomic situation (bankruptcies and fear of default), and how economic activities are done on the spot. This implies that, from the standpoint of specialists in the World Bank, the austerity measures dictated by the IMF are much too standardized to be able to have a positive effect in a particular setting. Stilglitz gives three examples in which the IMF policy failed: Thailand, Indonesia, and the former Soviet Union. At the same time, he underlines that the IMF always has the support of the US Treasury Department for the implementation of its policies, and this raises the question as to whether the IMF is, indeed, as "impartial" as it pretends to be.

First, let us consider Thailand. Together with other East Asian countries (Korea, Hong Kong, Singapore, and Taiwan), this country "came off a miraculous three decades: incomes had soared, health had improved, and poverty had fallen dramatically. Not only was literacy now universal, but, on international science and math tests, many of these countries outperformed the United States. Some had not suffered a single year of recession in 30 years."[26] Yet, on July 2, 1997, the global economy crisis started in Thailand. The seeds of this calamity, Stiglitz continues, had already been planted in the beginning of the 1990s, when East Asian countries, under international pressure from, among others, the US Treasury Department, had liberalized their financial and capital markets. There was absolutely no reason for this liberalization, since they did not need to attract more funds (savings rates were already 30 percent and more).

In all these countries, these changes provoked a flood of short-term capital – capital that looks for the highest returns in the shortest time – and led in Thailand to an unsustainable real estate boom, a bubble that was to burst in the shortest time: "Just as suddenly as capital flowed in, it flowed out. And, when everybody tries to pull their

---

[26] Stiglitz, "The Insider."

money out at the same time this causes an economic problem, a big economic problem." So, the root cause was not imprudent government, but an imprudent private sector – "all those bankers and borrowers who'd gambled on the real estate bubble."[27] The IMF, however, blamed the government and imposed its stock remedy: fiscal austerity (balanced budgets) and tighter monetary policies (including higher interest rates). Sitglitz says he was skeptical about these measures, for

> under such circumstances, I feared, austerity measures would not revive the economies of East Asia; it would plunge them into recession or even depression. High interest rates might devastate highly indebted East Asian firms, causing more bankruptcies and defaults. Reduced government expenditures would only shrink the economy further.[28]

And this is exactly what happened.

Stiglitz uttered his concerns to some senior staff members of the IMF, but they responded that the board of executives left them no other choice than to impose austerity measures – whereas members of the board complained that the staff pushed them in that direction. Furthermore, everybody in the IMF assured him that if certain measures turned out to be contractionary, they would reverse the policies. "This sent shudders down my spine," Stiglitz says, "for one of the first lessons economists teach their graduate students is the importance of lags: it takes twelve to 18 months before the change in monetary policy shows its full effects."[29] The effects of a miscalculation can only be observed when it is too late. This brings Stiglitz, who has himself been a professor of economics in Oxford, Stanford, Yale and Princeton, to declare that the IMF never succeeded in recruiting any of the best students of these universities. When finally informed by the IMF that all it was asking from the East Asian countries was that they balance their budgets in the face of recession, he almost became desperate. He recalls that the Clinton administration fought a battle with Congress to allow the US to have some deficit spending in the face of

---

[27] Stiglitz, "The Insider."

[28] Stiglitz, "The Insider."

[29] Stiglitz, "The Insider."

recession, and that this was precisely what economists had been teaching for more than 60 years to their graduate students: recession can only be withstood by means of momentary deficit spending. The IMF, however, seemed not to have understood this lesson.

He then turns his attention to Indonesia, with its multiracial population, where the crisis had spilled over. As a representative of the World Bank, he had, at a meeting in Kuala Lumpur, advanced the idea that an excessively severe monetary and fiscal program in Indonesia could lead to social and political turmoil. Michel Camdessus, then managing director of the IMF, ignored this warning and argued that Indonesia needed a short-term pain in order to emerge from the crisis stronger, as this had been the case with Mexico. Yet, Stiglitz exclaims, there is no analogy between these countries. Mexico became stronger not thanks to the austerity measures of the IMF but thanks to its membership in the NAFTA (Free Trade Agreement between US, Canada, and Mexico). There happened to be an economic boom in the US, and so Mexico could profit from a surge of exports to the US. But Indonesia's situation is different, for its principal trade partner is Japan, and precisely at that moment, Japan also suffered from a recession. Here again, Stiglitz observes a lack of in-depth analysis. Indonesia was in a much more explosive social and political situation than Mexico, and the IMF overlooked this.

> A renewed ethnic strife would produce massive capital flight (made easy by relaxed currency-flow restrictions encouraged by the IMF). But none of these arguments mattered. The IMF pressed ahead, demanding reductions in government spending. And so subsidies for basic necessities like food and fuel were eliminated at the very time when those subsidies were more desperately needed than ever.[30]

By January 1998 the economic situation in East Asia had become so bad that the World Bank's vice-president for Asia spoke of a calamity in that part of the world. Yet the US deputy Treasury Secretary told him not to dramatize the situation. This made Stiglitz muse over what the IMF and the US Treasury Department are in fact doing. Are they really serving countries with difficulties in the world, or are they pursuing their own interests, even by destroying the local social fabric

---

[30] Stiglitz, "The Insider."

if necessary? What happened in Russia is a case in point. After the fall of the Berlin Wall two schools of economics in the US began to study what should be done in the event that the Soviet Union disintegrated. One school, having historical knowledge of the Russian situation, insisted on the need to develop an institutional infrastructure to regulate the market economy – such as legal structures that enforce contracts, and regulations that make a financial system work. The other school opted for shock therapies and massive privatization. The IMF and the US Treasury Department were eagerly receptive to what the latter school had to say, and the result is known. Russia began a sell-out of its state owned enterprises, of which only some mighty tycoons took advantage, whereas the rest of the population was reduced to poverty. Russia's money had gone to Swiss banks and other fiscal paradises.

Riccardo Petrella on the Pitfalls of Globalization

Thus far, I have treated globalization mainly from a geopolitical standpoint. I have also presupposed awareness of the fact that telecommunication has come to play an increasingly important role in the "world as global village." Without telecommunications – faxes, e-mails, internet, and cell phones – one could hardly communicate so rapidly with, and receive information from, geographically distant regions of the globe. I did not dwell on this electronic infrastructure since a lot of studies have already focused on this issue, but also because these studies tend to exalt an already unified world,[31] whereas in reality this allegedly "unified world" is full of disparities. It is only by calling attention to these disparities that ethical concerns come to the fore.

In Stiglitz we have seen how fiscal politics are far from innocent, and that they often thrive on power struggles. At the end of his assessment Stiglitz returns to this question. As an American with a great deal of expertise with regard to economic policies, he cannot help but ask why the dealings of bureaucrats in the IMF are wrapped in such extraordinary secrecy – unwilling to listen to others or of letting them-

---

[31] R. Schreiter, *The New Catholicity: Theology between the Global and the Local* (Maryknoll: Orbis 1999).

selves be questioned. Could it be, he asks, that underneath their policy of lending money to countries in need there is the hidden agenda of fortifying the economic and financial position of the superpowers? And that this accounts for the undemocratic character of the institution? "Economic policy is today perhaps the most important part of America's interaction with the rest of the world. And yet the culture of international economic policy in the world's most powerful democracy is not democratic."[32]

In his groundbreaking essay "the pitfalls of globalization" (*Ecueils de la mondialisation*) Riccardo Petrella, professor of economics at Louvain-la-Neuve (Belgium), wrestles with this same problem of the undemocratic decision making processes in the financial and economic centers of the world. For him, the capitalistic "world of affairs" is not democratic, but totalitarian; "it elevates criteria employed in capitalistic economics to the standard and norm of what is good, useful, and necessary in the economy *and also elsewhere.*"[33] Consequently, the nation states are forced to live up to the requests of the "world of affairs," and nearly all states comply with it:

> they regard it as their principal goal to promote the integration of their country into the global economy. All things are subordinated to this finality: investment policies, technological innovations, policies of labor market, schooling, and universities, rules of commerce, fiscal policies etc.[34]

This is what the old core member countries of the European Union have been doing; it is also the aspiration of the new members who formerly were part of the communist Eastern Bloc.

Since higher performance in technology is the motor of economic growth, technological advance has become the ally of the neo-liberal free market. This leads to an enhanced competition among universities (some of their faculties having links with industries), and specialization in electronic means of communication. It also encourages the

---

[32] Stiglitz, "The Insider." Cf. ftnte. 25.

[33] R. Petrella, *Ecueils de la mondialisation: L'urgence d'un nouveau contrat social* (Montreal: Editions fides / Quebec, Musée de le civilisation 1997), 8. Italics mine.

[34] Petrella, *Ecueils de la mondialisation*.

creation of high quality services and manufacturing of high quality goods. In short, there hardly exists an escape from integration into the global market. This state of affairs is not only presented as a fact, Petrella adds, it is also supported by three ideological principles that have remodeled the economic and sociopolitical system of our countries in the last twenty-five years: the liberalization of the market, the deregulation of the economy, and the privatization of key services.

Liberalization is the supreme dogma from which the other two dogmas derive. This all started with the uncoupling of the dollar from the gold standard under President Nixon in the early 1970s. From that time onwards, the flow of money could ease in and out of the US with unprecedented facility. Free movement of capital throughout the whole globe became the hallmark of business. Moreover, this freedom defines all other freedoms: freedom of property, freedom of enterprise, freedom of commerce, freedom of innovation. Infringement on the free market also implies infringement on all other freedoms. So, the state is expected not to place any hindrance upon these freedoms. On the contrary, it must endorse this trend by furthering the privatization of all that possibly can be privatized: "banks, insurances, air lines, trains, metros and tramways, water, gas, electricity, hospitals, universities, schools, professional formation."[35]

According to this ideology it is no longer the local state that oversees politics; this role has been taken over by the financial centers – the IMF, the World Bank, and National Banks. They tell us what the state must do to obtain zero inflation, and a balance of payment equilibrium; they also insist on reducing fiscal pressure on capital to attract private investments, and on cuts in public and social expenditures. In 1996 at the meeting of the "World Economic Forum" in Davos (Switzerland) the president of the German Central Bank made it clear that "the political leaders must realize that in the future they will be subject to the control of the financial markets."[36]

The financial world, thus, arrogates to itself the right to intervene in the internal affairs of the state, thereby forgetting – Petrella adds – that (according to a study by the Bank of England in 1995) only 10 % of the financial transactions go to the creation of new wealth whereas the rest is purely speculative money – speculating on the difference

---

[35] Petrella, *Ecueils de la mondialisation*, 16.

[36] Petrella, *Ecueils de la mondialisation*, 18.

between real and anticipated prices in various currencies. Yet, the financial centers are eager to have a say in the real economy from which they are, in fact, dissociated.

At the same time, the world of commerce is eager to show its clout. The WTO puts forward various clauses – social, environmental, and democratic. It arrogates to itself the right to use the weapon of economic blockage whenever a country disrespects democracy and human rights (whatever this might mean), or when it does nothing to prevent environmental depletion, or when it neglects the basic rules of social rights. Yet these clauses, Petrella observes, are full of ambiguity. It might seem as if the WTO is concerned with issues going beyond the purely economic, yet, it by no means possesses the instruments for mending these abuses. He says: "One cannot confer to commerce and trade the role of regulating the social, human, and democratic development of the planet."[37] These matters pertain to the community of world citizens. Only a new social pact among them – and not the cult of competition – will be able to resolve questions such as the right to work, sustainable develoment, and respect for political and civil rights.

All this shows that the role of the state is seriously undermined. It is no longer up to the parliament to fix their agenda; this task now falls to the private sector. Business groups, like Bangemann, have already sent recommendations to the European Council, the main decision-making body of the European Union, on how to shape Europe into a global information society, thus keeping this important decision entirely in the hands of the private sector. This not only deals a deathblow to the actual functioning of the nation state; it also exposes the citizens to the management of industrial and financial centers. The citizens are no longer treated as members of a social community with civil rights, but as commodity-like resources, to be used, replaced or laid off at will. Unemployment and poverty of the "socially excluded" become a serious problem in the US and also in Europe (in 1994 13.9 million poor were registered in Great Britain among a population of 60 million).

Moreover, the stress on individual performance is going to erode the sense of human solidarity. The social security system is seen as too costly. Whoever falls "out of the boat" will be left behind. This is

---

[37] Petrella, *Ecueils de la mondialisation*, 21.

the "logic" of neo-liberalism which is already well on its way to dismantling the European welfare system. This dismantling is being justified as follows: citizenship, it is said, cannot be the basis for entitlement to social rights. Such a right can, as a matter of fact, never be permanent: it must be earned: it can be granted but also taken away. When insufficient finances are available for public spending, one looses one's claim to social benefits. This rule of thumb, Petrella remarks, is full of contradictions, because, for all of the complaints about the shortage of money, the financial markets take pride in their financial health.[38]

The dismantling of the welfare state in Western Europe is only one example. Whole regions of the world – most of the countries in sub-Saharan Africa – are left out of the boom of economic activities. Or, worse, the liberalization of markets obliges them

> to orient their economy towards the production of goods destined for export, as this is almost totally the case with the agricultural produce, food, textile, energy, etc. All this results in the augmentation of poverty in these countries; it largely increases the misery and hunger in the world.[39]

With this background in mind, Petrella launches an alternative plan for doing economics, one which first of all calls into question the premises of neo-liberalism. In 2020 the world population will reach 8 billion, and the neo-liberal economy will not care about the poorest of them. So, it is nonsense to invite all the nations of the world to step into the neo-liberal global market. What really ought to be done is to determine the principles, rules and institutions to guarantee that "those 8 billion people become citizens capable of satisfying their basic needs in matters of drinking water, housing, food, energy, health, education, information, transport, communication, artistic expression, and participation in the decision making processes of the community."[40] The question is thus: "On what basis and through which means will one be able to produce the wealth of the world community?"[41] Real

---

[38] Petrella, *Ecueils de la mondialisation*, 30.

[39] Petrella, *Ecueils de la mondialisation*, 32.

[40] Petrella, *Ecueils de la mondialisation*, , 39.

[41] Petrella, *Ecueils de la mondialisation*.

concern for this "world community" is not to be expected from an ideology that is only interested in the creation of private wealth.

The issue of water is a case in point. One cannot leave the exploitation of water in the hands of private companies that use this precious property of the earth as a commodity to be sold on the market in order to increase the capital of a predatory company. Water exploitation must be communally organized, by all those who live around an important river, for example: inhabitants, peasants, industrial enterprises, environmental action groups, public authorities, and the tourist sector. Only a communal management in view of the common good can really take care of this patrimonial good.

The new economic project must be based on a social contract among the citizens of the earth. At the same time efforts must be made to disarm the neo-liberal financial forces through worldwide coordinated actions undertaken by progressive economists. Four strategies must be developed.

1. The introduction of a Tobin tax (0,5% on financial transactions), the revenues of which will go to a Global Fund for Citizenship that will use them to finance a fair distribution of water on a world scale, and to supervise other domains where the global communal wealth of the earth is at stake. Levying this tax is technically possible, provided that the G7 decide upon its introduction collectively.

2. The elimination of the 37 fiscal paradises that directly contribute to the "increasing criminalization of the economy (fiscal evasion, speculation, drugs traffic, illicit trade in weapons)."[42]

3. Abolition of the secrecy surrounding the banking industry. This is a precondition for developing "a progressive fiscal policy, based on social justice and solidarity among individuals and generations."[43]

4. The credit rating of countries must no longer be left in the hands of private firms of financial experts who in the privacy of their offices determine which countries will be on the top of the list of creditworthy nations. In July 1996, for example, Italy took decisive steps to cut in state expenditures. On this account its credit rating rose from A3 to AA1.

---

[42] Petrella, *Ecueils de la mondialisation*, 42.

[43] Petrella, *Ecueils de la mondialisation*, 43.

These measures must be accompanied by the creation of a Global Council for Economic and Financial Security. Its major task would consist in "redefining the rules of a new global financial system (the Bretton Woods of the 21st century) and in seeing to it that its funds go to development and well-being of the whole world population."[44] In the new financial order technologies should be developed, not just for profit, but to allow human beings to satisfy their basic needs on a world scale. These important measures would put an end to the growing gap between wealthy top billionaires and the destitute masses.

Fornet-Betancourt: Asking Philosophical Questions about Globalization

Raúl Fornet-Betancourt, a Cuban philosopher who works in Germany for the Scientific Institute *Missio Aachen*, bases his analysis on a subversive reading of Hegel's *Phenomenology of the Spirit*. Hegel wanted to grasp the "spirit" of an epoch through the various – often contradictory – changes that took place in the transition from mercantilism to the bourgeois free market. Fornet-Betancourt pursues the same aim. He wants to lay bare the "spirit" that propels the further transition from bourgeois free market to the actual phase of globalization. But unlike Hegel (and taking his lead from Marx) he does not exalt this new "spirit" but is rather critical of it.

Nonetheless, he shares with Hegel the same empirical starting point: one has to start from an analysis of the new facts in order to deduce from them the new "spirit." These facts are: 1. A permanent expansion of knowledge and technology in the service of steady economic growth.[45] 2. A boom in the means of electronic communication that facilitates action from a distance. 3. Dominance of transnational actors over the dealings of the nation states. 4. A drastic restructuring of the domains of finances, economy, and research, but also of forms

---

[44] Petrella, *Ecueils de la mondialisation*, 44.

[45] R. Fornet-Betancourt, "Die Globalisierung aus philosophischer Sicht," in R. Fornet-Betancourt (ed.), *Kapitalistische Globalisierung und Befreiung* (Frankfurt: IKO Verlag für Interkulturelle Kommunikation, 2000), 72.

of life.[46] 5. The shaping of a global world in which events in one part of it have a direct impact on all the other parts: globalization is both a factor of coordination and of fragmentation.

Fornet-Betancourt takes these facts from sociological studies but he regards them only as the context from which to delve into the "spirit" of the epoch. For him, sociological studies tend to turn a blind eye to the ideology of the free market, which they fail to carefully analyze. Fornet-Betancourt is a leftist philosopher trained in ideology criticism.

In fact, the term ideology has already surfaced in the studies of Stiglitz and Petrella. Stiglitz made it clear that the insistence of the IMF – in line with the WTO – on the liberalization of the market was not value free, but geared towards the political interests of the superpowers that benefit from it. Petrella, in turn, questioned the inevitability with which the ideology of the free market is presented, as if all the nation states had no other choice than to integrate their economies into the global market.

As far as Fornet-Betancourt is concerned, he explicitly calls attention to the deceptions of the free market ideology. Whereas globalization is promoted as a worldwide process, it is in fact nothing else than "a restructuring of the economy in the interests of the actual three major economic regions: the US, Europe, and Japan [with the new Tigers in South and Southeast Asia]."[47] One has rather to do with a "triadization" than with a "globalization" of the world. Even when this process is described as a growing "interdependence" of the world, this terminology conceals the asymmetry of power which is at work in it.

In addition to the techniques of concealment, Fornet-Betancourt also points to the free market's propaganda machine that endeavors to lure the whole globe into assimilating the worldview or "metaphysics" of neo-liberalism. With Martin Heidegger he defines "metaphysics" as the horizon from which we have to understand all of our relationships in the world.[48] He finds that this is exactly what neo-liberal ideology

---

[46] Fornet-Betancourt, "Die Globalisierung aus philosophischer Sicht," 70.

[47] Fornet-Betancourt, "Die Globalisierung aus philosophischer Sicht," 64.

[48] Fornet-Betancourt, "Die Globalisierung aus philosophischer Sicht," 75. More technically, "metaphysics is the historic background against which a decision is taken about the relations of the human persons with Being as such and as a whole," with reference to Martin Heidegger,

aims at: "with its totalitarian ideology neo-liberalism wants to determine the horizon from which we have to understand all our relationships in the world – including the relationship to that what we would like and ought to be."[49] Neo-liberalism annuls all previous definitions of the "good life." With a tremendous power of seduction it offers a new model of the "good life"– a model that is flly controlled by the economic logic of the system, and not by human persons (in spite of the appeal that is made to individualism in shaping one's life)."[50]

What is propagated is a real "anthropological revolution," one that is much more alarming than the social and ecological disasters that one is wont to associate with this new metaphysics. Even Habermas was not radical enough when speaking about the "colonization of the world in which we live," that is of our social and cultural environment. What is at sake is the "colonization" of our very hearts and minds: it is a transformation of the conditions of our lives: of our "becoming subjects" as human persons.

Fornet-Betancourt is deeply concerned about the demise of the "subject" as the ultimate decision-maker regarding the question of grounding a fully humane society. He fears that this responsible "subject" is going to be eroded, disfigured, and hypnotized. For instead of promoting a subject whose growth depends on community-oriented decentering of the Ego, what is encouraged now is a human subject focused on the acquisition of private property, and whose contacts with the world and to others take on a mercantile relationship.[51] Fornet-Betancourt is rather pessimistic about the future, for he understands perfectly that the neo-liberal ideology needs this "anthropological revolution" to assure its own hegemony. As such, no means will remain unutilized to achieve this goal. On the other hand, he believes that resistance to the system is possible. He refers to the mushrooming of protest movements, such as "alternative globalization from below,"

"Nietzsche: der europäische Nihilismus" (1940), in M. Heidegger, *Gesamtausgabe*, vol. 48 (Frankfurt: Klostermann 1986), 208.

[49] Fornet-Betancourt, "Die Globalisierung aus philosophischer Sicht," 76.

[50] Fornet-Betancourt, "Die Globalisierung aus philosophischer Sicht," 76.

[51] Fornet-Betancourt, "Die Globalisierung aus philosophischer Sicht," 77.

The World Social Forum,[52] and movements for the promotion of democracy and human rights.

He gives these new movements full credit. Yet, as a philosopher in the tradition of critical ethical humanism (Herder, Marx, Sartre, Levinas, Dussel) he invites these movements to a radical break with the neo-liberal way of life to whose tentacles they have already partly succumbed. How can a truly democratic society emerge, he asks, when the citizens have put up with being reduced to consumers? It is only by asserting themselves as responsible subjects that they will be able to stand up for their collective human rights. Or, to take another example, how can an alternative "globalization of solidarity" come off the ground, unless it is carried out by persons who regard praxis of solidarity as an essential and not just accidental part of their "being in the world"? This again presupposes a rediscovery of oneself as a responsible subject with empathy for the victims in history.

The deepest motive in Fornet-Betancourt's ethical consideration is the scandal of asymmetrical power relations. For him, the ethical debate on globalization must focus on this question: how is it possible that so many people are not given a chance to benefit from economic growth, while others live in sheer abundance? And, secondly, what has to be done to stop this scandal? The beginning of an answer to this latter question can surely be found in Petrella's program of a new social contract among the citizens of the earth.

By Way of Conclusion: The Legacy of the European Enlightenment

The thesis of this article is that economic globalization is basically a post-Second World War phenomenon, and not just the continuation of the economic expansion under European colonialism. To substantiate

---

[52] The World Social Forum (WSF) is an open space for discussing alternatives to the dominant neo-liberal processes, for exchanging experiences and for strengthening alliances among mass organizations, people's movements, and civil society organizations. The first WSF was held in 2001 in the southern Brazilian city of Porto Alegre. Subsequent meetings took place in Porto Alegre (2002), Hyderabad (2003), Mumbai (2003), and Porto Alegre (2005). It is attended by circa 100,000 people.

this view I have delved into the immediate antecedents of globalization: the US steered reconstruction of Europe and Japan (its hinterland included) after the Second World War. Instrumental to this are, besides the Marshall plan, the working of the Bretton Woods Institutions – IMF and World Bank – and the WTO. In connivance with each other these institutions set out to propagate the "free market" all over the globe. This spreading, however, is never disconnected from geopolitical interests of the US and, to a lesser extent, the G7. And this can, of course, lead to underhanded dealings and the implementation of hidden agendas. Especially with regards to the IMF it became evident that fiscal policies are hardly neutral and value-free. The Structural Adjustment Programs (SAPs) attached as strings to loans often serve the interests of the financial world more than the interests of the countries in need, at the expense of the real development of the poor (health care, literacy). This already raises the ethical question as to the extent to which Third World Countries are getting a fair treatment when they are forced by foreign planners to enter the neo-liberal global market.

Yet, our analysis also made it clear that European citizens are, in a sense, not better off. Here, too, the financial world dictates what governments have to do to incorporate their economies into the global market. At this point an erosion of democratic institutions can be observed as well as the citizens' reduction to the role of peonies on the chessboard of economic planning and the consumer market. It is time, therefore, for conscientized citizens to stand up and to protest against all sorts of attempts at using purely economic standards and norms to define what the "good life" is about. They can hereby fall back on the European heritage. True, the *homo economicus* is an offspring of the European Enlightenment. Yet, the Enlightenment program cannot be reduced solely to the imposition of economic logic. It also, and perhaps more so, comprises the culture of open and public discourse on human values and norms. European Enlightenment is also the cradle of the birth of democratic societies in which the citizens discuss the social arrangements that must be made to guarantee the common good in an egalitarian society. It is this aspect of the European Enlightenment that nowadays continues to inspire all those who commit themselves to the emergence of an alternative "globalization from below." This is the case with Petrella's program of a new social contract among the citizens of the earth, and with the activities of the World Social Forum.

Norbert Hintersteiner

The Postcolonial Claim for Culture: Inculturation and Africanism

In the second half of the twentieth century, intercultural theology has searched for appropriate means to address the intercultural problematic created by the expansion of Christianity into Africa. It saw these means in the proclamation of culture through the construction of local religious identities and African theologies, developing along the lines of inculturation and postcolonial discourse. This essay seeks to show that inculturation not only belongs to and operates from within the historical context of the postcolony, but also that its deliverances are unintelligible outside the discursive practices by which the postcolony itself is constituted. Since Africanism as a cultural claim is operative in both discourses, I argue that inculturation represents a discursive "postcolonial" African response to the intercultural colonial problematic.

Preliminary Remarks

First, let me indicate why I think it is necessary to link inculturation to postcolonial discourse. There are several reasons why such a link is required: thematic, political and methodological. Many of the thematic concerns regarding inculturation are shared by postcolonial theory. Both discourses tend to be oppositional; both are concerned with the impact of colonialism on the culture, traditions and worldviews of formerly colonized territories and with the reactions and responses of colonial subjects to their historical plight. Politically both seek to make sense of how the current global political and cultural situation can be understood as, in some crucial respects, the result of previous colonial relationships.

Methodologically, if inculturation is to avoid theoretical redundancy, it will need to be conscious of its own discursive context in the way that postcolonial discourse is since many of the themes which it addresses such as: culture, the interface between indigenous knowledge and Western systems of thought, the relation of the past to the present, liberation, difference and otherness, etc., have all been thoroughly debated in postcolonial theory.

Because inculturation has ignored developments in postcolonial theory, it repeats certain errors of identity, culture, and the nature of colonialism itself. It also remains uncritical of the ways in which it continues to be dependent upon colonialism, the ways in which it produces the colonial. Only by exposing itself to some of the critical insights of postcolonial theory, will it be able to rid itself of its self-willed naivety. To expect inculturation to be consciously and critically cognizant of its postcolonial context is to expect it to speak with both integrity and intelligibility: integrity because as part of the historical context of inculturation, postcolonialism cannot honestly simply be set aside; intelligibility because the possibility of inculturation itself and thus its significance as a project depends on the history of colonialism out of which the postcolonial has emerged as both memory (anamnesis) and protest.[1] Furthermore, linking inculturation to postcolonial theory is also a way of showing how the former is a historical outgrowth of a protracted discursive process, providing the grounds for a possible account of its genealogy and of how it is unconsciously positioned by colonialism.

If it is true that all human utterances are shaped by their social and historical context, then to insinuate a colonial and postcolonial background for inculturation is to make out some of the ways in which it is shaped by its context.

What, then, is the relationship between inculturation and postcoloniality? Were the answer to this question to depend solely on the rather infrequent invocation of the concept of postcoloniality, then it might, at least on the face of it, seem that there is little connection between these two discourses. Such disconnection might indeed seem to be "ideologically" confirmed by the historical emergence and association of the practice of postcolonial discourse within the Western academy and its paradigmatic *ratio*. As such it can be dismissed as simply one more instance of neo-colonialism.

Here I wish to set the context for the ways in which inculturation may be understood as part of a more general set of articulated discur-

---

[1] On the concepts of integrity and intelligibility in theology's relation to other disciplines, see D. Ottai, "Christian Theology and Other Disciplines," in *The Journal of Religion* 64/2 (April 1984): 173-77.

sive practices formed and represented via the rhetorical figures of postcolonial discourse, Christian theology, and Africanism.

Postcolonial Discourse and Inculturation

I will begin not by offering a positive definition of postcolonial theory – a largely fruitless task if we take seriously the extent of the contestation over the meaning of the term – but by outlining some of the chief objections that have been advanced against it. I wish ultimately to argue that the pitfalls of postcolonial theory describe the discursive character of a practice whose identity is methodologically comprised of a complex blend of contradictions, conflicts, antinomies, compromises and acts of resistance. Postcolonial discourse is not free of all of these ambiguities since it is the case that the realities which it describes and explains were themselves fundamentally constituted by them. Second, I shall raise the specific question of how inculturation can be positioned in relation to postcolonial theory. My interest is to show that inculturation is a species of postcolonial discourse which operates through a certain cultural claim, for example as a mode of African self-identification, and whose character is necessarily mediated through some of the basic tensions and ambiguities of postcolonial theory itself. Third I shall deal with some theological challenges and opportunities which my characterization of inculturation presents.

Objections to the Postcolonial Discourse

First, do we now live in a postcolonial world, and if so, in what way, and if not, in what respect is the claim that we do misleading? The term "post" literally designates an "after" and intimates a real "beyond" and thus seeks to say something about the end of formal colonialism and its political and cultural aftermath. However, its current signification is complicated by the fact that since the official retreat of colonialism, the global realignment of economic and social forces in international politics (so-called globalization) continues to be marked by deep inequities in the distribution of power and wealth. Formerly colonized countries have disproportionately carried the burden of these injustices. Scholars today hold that the history of the injustices which these inequalities have produced can more or less be traced back to colonial times. Indeed, globalization itself can be seen as a historical product of certain long standing processes which have their basis in colonial relationships. After all, colonialism itself was a powerful globalizing project which – through religion, specifically Christianity, and the political economy of capitalism and cultural domination – literally extended to the very ends of the earth. No doubt, for this reason globalization is regarded by many of its critics, especially in the "Two Thirds World," as an agent of neo-colonialism.

On this view, a view that I roughly share, globalization operates in an essentially deterritorialized mode to iterate, repeat and reproduce the social, economic, and cultural imbalances which once characterized imperial rule without the territorial and spatial ambitions of earlier forms of colonialism. Thus to describe globalization as an agent of neo-colonialism is to understand the latter as consisting of the means by which a past history of oppression is iterated, how the effects of that iteration are configured and deployed into new patterns of global domination and the tactics and strategies of resistance that it consequently engenders. Of course, none of this should in any way be taken to suggest either an unbroken line of continuity between globalization and colonialism or some sort of direct, unqualified recapitulation of an ontologically actualized history of power which can only now be reproduced – without cancellations and recreations – in the present.

My main point is that the "post" in postcolonial discourse is far from delineating a movement of complete transcendence of the boundary between different chronotopic mutations of the same history of power which is also the history of the same; it locates the possibility of redescribing new power relationships in terms of the "after" intimated by the "post" thereby making it possible for us to take seriously both their past and as well as their present. The "after" can only be understood through its generative "before" and its outworking in the present. It is perhaps for this reason, to provide one example that Abiola Irele's discussion of the nature of African discourse begins with some of the earliest moments of protest in the eighteenth century and extends to the present.[2] A second objection against the term

---

[2] A. Irele, "Dimensions of African Discourse," in K. Myrsiades and J. McGuire (eds.), *Orders and Partialities: Theory, Pedagogy and the Postcolonial* (New York: SUNY 1995), 17.

"postcolonial" is its provenance and continued citation at Western academies in the metropolitan centers of Europe and America. Although colonial knowledge of the other was produced in many places outside the academy – government records, memoirs of explorers, the correspondence of colonists, after dinner speeches, etc., – and although the colonial archive is therefore, far more extensive than is represented by scholarly productions, it was above all in the academy that the most assiduous and systematic attention was given to rewriting the history of colonial others in order to make it correspond to and buttress the interests of imperial masters.

Disciplines such as history, anthropology, theology and even ecology came to play an important role in providing intellectual justifications for the postcolonial project. It was in the academy that the colonial subject became an object of study and new forms of knowledge became possible. Anthropology itself, it has been observed, acquired its theoretical sophistication in this context. Given all this, some have argued that postcolonial theory privileges the disciplinary practices associated with the history of Western power. It is the connection between knowledge and power encoded in the word discipline itself which allows for the privileging of the products of the Western academy.

If we inquire into the form of this privileging three things stand out. First is the privileging of accounts of knowledge of colonial relationships at the expense of indigenous and native worldviews. The term colonial in the "postcolonial" exhibits this. Second, the term "post" privileges a certain history and its mode of historical consciousness as well as its techniques of organizing history by breaking it up into periods; it privileges time by reducing what is significant about the other's past to what is only datable from the moment of this other's encounter with colonialism; and it privileges it by demeaning any attempt to recover anything that existed prior to that encounter as essentialist nativism – and all this at the expense of the power dynamics that constituted the actual relationships which were the material expression of that encounter in the first instance. Third, postcolonial theory privileges the elitism of its practitioners who, for the most part, tend to be white, predominantly male, Anglo-American and middle class. Contrary to what the prevailing culture of political correctness and its liberal ethic of an often contrived multicultural diversity in the university might lead us to believe, this elitism is not offset but is rather reinforced by the considerable presence in the Western academy of diaspora intellectuals – such as `Two Thirds World` Theologians in Europe – from formerly colonized countries some of whom have made substantial contributions to the rise and development of postcolonial theory.

There are other objections that have been leveled at postcolonial theory such as that it is a homogenizing, essentializing and universalizing discourse; homogenizing because it ignores the manifold variety of colonial histories; essentializing because it regards the identities of all colonial subjects as metaphysically possessed of a single unifying essence; and universalizing insofar as it proposes a generic representation of colonialism which covers all instances in all places.

All these objections would seem to suggest that the term "postcolonial" is unserviceable and should thus be jettisoned. I wish, however, to argue a very different case here.

First if we take seriously the ambiguities, tension and antinomies that constitute the basis for the above objections we shall see that virtually all oppositional discourses – but especially those sponsored by academics and other intellectuals – are historically positioned by the quality of a certain movement of time, a historicism, if you wish, in which their existence can no more be explained outside the presupposition of Europe's encounter with the other than the historical mutation of that encounter into present relations of global domination can be wished away. Either we accept the impossible idea that nothing has changed since the first encounter took place or we recognize that colonialism was itself a network of historical movements which divided time in terms of a "before" and "after," a division which was not unknown to its victims. To deny any division between the "before" and "after" of colonial time in the name of political sensitivity is not only to freeze colonial relations in the synchronic space of an ever present domination, it is also, in the end, to display the most condescending political insensitivity. Does not such a denial privilege the colonial by insinuating its eternity? This in fact would seem to be the reverse side of an eminently modernist strategy. Modernism, in its fear of the past, installs the present and the future as the eternity of endless progress.

If politics and power are ceaselessly played out in historical time, if human existence is always bounded by time and produced in and through time, then genuine political sensitivity can only take the form of sensitivity to the work of time.³ The denial of the "after" of the "post" in postcolonialism is also politically dangerous because it freezes the agency of the colonial subjects by evacuating it of any *trans*formative possibility. If those who were colonially subjugated did in fact confront colonialism through various acts of the cunning of indigenous thought such as feigned accommodation, open revolt, mutiny, struggle, and resistance, then either their efforts were productive of some change or colonialism always triumphed. The first option is attested to by the demise of direct official colonization which, it turns out, happened in many places against the will of the colonizer. That this demise involved, as we have already hinted, the forced metamorphosis of colonialism into newer forms of domination should not be allowed to obscure the fact that the space vacated by the former became the opportunity for the emergence of new societies, new cultural experiments and new political institutions. It is the emergence of these that constitutes the postcolony.

Locating Inculturation: Religion and the Post/Colonial

If one accepts these arguments regarding postcolonism, then the second option about the perpetual triumph of colonialism against the insurgence (agency) of the colonially subjugated falls away, while the need to locate inculturation firmly in the postcolony arises. But to situate inculturation in the postcolony in this way is to define it in terms of a trajectory of the "before" and "after" of colonialism.

In particular, it is to give inculturation the practice as a postcolonial identity whose genealogy originates, for example, in Africa's cultural confrontation with Europe's negation of Africa's difference and otherness and whose present form is a discursive reassertion, within the context of the end of official colonialism, of that same difference and otherness. Inculturation represents the specifically religious or theological reassertion of such a cultural memory.

For example, it is predicated on the fact that one of the most distinctive features of the postcolonial situation in Africa today is the

---

3   On the work of time see J. Fabian, *Time and the Object: How Anthropology Makes its Other* (New York: Columbia University Press, 1983).

massive presence of Christianity. Such a substantial presence did not, of course, always exist. When one peruses the missionary record one is struck not only by the violent charges of intractable heathenism but also by the frequent complaints of many missionaries regarding the resistance of natives to convert to Christianity.

Today the story is quite different: conversion has become a routine occurrence as is evidenced by the astonishing growth of African Instituted Churches (AICs), the persistent grip of "traditional" forms of denominational Christianity and the overwhelming appeal of Pentecostalism throughout the continent. Whatever gradual role Africans themselves played in popularizing Christianity, it seems clear that the presence – though not necessarily the current numerical strength – of Christianity in Africa is in some significant measure a historic testimony to the success of missionary effort. Of course, this statement pertains only to the contribution of missionaries in introducing Christianity but not to the present-day shape and content of the latter's African identity.

Today, the quest for African identity lies at the heart of the project of inculturation understood here as the attempt by Africans to create a form of Christian self-understanding that is informed by an "anticolonial" recuperation of their own varied cultural traditions. Its "anticolonial" thrust and, as I shall argue here, its location and largely implicit participation in the discursive practices of postcolonial theory, tie it to the history of colonialism.

As is well known, invoking the figure of the missionary and the establishment of Christianity in Africa necessarily involves recalling the largely positive relationship between Christianity and colonialism as the formative setting of Africa's historically fraught encounter with modernity, for it was in the context of colonialism that missionary activity came to fruition. Furthermore, to recognize the connections between missionaries and colonialists as well as the far-reaching presence of Christianity in Africa is to refuse a false secularism that has infiltrated both local and global official (elitist) perceptions of Africa. According to these perceptions the most significant historical problems of Africa pertain to the failure of the political state, the problem of development, the allocation of resources, the proliferation of civil wars and the introduction of mimetic democracy. Of course, what these perceptions mask is the fact that none of these problems is fully comprehensible without the acknowledgment of the constitutive role religions, Christianity, Islam, and African traditional religions, have played in defining the terrain on which colonial relationships were performed and out of which the postcolonial itself emerged.

The reality is of course that religion has been and continues to be a colossal force for social transformation – sometimes as a protest against colonialism and sometimes as a response and adjustment to the failure of the African experiment. If religion has always been constitutively central to colonial and postcolonial relationships, then clearly the postcolonial or the postcolony is structured by religious imaginary.[4]

While this does not authorize the conclusion that the colonial project was itself a religious project, I want to suggest that in Africa both the moment of colonialism as well as its "aftermath" – now popularly referred to as the "postcolonial" – were profoundly marked if not driven by the conjectural dialectic of religious and political motives through which it operated and was constituted. To assign a religious identity to the postcolonial means taking this "dialectic" seriously; thus the privileging of political and economic accounts in official perceptions of Africa often obscures the fact that the history of the postcolony is at the same time the history of its problematical constitution as a more or less thoroughly religious entity.

The principles of its configuration, the social and cultural institutions that mediated it into being, the "doxological" statements that enunciated its necessity, the discursive archive in which is inscribed its formative memory, the objects of its popular and academic attention and the hermeneutical modalities of its self-expression are all, in one way or another, fundamentally defined by a constitutively generative religious imaginary.

I call this "Colonial Christendom." Let us take "Colonial Christendom" provisionally to mean simply the conjunction between colonialism and Christianity. For the moment, I simply want to posit "Colonial Christendom" as a complex and largely positive relation between colonialism and Christianity. I mean by positive not only that

---

[4] The postcolony is a representative code, a sign of the historical institutionalization of the end of direct colonization as the (re)production of multiplicity in forms of life. On the postcolony see, A. Mbembe's definition in his *On the Postcolony* (Berkeley / Los Angeles: University of California Press, 2001).

the relation in question is characterized by a certain historical facticity but also that it was generally constituted by the "happy" interplay of the logic of a reciprocal transference of the otherwise different motives, impulses and goals of each side of the relationship into the everyday content of that relationship thereby producing a sort of dialectic of mutual interests: to civilize (colonialism) and to missionize that is, to convert natives from paganism to Christianity. Lest I am charged with a simplistic view of relations between missionaries and colonialists, I want to stress here the contingent, indefinite, excessively multiple and ultimately slippery nature of the motives, impulses and goals of both missionaries and colonialists both in relation to each other as well as in relation to colonized subjects.

Of course, the historical consciousness in whose name this religious imaginary functioned does not answer to a singular identity in any straightforward manner. Colonialism was only a part of it. But then so were the strivings (sometimes unto death) of the many missionaries who, on God's behalf, assumed the "white man's burden."

It was this conjunction that marked the encounter between Africa and the West, an encounter which involved strenuous efforts by missionaries to convert and to "civilize" natives by requiring them to set aside their social and cultural modes of being.

I am interested here in the reciprocal over determination of Christianity and colonialism in this encounter. This reciprocal over determination means two things: that the establishment of Christianity in Africa was often shaped, conditioned and mediated through colonial rationality and in turn colonial rationality was recurrently shaped, deployed and propagated by the Christian mission.[5] This historically contingent relationship has been perceived in Africa as largely negative for it instituted and actualized regimes of cultural, political and historical power which produced the social structures within which missionaries, colonialists and natives encountered each other and whose effects were the alienated relations which constituted the substance of that encounter.

---

[5] Mudimbe has gone so far as to speak of an "isomorphic" relationship between colonialism and Christianity. Cf. V.Y. Mudimbe, *Tales of Faith: Religion as Political Performance in Central Africa* (London / Atlantic Highlands: The Athlone Press, 1997), 148f.

Mudimbe has drawn attention to the various ways in which the category of the negative in African discourse is a response to Africa's negative encounter with its European other. He identifies three major moments of negation. The first involves the negation of African identities, the second, following Hegel, denies the possibility of African history and the third posits a totalizing logic consisting of Greek rationality, Western science and Christian ethics which excludes all other cultures that do not conform to it.[6]

That colonialists and missionaries abhorred and despised the social institutions and cultural beliefs of their subjects is now well known, as also, is the fact that both Christianity and colonialism were socially, culturally and historically disruptive. Both the mission to civilize which was part of the basic framework and driving principle of colonialism and the desire to convert natives to Christianity, the fundamental *telos* of missionary activity, sought to displace and reorganize African spaces in the name of new orders of social and cultural existence derived from and essentially modeled upon Europe as the inherent (and thus only) paradigm of authentic human sociality. In the areas of symbolic exchange, European cultures, religions and philosophies were rigorously proposed as the new categories for rethinking and apprehending reality, and through its power, Christianity ensured their gradual acceptance and appropriation.

In Search of a Postcolonial Response to a Cultural Crisis

What I am interested in here is the African response to all this. I want to argue that inculturation represents a discursive "postcolonial" African response to the "intercultural problematics created by the expansion of Christianity to Africa."[7] In other words, I am interested in inculturation as one way in which Africans have been critically responding to the sundry ways that missionary "ideology" and praxis has instituted new patterns of alienating cultural experiences which have eventually shaped African Christianity.

---

[6] Mudimbe, *Tales of Faith*, 147-48.

[7] Mudimbe, *Tales of Faith*, ix.

To take this seriously is of course to make sense of the distinction between the missionary contribution to the founding of Christianity and subsequent African elaborations of it and thus to reject the supposition of a possible historical rupture between the two. Inculturation is necessarily and simultaneously oriented in two different historical directions; the history of missions and the African reactions it elicited on the one hand, and on the other, the appropriation of both by contemporary African theologians.

The project of inculturation testifies to a crisis situated somewhere between the founding of Christianity and its subsequent elaborations by indigenous peoples so that any crossing from the one to the other turns out to be problematic.

Philosophically as well as theologically this crisis is one of consciousness, knowledge, rationality and cognition. Of course, in so far as all knowledge is necessarily reflective of the social conditions of its production, of the fact that the consciousness through which knowledge is mediated is always a cognized cultural product then the crisis is ultimately also a social and cultural crisis. The crisis originated in the radical interrogation and devaluation of traditional modes of thought by and through the colonial project. Writing on Nigeria – although his account is *mutatis mutandis* applicable to many parts of Africa – Olufemi Taiwo, has argued that one of the effects of colonialism and Christianity was to alter, disrupt and destroy what he calls "indigenous modes of knowledge production."[8] Taiwo notes that although the consequences of these disruptions on local economic and political structures have been the subject of much discussion, their significance for culture has been largely ignored. Thus Africanists have succumbed to a sort of "recurrent reductionism" whereby culture and cultural products are accorded the status of epiphenomenal manifestations of more structural (economic and political) orders.

Yet it is precisely in the realm of culture that the effectiveness of the colonial agenda is best evaluated, for it was there that new epistemic structures were created, new ways of being human were prescribed, new modes of perceiving and describing the world were preached and enforced and it was also there that the new myths of

---

[8] O. Taiwo, "Colonialism and Its Aftermath: The Crisis of Knowledge Production," in *Callaloo* 16/3 (1993): 880-904.

Christianity imposed a new moral consciousness and new forms of identity.

Indeed, the transformative success of the colonial project both in its economic as well as its political aspects was due to its ability to "prey upon local idioms to infiltrate the consciousness of the people and thereby secure wide acceptance for the concepts of justice and morality they [the political and economic aspects of colonialism] presuppose."[9] Perhaps one reason why the fate of traditional or indigenous modes of knowledge in modernity warrant serious critical attention is that anyone or any system that gains hegemonic control over them either by redefining them negatively as primitive, "other" and uncivilized or by transforming them into new social constructs and cultural practices via conversion and civilization as both missionaries and colonialists did, will have acquired the power not only to refuse the subjects of these traditional modes of knowledge the autonomy and to mint their own identities in their own idiom but also the power to force upon them foreign myths and metaphors for understanding reality. Lest it be thought that this amounts to nothing more than the projection of a hypothesis regarding what might be the case if only certain historical conditions obtained, I want to suggest here that contemporary arguments about the nature and status of indigenous knowledge along with the moral economies they presuppose and express are essentially about how, in modernity, political and economic power has been exercised through "ideology" or through the control of human identities and the means by which the latter are socially produced.

The colonial context provides some of the most direct examples of the operation of this sort of "ideological control." The devaluation of indigenous knowledge to which I have already referred can be seen as part of the pervasive attempt to clear up an epistemic (and thus cultural) space for such control. If the effects of colonialism and the missionary enterprise were as all-encompassing, insidious and even irremediable as many thinkers have suggested, and if it is the case that today we experience modernity (irrespective of our geographical location) as the totalizing impossibility to think other realities without the culturally and politically complex mediation of the domination of the

---

[9] Taiwo, "Colonialism and Its Aftermath," 894.

world by the West, then the question that confronts us pertains to that of opposition and resistance.

Inculturation and the Rethinking of African Identity

I have already hinted that African discourse emerged as a critical response to colonialism and Christianity. Let me now approach the African response to the effects of colonialism on African rationality in two ways. First I want to characterize it in broad terms, that is, in terms of Abiola Irele's notion of "dimensions of African discourse."[10] What is said about African discourse here covers a wide range of theoretical concerns: politics, literature, philosophy, theology and other symbolic products. Second, I want to narrow my characterization in order to focus specifically on inculturation. In this second move I shall argue that inculturation is a species of a much larger discursive practice made up of a variety of African efforts to rethink African identity.

Dimensions of Africanism

Irele describes various dimensions of African discourse in terms of the structure of this discourse as response. First of all African discourse – going back to some of the earliest moments of the African-European encounter – enunciated itself in oppositional terms, it took on what Irele calls "a movement of contestation" in which black humanity discursively pitted itself against the historical claims of Europe. The most distinctive thing about this aspect of the discourse was that it confronted one form of racial consciousness – white supremacist "ideology" with another – black/African nationalism. In this phase of its history, race and culture were effectively collapsed into each other.[11]

---

[10] Cf. A. Irele, *Dimensions of African Discourse*.

[11] Irele, *Dimensions of African Discourse*, 18. Although Irele does not make this point, it seems to me that the conflation of race and culture by Africans can be read as a mimetic practice whose conditions of possibility were already delivered and actualized in the manner in which Europeans themselves defined race: race was culture; race was all.

Whether through autobiography or through poetry (and historically, morally and metaphysically) Africans created a "poetics of aggression" which was and still is "adversarial in posture," "polemical in significance" and "combative in form."[12] Second, the African critique of colonialism consisted of an interrogation and critical assessment of Western civilization itself, its historical claims, its beliefs about and place in the world. Third, Irele argues that African discourse has been characterized by "a form of romanticism" or "an aesthetic traditionalism" whose two pillars are the assertion of a collective will and a historical recollection and reaffirmation of indigenous cultures, languages and worldviews. We can readily discern here the basis of the emergence of both the discourse of nativism as well as various forms of African nationalism. Thus as recounted by Irele, Africanism (another of his terms for African discourse) is much more than just a protest against the negation of African beings; it also represents a re-historicization in African terms of African traditions and cultures. Fourth, this Africanism has been carried forward by means of a refusal to privilege Western languages, literature and the "thought systems of the colonizer."[13] Fifth, Africanism is thoroughly "historicist" in its political practices, that is, the forms and content of its resistance are not constructed by abstract or theoretical idealizations of the Africanist project but by the politics of place and context. Sixth, running through all of the above moments of African discourses is a powerful thrust towards emancipation. Indeed, emancipation or self determination in politics and as well in culture is the ground motive that defines an African difference and organizes the forms of its resistance. Each of these features of African discourse, I shall argue, is not only exemplified by postcolonial discourse but also by inculturation.

Inculturation and Africanism

Let me, therefore, by concluding, suggest some of the ways in which inculturation is a species of the sort of Africanism I have been discussing. In doing so I do not, however, want to create the impression that

---

[12] Irele, *Dimensions of African Discourse*, 17.

[13] Irele, *Dimensions of African Discourse*, 21.

practitioners of inculturation have consciously carved out a distinctive discursive space within Africanism. In fact, one of my arguments is that African theologians generally and practitioners of inculturation in particular have, paradoxically, have tended to elide context and location while at the same time and rather uncritically operating with a very high view of both. This is self-evident in African theology's failure to engage scholarship in other areas of African studies.

In what respects, then, is inculturation an expression of Africanism? First, there can be no doubt that inculturation is an oppositional discourse whose goal is to resist and displace the epistemic claims of a Western-inflected Christianity. While African theologians have not been upfront about the relationship of their arguments against colonialism to similar arguments in other areas of African thought, it is clear that their aggressive methodological polemics against missionaries and, indeed, against all forms of Western theology correspond to the polemical and combative thrust of Africanism itself. Like the latter, the oppositional character of inculturation which these polemics inherently embody is predicated upon and is productive of a form of racial consciousness that assimilates culture into race and vice versa. As we shall see, it is because of this that nativism becomes an important feature of the identity of inculturation. Inculturation is predicated upon racial consciousness because it takes as a given that the dispute between Africa and the West is a racial dispute or at least one in which race epitomizes the essence of otherness and thus marks the parameters by which difference is contested and negotiated. It is productive of racial consciousness in so far as race, otherness and difference are not only assimilated into each other but are also consciously renegotiated in the light of the failure of inculturation to completely resist the effects of its "European other." Indeed, the very existence of inculturation as a kind of *espace métissé* attests to this failure and throws some aporias in the path of inculturation.[14] To assign methodological significance to the polemics *qua* polemics of inculturation is to do two things: first to postulate an epistemological basis for the acts of resistance which they call for and second, to recognize the extent to which these polemics organize a whole discursive field. From this perspective, it is wrong to reduce these polemics to the level of their tactical

---

[14] Mudimbe defines *espace métissé* as "a new mixed cultural order." See his *Tales of Faith*, 145.

and strategic function. It is important to worry about the relation of polemical discourses to knowledge because such discourses are often dismissed by academics as nothing more than "polemics."

The second way in which inculturation participates in Africanism is through its commitment to deconstruct the epistemic systems and beliefs of Western theology. We should of course be careful here for it is misleading to say that African theologians have been reading canonical works of Western theology and philosophy in order to apply to them the methods of deconstruction as one finds these in postcolonial writings. The deconstructive operations of inculturation are primarily political rather than textual – even where these are mediated though novels, poems and other written works. The text, understood here somewhat narrowly, is but a critical instrument with which to call into question some of the most fundamental aspects of Western culture; its view of humanity and justice, its modes of social organization and its theological and philosophical constructs. Thus for example, African theologians have consistently drawn attention to the contradictions and ambiguities of Western ideas of the human which excluded the humanity of non-whites or modes of Western social organization which lionized the individual often at the expense of community or, again, notions of Western justice's "universality" which was part of philosophical and mainline political orthodoxy although its conscious application was always carried out partially and in the interests of a few privileged colonialists. It seems, much of what African theologians have said about all this, has in general been rather unsophisticated, but I think that the contradictions and antinomies to which their polemics point are real enough.

At the specific level of theological practice it is possible to instance the work of someone like Charles Nyamiti[15] who has been reworking major Christian themes through African idioms, models and metaphors as embodying the sort of deconstructive operations that I am attempting to identify here. Without explicitly engaging the major texts of Western theology Nyamiti reworks central doctrinal *topoi*

---

[15] See the following works by C. Nyamiti, *The Scope of African Theology* (Kampala: Gaba, 1973); *The Way to Christian Theology for Africa* (Eldoret: Gaba, 1975); *African tradition and the Christian God* (Eldoret: Gaba, 1977); *Christ as our Ancestor: Christology from an African Perspective* (Gwer: Mambo, 1984).

such as God, Christ, Church, Holy Spirit, Eucharist, etc., by grounding them in indigenous structures of meaning thereby introducing into African theological discourse a constitutive suspicion about, on the one hand, the social and cultural relevance of the grammar, rhetoric and content of Western theology to non-Western contexts, and on the other, given the history of colonialism, about its political and social commitments *vis-à-vis* those contexts. This suspicion is part of the polemical structure of inculturation and is constitutive in the sense that from the very beginning it defined African theology as the expression of a sort of historical mistrust in Western Christianity, a mistrust whose justification is the history of missionary Christianity in Africa.

That the work of Nyamiti calls into question and displaces – or at least attempts to displace – standard Western categories by reconstituting their meaning in a rediscovered African idiom brings us to the third way in which inculturation is part of Africanism. In its positive, i.e. self-referential form, Africanism is, at least at one level, organized around what, as we have seen, Irele describes as "a form of romanticism" or "an aesthetic traditionalism." This is the attempt to recuperate the goods of a repressed, subjugated and travestied indigenous cultural memory. In inculturation this has taken the form of a celebratory "return" to all the elements of the African past before the advent of colonialism. This return is necessitated by a posited primordial purity of the African heritage and justified through the uses to which it is put to critique and remedy the alienating effects of a colonial modernity.[16] It is this "return" which has enabled the narratives of nativism and indigenism, both of which are central to inculturation. To be sure, there are all sorts of problems – essentialism, for one – with the notions of identity which such a putative return implies. What is important at this point is to see – and this is the fourth element of the Africanist identity of inculturation – that the nativist articulation of pure indigenism requires a more or less complete epistemological rupture with Western thought, its languages, literatures, philosophies and theologies.

Finally, inculturation is of a piece with Africanism in its emphasis on location and context. One of the pretensions of Western thought has been the idea that Western cultures are all shaped and driven by a

---

[16] Cf. R. Radhakrishnan, "Postcoloniality and the Boundaries of Identity," *Callaloo* 16/4 (1993): 750-71, for this understanding of the notion of "return."

universal rationality which can – and whose historical mission is to – subsume, purify and correct any aberrations such as are represented by non-Western cultures. The presumption was that these other cultures in their very "otherness" lacked rationality. This is a well known story which will not be repeated here. By emphasizing place and how all human cognitive and cultural practices are social conventions molded and shaped by the context in which they are produced, inculturation like the Africanism within which it is located, relativizes the universalist claims of the West. One important consequence of this is that the character of truth is no longer determined simply in terms of its supposed internal, that is, logocentric properties but in terms of its social functions as well. Truth becomes identified with place. Thus the adjective "African" in African theology or African philosophy takes on a conceptual significance which – both in the wake and aftermath of colonialism – refuses to deterritorialize thought because such deterritorialization obscures the fact that the spread of colonialism (at the level of thought, e.g. the colonization of native minds through Western ideas, as well as that of political practice) was itself predicated upon the acquisition of territories precisely in the name of the dominant territories of Europe.[17]

There are of course other ways of showing that inculturation belongs to the "after" of the history of the demise of that which enabled it in the first place. I said above that one of the strategies employed in its cultural dispute with the West is to invoke the possibility of a return to an African past undistorted by European contact. Although the possibility of such a return has been denied and affirmed by different theorists in postcolonial discourse, the fact that it is at all imagined in inculturation registers the latter's position within that discourse.

To summarize, I have been dealing with the relationship between inculturation and Africanism. I have tried to show some of the ways in which the enabling conditions of the former are to be found in the articulations of the latter and how the grammar of both is, in certain cru-

---

[17] On the relationship between thought and territoriality see G. Deleuze and F. Guattari, *What is Philosophy?* (New York: Columbia University Press, 1994), ch. 4.

cial respects, normatively structured by the lexicon of postcolonial theory. Since the above discussion has proceeded on a general and somewhat abstract level, I now wish to leave it to the readers' and local theological agents' concreteness.

Frans Wijsen

"The Future of the Church is in our Hands": Christian Migrants in the Netherlands

In his book *The Next Christendom*, Philip Jenkins has a section on "The New Europeans."[1] Looking at the rapid spread of mosques across urban Europe it would be easy to believe that Islam might be Europe's future religion, says Jenkins. Yet, a great many European immigrants are Christian, and they raise the prospect of a revitalized Christian presence on European soil. "People of African and Caribbean stock have revived Catholic communities in the metropolitan countries." Presently, "about half of all churchgoers in London are Black." Of course, "there is also the issue of harmonization." It is hard to predict "how far the children of immigrants will adopt the laxer and more 'modern' thought-ways of Europe." Yet based on the American experience it is likely "that new immigrants are commonly more religiously active than their forebears at home." Thus, "the process of secularisation is not yet that advanced, and for the next few decades, the face of religious practice across Europe should be painted in Brown or Black," says Jenkins.

In this brief paper I would like to deal with the following two issues: To what extent and in what way do the migrants' movements threaten feelings of identity and security? And how can theologians in Europe respond to these feelings? This paper comprises three parts. The first is sociological, addressing the first issue and focusing on integration and cultural identity. The next part examines the second question from the perspective of new mission theologies arising from projects providing a missionary presence among migrants. The third part deals with the same question from the perspective of migrant theologies arising from migrant movements. Finally, I will draw some conclusions.

In answering these two questions I rely heavily on the research that my co-workers and I have been doing since 1998 among Christian

---

[1] See P. Jenkins, *The Next Christendom: The Coming of Global Christianity* (Oxford: OUP, 2002), 96-99. All references in this paragraph are to page 99.

migrants in Europe, more particularly among African, Caribbean and Latin American Catholics in the Netherlands.[2] The Netherlands has a population of 16 million, of which 10 percent are non-Western migrants, roughly 50 percent of them being Muslims and 40 percent Christians. The expectation is that the group of non-Western migrants will approach 22 percent of the Dutch population by the year 2050.[3] Whether Jenkins' prospect of a predominant Black or Brown Christianity in Europe will come true is yet to be seen. The aim of this paper is not to review the debate on whether or not Europe is an exceptional

---

[2] See J. Maaskant, *Afrikaan en Katholiek in Rotterdam: waar kerk je dan?* (Nijmegen: Wetenschapswinkel, 1999); J. Maaskant, "Afrikaanse Katholieke Pinkstergelovigen in Rotterdam," in *Wereld en Zending* 28/4 (1999): 37-44; N. Adelesi, "Katholieke Migranten uit Afrika in Nederland," in N. Adelesi and F. Wijsen, *Afrika in het Jubileumjaar* (Nijmegen, 2000), 9-17; J.C. Guerra, "Interculturele kerkopbouw: Kerkvorming met Migranten," in C. Sterkens and J. van der Meer (eds.), *Kerk aan de stadsrand* (Budel: Damon, 2004), 191-214; J.C. Guerra, "Naar een theologie van de migratie. Context, perspectieven en thematiek," in *Tijdschrift voor Theologie* 44/3 (2004): 241-58; J.C. Guerra and F. Wijsen, "Multiculturele of interculturele liturgie?" in D. Broersen, *et al.* (eds.), *Ik loop hier stage* (Heeswijk: Dabar-Luyten, 2005), 85-102; J.C. Guerra *et al.*, *"Een gebedshuis voor alle volken": Gemeenschapsopbouw en kadervorming in roomskatholieke allochtonengemeenschappen* (Zoetermeer: Boekencentrum, 2006); J. Vernooij, "Going for Identity: The Case of the Creoles of Suriname," in A. Borsboom and F. Jespers (eds.), *Identity and Religion: A Multidisciplinary Approach* (Saarbrücken: Verlag für Entwicklungspolitik Saarbrücken, 2003), 155-84; J. Vernooij, "Migration and Interculturality: The Surinamese in the Netherlands," in R. Fornet-Betancourt (ed.), *Migration and interculturality. Theological and Philosophical Challenges* (Aachen: Wissenschaftsverlag Mainz, 2004), 199-224; F. Wijsen, "'Een vreemdeling is twee dagen gast ...': Afrikaanse Katholieken in Nederland en hun uitdaging aan theologie en pastoraat," in L. Boeve and J. Haers (eds.), *God Ondergronds* (Averbode, 2001), 161-74.

[3] See Wetenschappelijke Raad voor het Regeringsbeleid (Scientific Council for Government Policy), *Nederland als immigratie-samenleving* (The Hague, 2001), 48-53.

case and whether or not there will be a religious revival in Europe,[4] among others by the influx of Christian migrants from non-Western countries. My aim is a limited one, to open an emerging field of study, largely neglected by theologians in Europe, namely the study of Christian migrants, migrant churches and migrant theologies.

Integration and Cultural Identity

Most countries in Europe have become multicultural. In most cases this is a consequence of their colonial and missionary history, and its present form of globalization.[5] Promoting open markets also means the free traffic of ideas, goods and people. This was the case, in a planned way, with postwar migrant laborers who were invited to the Netherlands to contribute to economic growth as is still the case today for ICT technicians from India and nurses from South Africa. This is also the case, although unplanned, with economic and political refugees, who have been arriving to the Netherlands and will continue in the future to arrive in ever greater numbers.

The scholarly debate centers on the extent to which, and the way in which, migrants are integrated into our societies, and whether or not they need to integrate. Whereas several decades ago the dominant view was that ethnic minorities must integrate while retaining their identity, some scholars in the Netherlands now speak about a "multicultural tragedy" or a "multicultural illusion." They see growing segregation of ethnic minorities and stress the need for assimilation to the dominant culture in the Netherlands.[6]

Empirical research findings are ambiguous. Some researchers suggest that socioeconomic integration is a success, but the sociocul-

---

[4] See G. Davie, *Europe: The Exceptional Case. Parameters of Faith in the Modern World* (London: Darton Longman & Todd, 2002); P. Berger, *The Desecularization of the World* (Washington / Grand Rapids: Ethics and Public Policy Center / Eerdmans, 1999).

[5] See G. ter Haar (ed.), *Strangers and Sojourners: Religious Communities in the Diaspora* (Leuven: Peeters, 1998).

[6] See C. Huinders (ed.), *De multiculturele illusie: Een pleidooi voor aanpassing en assimilatie* (Utrecht, 2000).

tural gap between the indigenous people and foreigners is widening.[7] Other researchers claim that migrant movements do not form an essential alternative to the individualized and secularized Dutch lifestyle. Apart from the pillarization of education there is no indication of a reversal of the modernization process. The assimilation of migrants to dominant Western European cultural patterns proceeds more rapidly than is usually thought.[8]

In our own research we concentrate on non-Western Christians' identity interactions, more particularly on the conditions that permit such interaction and its effects. In the case of the conditions, the question is whether a clear, strong identity implies that Christian migrants close themselves to others. Or does a strong, clear identity guarantee openness to others – does it provide a springboard towards society? In the case of effects, the question is whether interaction with others means that migrants lose their identity, or whether it strengthens their identity. The fact that we concentrate on Christian migrants adds an interesting dimension to the scholarly debate. Is the non-integration of non-Western migrants attributable to the "ignorance of Islam," as some scholars suggest?[9] And is the integration of non-Western Christians facilitated by the fact that it takes place in a society which, while highly secularized, still has a dominant Christian culture?[10]

Our finding is that there seems to be a decline in institutional affiliation, hence growing individualization, in migrant communities as is the case for Dutch citizens. Yet in contrast to the latter, religion remains important to migrants and they adhere to non-Western norms and values. What they find difficult to accept is the liberal individual-

---

[7] See R. Rijkschroeff *et al.*, *Bronnenonderzoek Integratiebeleid* (Utrecht, 2003).

[8] See J. Becker and J. De Wit, *Secularisatie in de jaren negentig* (The Hague: Social and Cultural Planning Office of the Netherlands, 2000).

[9] See P. Cliteur, "Jemen in Nederland," in P. Cliteur and V. van den Eeckhout (eds.), *Multiculturalisme, cultuurrelativisme en sociale cohesie* (The Hague: Boom Juridische uitgevers 2001), 17-64; P. Fortuyn, *Tegen de islamisering van onze cultuur*, Utrecht: Karakter Uitgevers, 1997).

[10] See G. ter Haar, *Halfway to Paradise: African Christians in Europe* (Cardiff: Cardiff Academic Press, 1998), 82-86.

ism, widespread in Western societies, the idea that the individual is a rational human being and free to determine his or her own life. Counter to this image of human beings, they maintain that a person is not an individual but is always a member of a wider community, and that human beings are not free but have to be obedient to the will of God. This shifts the debate on multiculturalism from a conflict between Christian and non-Christian perspectives to a conflict between Western and non-Western perspectives. The non-integration of non-Western migrants is not only attributable to Islamic beliefs and practices.

In answering the first question, "to what extent and in what way do migrant movements threaten feelings of identity and security?" I will limit myself to feelings of insecurity in the relation between Dutch Christians and migrant Christians. Apparently, the gap between the two groups is growing. Why is this so? Psychological theories see the importance of religion for migrants as a source of security and identity in a context where everything is strange – religion as an identity marker, as can be observed among Dutch migrants in Canada, Australia and New Zealand. And often, identity categories have a boundary between the "self" and "others." Though in most cases people will have "multiple identities" or "polyphonic selves," in situation of distress people tend to identify strongly with one "self." Sociopsychological theories hold that a positive attitude towards one's own (religious or ethnic) group presupposes a negative attitude towards other groups. For example, the social identity theory claims that people are even willing to manipulate their image of the other negatively in order to enhance their own positive self-esteem.[11] The disadvantage of these theories is that they remain at the cognitive level of analysis.

In our own research we use Pierre Bourdieu's theory of practice, which pays more attention to social structures in its analytic framework.[12] Bourdieu perceives society as a pluralistic space of more or less independent fields (markets) where people or groups of people (actors) try to serve their own interests (make a profit) using various

---

[11] See H. Tajfel and J. Turner, "The Social Identity Theory of Intergroup Behavior," in S. Worchel and W. Austin (eds.), *Psychology of Intergroup Relations* (Chicago: Nelson-Hall Publishers, 1986), 7-24.

[12] See P. Bourdieu, *Das religiöse Feld: Texte zur Ökonomie des Heilsgeschehens* (Konstanz: UVK, 2000).

resources (forms of capital) partly in coalition and partly in competition with others. This explains why the inclusion in one field (e.g. politics) can be accompanied by the exclusion from another field (e.g. religion). Bourdieu's answer to the question about the growing gap between Dutch and migrant Christians would be quite simple: because the Christian migrants' share in the market of spiritual goods is growing, both quantitatively and qualitatively. Their numbers are increasing and their positions in the church become more influential, partly as a result of higher education. Hence Dutch Christians are fighting back to reclaim their share in the market of spiritual goods.

Whereas Western forms of Christianity were still dominant some twenty and thirty years ago and non-Western Christian minorities were accepted and cared for as "guests," or "strangers" that needed help, Western Christianity is losing its monopoly. As one of the informants in a migrant community put it "The future of the church is in our hands." One Dutch pastor complained:

> The Dutch parish is dead, but the migrant parish is full of life. It is almost impossible to find new mass servants, choir members or church council members in the Dutch parish, but in the migrant parish there are plenty of young people who are motivated to work as a volunteer in the church.

In the city of Amsterdam, 27 % of the churchgoers on Sundays in the year 2003 were migrants; 26% of all baptisms of children in the city of Amsterdam in the year 2003 were migrants.[13] In general, churchgoers in migrant churches are younger than those in the Dutch parishes. Migrants use their "spiritual capital" to improve their position in the church and – via the church – in society.[14] There is a real struggle going on for material and spiritual goods, not only for church buildings and church funds, but also of worldviews: against an individualistic, secularized image of humans and society and for a more communitarian, charismatic view. Interpreted in the light of

---

[13] See J. Massaar-Remmerswaal and M. Steggerda, *Statistiek van de allochtone gemeenschappen in Amsterdam: een pilot.* KASKI Memorandum nr. 331 (Nijmegen: KASKI, 2004).

[14] See Ter Haar, *Halfway to Paradise*, 83-84.

Bourdieu's theory of practice, insecurity is inherent in the market mechanism in the religious field.[15]

Migrants and Missionaries

The second question is: how can theology in Europe respond to these realities? My initial response is by looking at how pastoral agents in the field respond to them in practice. The collaboration between Dutch pastors in territorial parishes and migrant churches is still at an initial stage. This is no different in Protestant churches as the relationship between Dutch and migrant Christian communities is an uneasy and ambiguous one.[16] In the Roman Catholic Church, however, this is changing due to a new policy of the Dutch bishops to focus on "international" or "multicultural parishes."[17] At present, most collaboration has been going on between migrant communities and the Dutch missionaries who live and work in foreign countries and then return home to serve their own local church, and secondly, with the foreign missionaries who are beginning to come to the Netherlands. At present there are 83 foreign (Catholic) missionaries working in the Netherlands (there are 1013 Dutch priests working for the seven Catholic dioceses in the Netherlands; 788 Dutch priests work in parishes) and the number is rapidly increasing. It is a well-known fact that Dutch churches were extremely mission-minded, sending large numbers of missionaries overseas and establishing a wide network of supporting mission groups at home. Ever since World War II, and especially since Vatican II, this missionary effort has been changing dramatically be-

---

[15] According to Bourdieu, the religious field offers a heuristic model *par excellence* to analyze other societal fields, with the risks of misuse of power and even violence. See Bourdieu, *Das religiöse Feld*, 121-22.

[16] See J. van Butselaar, "An Uneasy Relationship: 'Old' and 'New' Churches in Western Europe," in K. Bediako *et al.* (eds.), *A New Day Dawning: African Christians Living the Gospel* (Zoetermeer: Boekencentrum, 2004), 179-200.

[17] See Guerra *et al.*, *Een gebedshuis voor alle volken*, 16-17. For a concrete example, see Guerra, *Interculturele kerkopbouw*, 198-210.

cause of the new mission theology, according to which every local church is primarily responsible for mission in its own country, but also because of a decline in priestly vocations.

Currently there is another major shift, characterized by the following phenomena. First, when missionaries return home many of them become involved with migrants in the suburbs of big cities. As former migrants, who know foreign cultures and speak other languages, this is quite understandable. Second, missionary institutes are starting to include non-Western members and to place them in mission projects in the Netherlands. This is happening in Amsterdam, Rotterdam and The Hague, as well as in most big European cities. Third, some Dutch dioceses are applying for church personnel to local bishops and religious congregations in the former "mission territories." In addition some political or economic refugees joined seminaries and serve Dutch parishes after being ordained to the priesthood.

There are numerous projects providing a missionary presence among migrants. Some missionary societies take responsibility for multicultural parishes. The Society of African Missions started an African parish in Amsterdam as far back as 1980; the Society of Missionaries of Africa (formerly the "White Fathers") and the Sisters of Our Lady of Africa (formerly the "White Sisters") started in the Hague in 1992; and the Society of the Holy Ghost (popularly known as the "Spiritans") started in Rotterdam in 1999. Their communities include non-Western, usually young and lively, members, priests and nuns. There is a huge variety of networks and centers supported by religious, such as the Network Religious for Refugees, supporting refugees "without papers" who are excluded from all basic Dutch social security services; the religious organization in Netherlands against the Sexual Trafficking of Women protesting against sex trafficking and employing illegal prostitutes in the sex industry; "Open Houses" such as the Missionary Centre in Heerlen and the Missionary Service Centre in Tilburg.

Missionaries working on these projects say that their "mission has come home." European missionaries originally took the gospel to non-Western countries. Yet, due to the process of secularization Europeans have forgotten about the gospel. Now non-Western people, the fruits of missionary endeavor in the former mission territories, are bringing the gospel back to Europe. After Vatican II mission was seen as "mutual missionary assistance between churches" but the assistance was not really mutual. For a long time churches in the so-called mission territories remained at the receiving end. This situation, however, is changing rapidly and Europe is being evangelized by non-Western missionaries. Thus in mission theology there is a shift from the paradigm of "mutual missionary assistance of churches" to the paradigm of "reversed mission."

Migrants and Multiculturalism

My second answer to the question, "how can theology in Europe respond to these realities?" is by looking at the migrant movements themselves and the migrant theologies that arise from them. Here again, the development of migrant theologies is still at an initial stage and the issue is more often put forward by native Dutch pastors than by the migrant churches themselves.[18] What can European theologians learn from non-Western Christians in Europe? The encounter with non-Western Christians confronts European theologians with their own particular church history. Between 1850 and 1950 Dutch society was highly pillarized, with almost 100 percent church affiliation and church influence in almost all spheres of life, from birth to death. People's lives were organized on the basis of the primacy of God's word (in Protestantism) or the teaching of the church (in Catholicism).

After World War II, and even more so after Vatican II and the student revolts in the 1960s, there was a rapid process of emancipation, going to the other extreme and making the Netherlands one of the most secularized societies in the world: human self-realization took the place of the proclamation of God's word. There was a shift from heteronomy to autonomy at all levels of church practice. Pastoral counseling became non-directive, focusing on human needs. Church development became community-based, stressing democratic leadership and an egalitarian organization. Catechesis and homiletics became experiential, stressing the receiver of the message rather than its content. Diaconal work became client-centered, focusing on the humanization of deprived people.

---

[18] See M. Janssen, "African Pastors and Life Stories," in Bediako *et al. A New Day Dawning*, 163-78.

This is where non-Western Christians rebel! They make European theologians aware that maybe they had gone too far, swinging from one extreme to the other, and they challenged them to work on a more balanced, integral or holistic approach, in which evangelization and humanization are seen, not as opposites but as two sides of the same coin. There is a shift from the primacy of God's word (heteronomy) over the primacy of human beings (autonomy) to a model that stresses interaction between God's word and human beings. Migrants advocate a more communicative theology solving questions concerning the relation between God, the church and the world. Despite hermeneutic traditions these basic questions remained unresolved, as growing fundamentalism shows. Among European theologians it was generally accepted that faith develops historically, that it is determined by its context and therefore changeable. Consequently theological and ecclesiastic language must be critical, hermeneutic and argumentative. What migrant theologies force European theologians to acknowledge is that European theology was only one way of practicing theology – relevant maybe to one particular context, but certainly not universally accepted.

Latino, African Diaspora, and Caribbean theologies are still in the process of being constructed in the Netherlands.[19] Yet what the emerging paradigms show is that they put migration at the center of theological reflection. Like liberation and feminism, migration is a perspective that cuts across all theological disciplines. Although migrant theologians stress that migration is the consequence of marginalization and thus dependence of "the rest" of the world on the West, they also stress the growing interdependence of peoples.

According to the instruction *Erga migrantes caritas Christi* (The Love of Christ towards Migrants),[20] published by the Pontifical Council for the Pastoral Care of Migrants and Itinerant People, "International migration must ... be considered an important structural component of the social, economic and political reality of the world today"

---

[19] See Guerra, "Naar een theologie van de migratie," 250.

[20] See S. Hamao and A. Marchetto, *Erga migrantes caritas Christi: Instruction of the Pontifical Council for the Pastoral Care of Migrants and Itinerant People* (Vatican City: Pontifical Council for the Pastoral Care of Migrants and Itinerant People, 2004). All quotes in this paragraph are from this text.

(No. 8). Although the instruction speaks about a practice of discernment (No. 65), it sees migration as an opportunity for community and dialogue (No. 2). "The ever increasing migration phenomenon today is an important component of that growing interdependence among nation states that goes to make up globalization" (No. 4); it is "a significant sign of the times" (No. 14). Thus, there is a task ahead for European theologians.

Conclusion

In answering the questions, "to what extent and in what way do migrant movements threaten feelings of identity and security?" and "how can theology in Europe respond to these feelings?," it should be noted, first of all, that European theologians must accept that Christianity's center of gravity has shifted to the non-Western world and also that the influence of non-Western Christianity in Europe is growing, both quantitatively and qualitatively. In terms of Bourdieu's theory, this shift will necessarily bring insecurity as European Christians lose the monopoly they used to hold. Indeed, the shift threatens their old identity, but to my mind rightly so. It is generating a new, probably more authentic "catholic" identity, namely a self-understanding among European Christians that they are part of a universal "world" church.

In answering the second question we pointed to the shift from mutual missionary assistance to reversed mission in mission theology, and from dependence to interdependence in migrant theologies. In missiology there has been a long debate about inculturation. Just as Christ became one of us through his incarnation, Christianity and Christian missionaries must find a place in non-Christian cultures. These theories were simply applied to the integration of non-Western Christians in Europe. Whereas some decades ago the question was how non-Western Christians could be integrated into Dutch parishes and congregations, now some scholars say that it is the other way round: how can Dutch Christians link up with vibrantly alive non-Western Christian communities?

Yet if the direction of the one-way street were merely to be reversed and European Christians ended up exclusively at the receiving end, this would not be a way forward! Therefore we advocate a shift from inculturation to interculturation.[21] There is an urgent need for a theology of intercultural encounter, a theology of interculturation – in short, an intercultural theology. While there has been a lengthy debate on a theology of religions or a theology of interreligious dialogue in Europe, in particular dialogue between Muslims and Christians in Europe,[22] theological reflection on the dialogue between people who share the same faith but come from different cultural backgrounds is still lacking.

There is of course the pioneering work of the Centre for Black and White Christian Partnership at Selly Oak since 1978, taken over by the Centre of Black Theologies at the University of Birmingham in 2002, which since then publishes the international journal *Black Theology*. But to the best of my knowledge, the studies in Europe are still in a descriptive and classificatory stage, not yet the more fundamental theological reflections as we know them from the Latino theology in the United States of America.[23] Undoubtedly, the need for inculturation theologies will continue, as the cultural decolonization and emancipation process continues, both in the Western and the non-Western world, including various migrant theologies such as Latino theology and African Diaspora theology but in present-day Europe there is an urgent need to go beyond the insular communities of "tribes" or "pillars," and develop an intercultural theology.

---

[21] See F. Wijsen, "Intercultural Theology and the Mission of the Church," in *Exchange* 30/3 (2001): 218-28; Guerra andWijsen, "Multiculturele of interculturele liturgie," 96-100.

[22] See G. Speelman *et al.* (eds.), *Muslims and Christians in Europe: Breaking New ground* (Kampen: Kok, 1993).

[23] R. Fornet-Betancourt (ed.), *Glaube an der Grenze: Die US-amerikanische Latino-Theologie* (Freiburg / Basel / Vienna: Herder, 2002).

PART II

WARS AND VIOLENT CONFLICTS

Siegfried Wiedenhofer

Towards a Theological Hermeneutics of Violence

In the context of globalization, conflict and violence can have a variety of different causes, such as political, economic and social.[1] Furthermore, the discussion of Samuel Huntington's idea that there will possibly be a clash of civilizations has demonstrated that in the future culture and religious differences may play a greater role as the causes of conflict.[2] As many conflicts result from mutual non-recognition, and recognition, as well as non-recognition, are closely connected to cultural and religious identity, it is very important that religions learn to come to grips with their particular traditions of violence and to find ways of living together in peace and mutual understanding. Religions normally put peace at the center of their beliefs and hopes;[3] and yet it is obvious that there is also a great potential for violence.

---

[1] Cf. A. Rapoport, *The Origins of Violence: Approaches to the Study of Conflict* (New York: Paragon House, 1989).

[2] Cf. S.P. Huntington, *The Clash of Civilizations and the Remaking of World Order* (New York: Simon & Schuster, 1996); J. Díez-Nicolás, "Two Contradictory Hypotheses on Globalization: Societal Convergence or Civilization Differentiation and Clash," in R. Inglehart (ed.), *Human Values and Social Change: Findings from the Values Surveys* (Leiden / Boston: Brill, 2003), 235-63; W. Link, *Die Neuordnung der Weltpolitik: Grundprobleme globaler Politik an der Schwelle zum 21. Jahrhundert* (Frankfurt a. M.: Büchergilde Gutenberg, 1998, 1999); H. Müller, *Das Zusammenleben der Kulturen: Ein Gegenentwurf zu Huntington*, 2nd ed. (Frankfurt a.M.: Fischer Taschenbuch-Verlag 1998, 1999); P. Norris and R. Inglehart, "Islamic Culture and Democracy: Testing the 'Clash of Civilizations' Thesis," in R. Inglehart, *Human Values*, 5-33; S. Rashid (ed.), *The Clash of Civilizations? Asian Responses* (Karachi *et al.*: OUP, 1997); B. Tibi, *Krieg der Zivilisationen: Politik und Religion zwischen Vernunft und Fundamentalismus* (Munich: Wilhelm Heyne Verlag, 1998).

[3] Cf. the summary given by S. Wiedenhofer, "Der Friede in den Religionen," in K. Garber *et al.* (eds.), *Erfahrung und Deutung von Krieg*

Religious Traditions Between Violence and Peace

The problem is not only that there are major differences between religions – which sometimes raises the question as to whether certain religions are potentially, or in reality, more violent than others – it is also that there are major differences within particular religions. For example, in Christianity, if we ask what the Bible says about violence we will receive very different and even opposing answers, in particular if we take into account the whole spectrum between violence and power.[4] In Genesis 6:11-13, for example, it is said, that the world is full of violence resulting from the sins of human beings:

> Now the earth was corrupt in God's sight and was full of violence. God saw how corrupt the earth had become, for all the people on earth had corrupted their ways. So God said to Noah, "I am going to put an end to all people, for the earth is filled with violence because of them. I am surely going to destroy both them and the earth.

It is part of God's wisdom to restrict the excessive amount of violence by means of violence that is exercised by law and legitimate authority:

> And for your lifeblood I will surely demand an accounting. I will demand an accounting from every animal. And from each man, too, I will demand an accounting for the life of his fellow man. "Whoever sheds the blood of man, by man shall his blood be shed; for in the image of God has God made man; (Gen. 9:5-6)

> "Everyone must submit himself to the governing authorities, for there is no authority except that which God has established. God has established the authorities that exist. Consequently, he who rebels against the authority is rebelling against what God has instituted, and those who do so will bring judgment on themselves. For

---

und Frieden: Religion - Geschlechter - Natur und Kultur (Munich: Wilhelm Fink Verlag, 2002), 97-111.

[4] It is theological encyclopedias that provide all relevant data. See also K.R. Chase, A. Jacobs (eds.), *Must Christianity be Violent? Reflections on History, Practice, and Theology* (Grand Rapids: Brazos Press, 2003); D. Martin, *Does Christianity Cause War?* (Oxford: OUP, 1997).

rulers hold no terror for those who do right, but for those who do wrong. Do you want to be free from fear of the one in authority? Then do what is right and he will commend you. (Rom. 13:1-3)

On the other hand, the God of the Old Testament is not only the God of mercy but also the God of revenge, wrath, jealousy and judgment. In Ex. 15:3 it is said "The LORD is a warrior; the LORD is his name." It is God who fought the wars against the enemies of Israel in order to provide the Promised Land to the people of the covenant as it is shown very impressively in the books of Joshua, Judges, Samuel and Kings:

So Joshua subdued the whole region, including the hill country, the Negev, the western foothills and the mountain slopes, together with all their kings. He left no survivors. He totally destroyed all who breathed, just as the LORD, the God of Israel, had commanded .... All these kings and their lands Joshua conquered in one campaign, because the LORD, the God of Israel, fought for Israel (Jos. 10:40.42).

Finally, there are a series of testimonies that show that God's true salvation and his eschatological accomplishment can only be mediated by nonviolent means like suffering, love, justice and peace:

Yet it was the LORD's will to crush him and cause him to suffer, and though the LORD makes his life a guilt offering, he will see his offspring and prolong his days, and the will of the LORD will prosper in his hand. After the suffering of his soul, he will see the light of life and be satisfied; by his knowledge my righteous servant will justify many, and he will bear their iniquities; (Is. 53:10-11)

This is how God showed his love among us: He sent his one and only Son into the world that we might live through him. This is love: not that we loved God, but that he loved us and sent his Son as an atoning sacrifice for our sins; (1 John 4:9-10)

You have heard that it was said, "Love your neighbour and hate your enemy." But I tell you: Love your enemies and pray for those who persecute you, that you may be sons of your Father in heaven. He causes his sun to rise on the evil and the good, and sends rain on the righteous and the unrighteous. (Mat. 5:43-45)

The situation is even more complicated if we consider church history. Not only are the sacred history of the Bible and the history of the Christian churches replete with violence, there is also a lot of violence that has been done to those deemed enemies (e.g. Jews, pagans, heretics and schismatics) in the name of the church.[5] In the Christian tradition there is a realistic point of view in which one tries to limit violence to some extent or, under certain conditions, to fight violence with violent means, as is the case with just-war theory and its application. In summary, in Christianity, we have testimonies of faith and testimonies of history that cannot be easily harmonized. Furthermore, it is not possible to simply reduce the differences in the Christian tradition to the gap between ideals and reality.

Beyond that, a general conclusion based on recent discussions is that there is a structural "ambivalence of the sacred" regarding the problem of violence and peace or violence and reconciliation.[6] In par-

---

[5] F. Buggle, *Denn sie wissen nicht, was sie glauben: Oder warum man redlicherweise nicht mehr Christ sein kann* (Reinbek: Rowohlt Verlag, 1992); K. Deschner, *Kriminal-geschichte des Christentums*, vol. 1-8 (Reinbek: Rowohlt Verlag, 1986-2004); L. Accattoli, *Wenn der Papst um Vergebung bittet: Alle "mea culpa" von Papst Johannes Paul II. an der Wende zum dritten Jahrtausend* (Innsbruck / Vienna: Tyrolia-Verlag, 1999).

[6] R.S. Appleby, *The Ambivalence of the Sacred: Religion, Violence, and Reconciliation* (Lanham: Rowman & Littlefield Publishers, 2000); cf. G. ter Haar and J.J. Busuttil (eds.), *Bridge or Barrier: Religion, Violence, and Visions for Peace* (Boston: Brill, 2005); G. Baudler, *Gewalt in den Weltreligionen* (Darmstadt: Wissenschaftliche Buchgesellschaft, 2005); J. Stenesh, *Rot on the Vine: The Many Dark Faces of Religion* (Portage: Cogno Press, 2005); C. Bultmann *et al.* (eds.), *Religion, Gewalt, Gewaltlosigkeit. Probleme - Positionen - Perspektiven* (Münster: Aschendorff, 2004); J.H. Ellens (ed.), *The Destructive Power of Religion: Violence in Judaism, Christianity, and Islam*, vol. 1-4 (Westport: Praeger, 2004): H. Maier, *Das Doppelgesicht des Religiösen: Religion - Gewalt - Politik* (Freiburg im Breisgau *et al.*: Herder, 2004); V.N. Makrides and J. Rüpke (eds.), *Religionen im Konflikt: Vom Bürgerkrieg über Ökogewalt bis zur Gewalterinnerung im Ritual* (Münster: Aschendorff, 2004); L. Weinberg and A. Pedahzur (eds.), *Religious Fundamentalism and Political Extremism* (London / Portland: Frank Cass, 2004); A.M. Al-Khattar, *Religion and Terrorism: An Interfaith Perspective*

ticular, it is at the interface of sacralizing politics and politicizing religion that violence best develops and prospers.[7] Therefore, to come to grips theologically with the problem of violence in religions in general and in our own religion in particular, it is necessary to interpret the tradition according to a theological hermeneutics. Only then will the interpretation of religious traditions be more than choosing those parts of tradition that best fit into one's own actual political or pastoral options. Every religion provides some orientation for its believers based on the Holy Scriptures, canonical texts, normative rites, emphasizing parts of traditions or particular authorities.[8]

The following short outline of a Christian hermeneutics of violence is based on a complex theory of religious tradition that contains a mutually determining logic, hermeneutic, and pragmatics of religious traditions.[9] This means that theological hermeneutics must cor-

---

(Westport: Praeger, 2003); A.T. Khoury *et al.* (eds.), *Krieg und Gewalt in den Weltreligionen: Fakten und Hintergründe* (Freiburg / Basel / Vienna: Herder, 2003); A. Lännström (ed.), *Promise and Peril: The Paradox of Religion as Resource and Threat* (Notre Dame: University of Notre Dame Press, 2003); J.D. May, *Transcendence and Violence: The Encounter of Buddhist, Christian, and Primal Traditions* (New York: Continuum, 2003); O.J. McTernan, *Violence in God's Name: Religion in an Age of Conflict* (Maryknoll: Orbis Books, 2003); J. Nelson-Pallmeyer, *Is Religion Killing Us? Violence in the Bible and the Quran* (Harrisburg: Trinity Press International, 2003); L.H. Steffen, *The Demonic Turn: The Power of Religion to Inspire or Restrain Violence* (Cleveland: Pilgrim Press, 2003); D.G. Bromley and J.G. Melton (eds.), *Cults, Religion, and Violence* (Cambridge / New York: Cambridge University Press, 2002).

[7] H. Maier (ed.). *Wege in die Gewalt: Die modernen politischen Religionen* (Frankfurt am Main: Fischer-Taschenbuch-Verlag, 2000).

[8] Cf. I. Pieper *et al.* (eds.), *Häresien. Religionshermeneutische Studien zur Konstruktion von Norm und Abweichung* (Munich: Wilhelm Fink Verlag, 2003).

[9] S. Wiedenhofer, "Tradition - History - Memory: Why do we Need a Complex Theory of Tradition?" in T. Larbig, S. Wiedenhofer (eds.), *Tradition and Tradition Theories: An International Discussion* (Münster: LIT Verlag, 2006), 375-98; S. Wiedenhofer, "Von der Grammatik religiöser Symbolsysteme zur Logik religiöser Traditions-prozesse." in

respond to the logic, hermeneutic and pragmatics of Christian faith. In other words, the theological interpretation of violence in Christian tradition has to match the basic contents and basic structures of Christian faith as well as the basic conditions of the Christian community of faith. According to classical catholic theological hermeneutics, what Christians have to believe is given by scripture and tradition interpreted in accordance with the faith of the Church and in particular the creed.[10]

A Christian Understanding of Violence

What does violence mean in relation to the Christian faith according to classical catholic hermeneutics? How do we interpret the plurality of belief testimonies as expressions of the one revelation of God? There are basically two general rules. First, interpretation has to occur in dialogue with the essential content and structure of Christian faith, i.e. in correspondence with the *regula fidei* as it is expressed in scripture and the creed, and secondly, interpretation has to take place in the unity of the faithful and in community with the church authorities. Setting the second rule aside, we will focus on the *regula fidei*. What is the comprehensive meaning of violence in Christian faith according to the rule of faith?

G. Melville (ed.), *Institutionalität und Symbolisierung: Verstetigungen kultureller Ordnungsmuster in Vergangenheit und Gegenwart* (Cologne / Weimar / Vienna: Böhlau Verlag, 2001), 165-80; S. Wiedenhofer, "The Logic of Tradition," in B. Schoppelreich and S. Wiedenhofer (eds.), *Zur Logik religiöser Traditionen* (Frankfurt a. M.: IKO Verlag, 1998), 11-84.

[10] S. Wiedenhofer "Hermeneutik III, Systematisch-theologisch," in *Lexikon für Theologie und Kirche*, vol. 5, 3rd ed. (Freiburg / Basel / Vienna: Herder Verlag, 1996), 6-7; J.K. Ratzinger, *Theologische Prinzipienlehre: Bausteine zur Fundamentaltheologie* (Munich: Erich Wewel Verlag, 1982); W. Kern *et al.* (eds.), *Handbuch der Funda-mentaltheologie*, vol. 4 (Freiburg / Basel / Vienna: Herder Verlag, 1988).

The *first interpretative step* is based on the *synchronic structure of the Christian faith*. Because *Jesus Christ* is the decisive revelation of God, he is the definite sign of salvation; he and his Gospel are not only the centerof the creed but also the *hermeneutical centerof the Christian belief in God*. As a consequence, to know what violence means in Christian faith the first hermeneutical step to be carried out is simply to read the *Gospel*. If we do this, we will discover that God is not the God of violence but the God of love and peace. By the powerless power of love and through the surrender of his Son, evil, death and violence are transformed into eternal life. Therefore, without any "sacramental" signs of nonviolence, neither could the Church perform its mission nor could violence be efficiently overcome. Therefore, pacifist movements in Christianity are true representatives of this central aspect of Christian faith. To summarize: Jesus Christ, the definitive sign of God, the "God with us" (Immanuel; Matt. 1:23) has not become violence, but peace (Eph. 2:14). The Church then is only following its mission when it continues the mission of Jesus Christ, being a sacrament of peace.

The *second interpretative step* is also based on the *synchronic structure of the Christian faith*. Because the Christian confession of faith is the *triune confession of creation, salvation and fulfilment,* the question concerning what violence dogmatically means also has to be answered in the *context of creation, of redemption and of fulfilment*. In the *context of creation,* violence can have different meanings. On the one hand, it is part of the order of creation according to God's will. In this sense violence can be a rational means to maintain legal order. It is upon this belief in creation, that the constitutional state's monopoly of violence is theologically grounded. There is a legitimate violence of the legitimate authority in service of justice and law. Yet according to Genesis 1:28, every dominion assigned to humanity is as God's vice-regent, steward or manager. Consequently, every exercise of legitimate violence has to be transformed from domination into a taking care of the subordinate. On the other hand, violence is seen as one of the most serious consequences of the absence of God, i.e. from the sin of the creatures. As such, it has to be understood in the context of unbelief, self-annihilation, deadly rivalry and demoniac compulsion. Placed into the *context of redemption and fulfilment,* violence appears already broken and overcome by God's love. There is hope amid the abundance of violence; there is, from place to place and from time to time, effective signs and anticipation of the eternal life, the definitive end of all violence. It is upon this belief in redemption and fulfilment that pacifism is theologically grounded. Christian pacifism is the "sacramental" sign of the founding experience made by Jesus Christ, that the power of evil and violence cannot be overcome by power and violence but only by suffering, surrender, patience and love and that it has been overcome definitely by God himself by tolerating and undergoing violence in the crucifixion of his son Jesus Christ.[11] Inasmuch as fulfillment is not yet achieved, the power of violence is broken yet the violence of the old world is still there. In this time in between, the Church's mission is to become a more effective sign of redemption, i.e. of peace, justice, patience, tolerance and reconciliation. In strict correspondence to the sign of salvation, the Church only has to faithfully represent the cross of the savior; her primary testimony will be a nonviolent one. Christian pacifism has therefore to play a very important role in the church.[12] In contexts of suppression and war, a restriction of violence through means of legal violence and resistance might be necessary. Just war theory, which is the ethical thematizing of this situation, and pacifism are therefore not alternatives in that only their pragmatics differ. Furthermore, they need each other to be adequately understood. For example, it often depends on the context or on the particular mission, whether a Christian supports a pacifist standpoint or a just war theory. As a result, they must both accept and maintain the dialectical tension between these two positions as the struggle between the supporters of Christian pacifism and the representatives of a Christian just war theory is a productive and necessary conflict in the church.[13]

The *third interpretative step* is based on the *diachronic structure of the Christian faith* is, as the creed shows, a *way that leads from creation to fulfilment*. Hermeneutically this means that every testi-

---

[11] Cf. J.-L. Marion, "Das Böse in Person," in *Internationale katholische Zeitschrift "Communio"* 8 (1979): 243-50.

[12] For nonviolence as the basic means of interreligious dialogue cf. D.J. Krieger, *The New Universalism: Foundations for a Global Theology* (Maryknoll: Orbis Books, 1991).

[13] Cf. the attempt of R.B. Miller to bring pacifism and just war theory into a dialectical relationship: R.B. Miller (*Interpretations of Conflict: Ethics, Pacifism, and the Just-War Tradition* (Chicago: University of Chicago Press, 1991).

mony of faith within this vast history is only understood correctly when it is understood as part of the whole history. No isolated part of the tradition of Christian belief is an adequate expression of revelation. Every part of tradition is a sign of the revelation of God to the extent that it is a part of the whole history. In this sense political, economic, social and cultural history is part of our theological understanding of violence. We have to interpret experiences and phenomena in light of the Gospel in order to learn how to see them as signs of God's judgment and grace. And we have to interpret the Gospel in light of our experiences today in order to learn about their universal meaning and promise.

It is clearly the connection between the particularity and universality of religious experiences that provides a substantial part of the background for the dark side of the history of religions; for the fanaticism and dogmatism, the self-righteousness and self-absolutizing which has had such dire consequences for "unbelievers," heretics, freethinkers and outsiders, and which has left such a bloody trail of injustice throughout the history of Christianity. The universal claims and mission of historical religions can all too quickly lead to fallacious claims of absoluteness, born of the self-assertive fantasies of a particular historical community. Indeed, a long, painful learning process has been required before it was possible for these communities of faith to purify their universal claims to truth and salvation from self-righteousness and fanaticism.

For example, through long stretches of its history, Israel simply identified the power of its God Yahweh with its own self-assertion and put this identification into practice as bloody "holy wars" against its enemies. Jewish suffering in the Exilic and Post-Exilic Periods (sixth to second century BC), however, created the opportunity for a new faith response to develop; which found its confirmation and culmination in the Cross of Christ. When Israel had apparently lost everything that had been a source of pride and tangibly embodied its election (land, kingdom, Temple), it was then that despair drove them to the realization that everything is a gift from God. The devout believer realized that God's chosen sign is a sign only if it points beyond itself to that which it is intended to bear witness to. As such, the universal truth claim of being God's chosen witness in the world is not one in the mode of possession but rather one in the mode of testimony. Based on this situation, Israel came to realize that war and aggression cannot be the proper setting and medium for God's saving acts in history, it is rather a messianic peace. Since faith in the fidelity of Yahweh was maintained throughout the experience of the Exile, the God who had first thrown the Egyptians and then the Philistines and Canaanites, horses and horsemen into the sea (Ex. 15) became the God who sets his omnipotent love to work so as to move the peoples of the earth to beat their swords into ploughshares and their spears into pruning hooks (Is. 2:1-5; 7:14-17; 9.1-6). And finally, it was in this context that the idea of election was purified from all implications of self-assertion and self-righteousness and transformed into the idea of mission and service to others. Being elected as a historical sign and witness to the almighty God ultimately means nothing other than the vicarious ministry of suffering, of being an impotent witness to love and of service – as is witnessed by the songs of the Suffering Servant (Is. 42:1-4; 49:1-6; 50:4-9; 52:13-53:12).

Inasmuch as the Crucified one stands at the center of the Christian confession of faith in God, and inasmuch as he has become the very sign of God himself for Christians, the sign in terms of which all other signs and images of God are measured and legitimatized; the Christian mission and witness are likewise to be measured by this sign of the cross. Discipleship in the steps of Jesus and the nonviolent "tolerance" of the Cross constitute the only form in which the truth and the salvation to which the Church is called to give witness can become universal. If the crucified Son of God stands at the center of the profession of faith in God, then it is forbidden for the general body of the faithful, as well as for theologians, to reckon who is greater (Mark 9:33-37, 10:42-45) – Christianity, Judaism, Islam, Buddhism, Hinduism etc. For indeed, the Christian knows that he or she is borne by the love of Christ, in whom the love of almighty God has become visible, who alone can deliver Himself up without losing Himself, and who precisely in this oblation awakens freedom, response and life in others. Communicative openness in solidarity, without losing oneself – that is the promise which is held out by Christian faith and which has yet to be made substantial in interreligious dialogue.

The *fourth interpretative step* is based on the *unity of God which* implies the *unity of revelation and truth* and the final *unity of faith and reason*. This means that theological interpretation must also be able to communicate with non-theological theories of violence, like theories of aggression, in order to verify theological knowledge by reason and to criticize ideological theories of violence based on faith experiences. On the one hand, it is faith that enlightens reason and liberates it from the captivity to the power of evil. On the other, it is reason that reveals the universal promise of faith and widens its insights to the entirety of life.

It is only through these multiple approaches that the comprehensive sense of violence according to the Christian faith can be brought to light. The identity of the Christian contribution to the problem of global conflict and violence can only be safeguarded when the theological hermeneutics used correspond to the basic content and structure of the Christian faith. The findings of this hermeneutics can no longer be brought into a coherent system of doctrine. Semantically, many tensions will and must remain. It is pragmatically, i.e. in the differentiated wholeness of the practice of faith that the consistency of the Christian answer to the problem of violence has to be achieved and held.

Hans-Joachim Sander

"You Love Life and We Love Death": A Crucible Difference Concerning God's Power in the Aftermath of Terror

Identities are dangerous ideas. To know what one's life is all about is a source of great power, a power which grows if this knowledge includes what others' lives are all about. Identities need "the will to identity," that is, the will to identify others and the will to be identified by others. In this sense, identities are powerful relations between people that have political and cultural importance. They bring people into relation independently of the fact of whether people want to be in relation to others, relations which may include the use of force. At the same time identities are unavoidable concepts in the search for a place in history, society, culture and religion. One cannot avoid searching for an identity, yet as soon as an identity is established, the potential for violence is born.

Europe and the Europeans are crucible examples of violent identities both as aggressors and as victims. In colonial times, Europeans found their identity by "civilizing" other people without excluding the use of force when deemed "necessary." Convinced that they had a sort of supernatural right to such an identity, the Europeans also created new identities for other people. They considered colonial identities to be God's will and their global mission as a response to being called by God. At present, Europe and Europeans are confronted with violence partly resulting from their own violent identity in the past; and this violence itself seems to be supported by God's will. After the disastrous bombings in Madrid on March 11th 2004, a video tape was found presenting a message from the terrorists (or from people backing them) that declared itself as a warning but was clearly a threat. At this point, I want to concentrate on the logic of identity in this message. The tape declares: "You want/love life and we love/want death."[1] This demonstrates a twofold logic on the basis of differences: you-we and life-death. The identity of the people behind the "we" is

---

[1] *Handelsblatt* (March 15, 2004), 3.

completely different from the identity of the people being referred to as "you." Secondly, this difference is a question of life and death.

Such a twofold logic of identity is important for understanding the problem of God in a world of conflicts. God is a religious concept which is able to define the difference between "you" and "we," an authority to establish identities and to use it as a lethal power. If one is looking for God-talk which can overcome a violent identity, one has to understand how religion can be used to establish violent identities.

Using Religion to Create Violent Identities: The Logic of Resentment in Leering Souls

In all religions, one can observe the combination of violent identity formation with the use of God's name or religious beliefs. A recent example in Christianity is the bombing attack on a federal building in Oklahoma City in April 19, 1995. 168 people were killed most of whom children from the kindergarten were located in the building. The man responsible for the attack, Timothy McVeigh, was linked to the violent culture of US militia groups. In the weeks before the bombings he made a couple of phone calls to a community known as Elohim City. This is a community belonging to the "Christian Identity" religious movement. McVeigh subscribed to the Christian identity newsletter "The Patriot Review." Furthermore, it seems that his attack was inspired by the novel "The Turner Diaries." McVeigh used an explosive mixture of substances as described in Pierce's novel.[2] Its author, William Pierce, openly criticizes the Christian Community and has founded his own religious movement, the Cosmotheist Community. Nevertheless, his novel is close to the ideas of the Christian Identity. Another example of a violent, religiously backed Christian identity is the antiabortion terrorist Eric Robert Rudolph. He is suspected of being responsible for the bombing during the Atlanta Olympic Games in 1996 and was sentenced for attacks on abortion clinics in Birmingham and Atlanta. In the world of the US antiabortion movement, Americans are called urgently to act as true Christians. For ex-

---

[2] Cf. M. Juergensmeyer, *Terror im Namen Gottes* (Freiburg: Herder, 2004), 54-58.

ample, the Christian identity of the US is an important factor in the campaign for the upcoming presidential election.

Very often one observes a conversion in the careers of religiously motivated terrorists. For some time they follow a life that at some points begins to disgust them. After their conversion they realize the reasons why their lives were disgusting and they find out what the true meaning of their existence is. For these people their process of searching for an identity is finally successful and religion gives them the chance to establish a stable identity. They develop the capacity for violence because they have found their identities. The reason for their violence is not because they are still searching and longing for a stable identity; rather, violence is a result of the experience of power derived from a stable identity. Terrorists are not searching for existence; they have found a purpose for their lives. They have the experience of being in control of their lives and this gives them the power to control others by means of force and violence. They are very clear about who they do not want to be. They have developed spiritual strategies to sacrifice themselves by realizing what their lives are all about. One cannot become a crusader simply by going on a crusade. The first step to be taken is to put up the cross and to convert to a truly religious identity. In such cases of a stable identity the difference between "we/myself" and "the others" has more power than under normal circumstances. This difference does not only function as a means of making social distinctions with regard to one's own identity, it also functions to create a contest in which identities compete to be stronger and more truthful. It has the power to declare war. Violence becomes necessary because other people are other than they ought to be, they are exactly what they shouldn't be or become. If "we" are really who we are, others cannot be allowed to be who they are which is other than who we are.

Religions are not responsible for this declaration of war but their symbolic systems are useful heuristic devices as they help to explain why one must not become what others have become. Their identities are weak identities because they are sinners, atheists, liars, murderers etc. So, by explaining which identities are strong ones, religious symbolic systems offer clues as to what kind of identity is a weak one. This is an inevitable process for every religion because religions must also teach one how to live an ethical or moral life. Religions cannot avoid presenting strong identities and showing how a strong identity can be developed.

As soon as the difference between a weak and strong identity is linked to the difference between "we" and "they," power is created. By controlling him or herself with the help of a strong identity, one can develop the power to control others who have weaker identities. By knowing the reasons why others are weak such a person can take the high ground. On the other hand, others are conceived as weak because they cannot realize why and how another person has established a strong identity.[3] The "we" will always be stronger them the "they." This situation of the weakness of the others and the strength of "our" identity is tremendously dangerous. It follows the logic of resentment and tends to become a vicious circle and a self-fulfilling prophecy. The strength of strong identities depends on their ability to demonstrate the weakness of the identities of others. Their weakness must be made obvious in order to give power to the stronger side. By having a strong identity I am able to demonstrate that they are weak. Violence and force are certainly means for such a demonstration; they demonstrate strength by creating weakness on the other side. The triumph over the other proves that I am following the right path and that I have established a strong identity. Nietzsche called this logic of resentment *die schielende Seele* ("the leering soul").[4] A leering soul is focused on the weaknesses of others and depends on this weakness.

Unfortunately, this logic is always possible because there is always weakness among people. Colonial Europe knew too well how to use the weaknesses of the peoples it colonized. It made profit out of political, military, cultural and religious weaknesses of these people. This knowledge made Europeans the masters of the world and shaped their modern identities. They could always respond to criticism by arguing that they brought civilization and technology to an underdeveloped world. Yet today, after a murderous century with two world wars

---

[3] In an interview with Mark Juergensmeyer, Mahmud Abouhalima, who was sentenced to prison for being involved in the first attack on the World Trade Center in 1993, declared: "I have lived their life but they did never live my life and so they will never realize how I live or think." For him secular, non-religious people "move like dead bodies." (Juergensmeyer, *Terror*, 102 [German edition]).

[4] F. Nietzsche, *Zur Genealogie der Moral*, Kritische Studienausgabe, ed. by Giorgio Colli and Mazzino Montinari (Munich / Berlin dtv: de Gruyter, 1999), 272.

and under the conditions of a globally connected world, the weaknesses of Europeans has become obvious, or at least of the famous "old Europe." The old identity cannot guarantee strength any more. Its violent character during the colonial age can no longer be the basis for pride and power. It casts a shadow over the past. Their new identity, born from the peaceful unifying process of the European peoples is not yet firmly established. Europe is still searching for a new identity to give it strength. It cannot hide that it has a weak identity and that it has not yet found a strategy for being strong on the global scale. So the old logic of resentment has a new victim. The people who have produced the video tape linked to the Madrid bombing in March realized that there are weaknesses in Spain and Europe in general and they knew how to use the logic of resentment "you want/love life and we love/want death." The fact that "they" love life is a sign of weakness. Thus, those who love death demonstrate strength. As long as the "you" love life, they cannot live up to the strength of the "we" who love death.

This grammar of a violent identity is a source of great power. At this point, one can introduce God into such an identity. God is always a factor that affects power; he empowers people and does not push them to be weak. He is a creative rather than destructive force. Therefore, one can link a strong identity with God; one cannot use his power as a weakening factor. If his name is linked with weakness or if weakness is presented to God then this weakness belongs to a strong identity or will be a clue to strengthening identity. In general and under normal conditions such a God can function as a humanizing factor in history, society, culture. Yet, in the case of a strong identity deeply dedicated to violence is different; here, on the basis of naming God, one betrays oneself and others with regard to the violence that one is responsible for. If this violence guarantees strength and the alternative to this violence is only weakness then God cannot be introduced to oppose this violence. It is not necessary to look upon violence as God's will. The video tape after the Madrid bombings doesn't say that God loves death. It says that these bombings are answers to the crimes in the wars in Afghanistan and Iraq and that there will be more answers "if it is God's will." God's part is not the death these bombings lead to. God's part in this game is by empowering the people who love death. He is not a deadly but a strengthening factor. Therefore, it is not necessary to know God's will. It suffices to call upon God to overcome one's own weaknesses. The result is that one cannot argue with reference to God's name against religiously violent people. They experience God as a power which strengthens their identity and no theology can establish an authority to conceive them that God has the power to weaken identities. This is a rather unpleasant result. Is there an alternative?

Plural Identities: Opposition to the Logic of Resentment

In the battle between the strong and the weak, God takes the side of the strong. As such a theological argument against the logic of resentment cannot deny the basic option in this logic. One has to argue against the second option which identifies the other as weak. In the logic of resentment God takes the side of the "we" against "the others." In arguing against this logic God's place in this difference is the difference itself. God does not stand against the strength of the "we" but at the same time he does not stand against the strength of the others. He stands against a relation which links "our" strength to the weakness of others. This is the position of a God who is love and yet this leads to a difficult position; this God is not useful in establishing an identity. He destabilizes an established identity and he is a power which empowers a plurality of identities. This plurality seeks strength in other identities. There is a biblical example for the plurality in Christian identities:

> For if I preach the gospel, I have nothing to boast of, for necessity is laid upon me; yes, woe is me if I do not preach the gospel! For if I do this willingly, I have a reward; but if against my will, I have been entrusted with a stewardship. What is my reward then? That when I preach the gospel, I may present the gospel of Christ without charge, that I may not abuse my authority in the gospel. For though I am free from all men, I have made myself a servant to all, that I might win the more; and to the Jews I became as a Jew, that I might win Jews; to those who are under the law, as under the law, that I might win those who are under the law; to those who are without law, as without law (not being without law toward God, but under law toward Christ), that I might win those who are without law; to the weak I became as weak, that I might win the weak. I have become all things to all men, that I might by all means save

some. Now this I do for the gospel's sake, that I may be partaker of it with you. (1 Cor 9:16-23)

Paul's mission statement leads to a strange result in terms of identity; a Christian needs a plurality of identities to become a true Christian. Others have something or are somebody necessary for Christians to take part in the Gospel. Christians cannot meet the other on an established basis; they have to meet the other on their basis in order to establish a Christian identity. Paul met the Jews not as a Christian, he met those not under the law not as someone under the law, he met the weak not in strength. If one puts this into the difference of weakness and strength then this missionary position becomes a key argument in opposition to the logic of resentment. Paul confronted himself with the strength of the other because his being Christian relied on their strengths. The strength of the Jews is that they are Jews, the strength of those not under law is that they are not under the law; the strength of the weak is that they are weak. Paul accepted the strength of the other as something he needed to become Christian – that he may partake of the gospel.

This is a logic in opposition to the logic of resentment. To become strong one needs the strengths of the other. Otherwise one is dominated by one's own weaknesses. In relation to the religiously violent people this leads to a difficult question: What is the strength of those religiously violent people? One answer is possible: that they do not fear death.

Loving Life and Accepting Death: A Logic of Empowerment in a World of Conflicts

The videotape of those who claimed responsibility for the Madrid bombings states: "you love life and we love death." The fatal error in this argument is the logic of resentment. On the basis of this logic loving life becomes a weakening factor and loving death is a lethal weapon. There is no way that one can argue with a God of love in favor of this position. Unfortunately, nor can one argue with such a God against this position.

Paul's plurality of identities changes this picture. There has to be a basis in terms of identity to meet those religiously violent people and this has to be strength in their identity position. Putting the positive into a negative formulation this strength becomes obvious: "you do fear death and we do not fear death." There is truth in such a position which is important for Christians in presenting their Gospel. People who fear death cannot sacrifice themselves for others. People who do not fear death are able to give up their lives for others. With such a position it is possible to overcome the weakening factor of a loving life. Those who love life should not fear death. There is a type of death that shows a love for life. The sacrifice on the cross is such a death. At the very heart of the Christian tradition one can argue against the religiously motivated violence in the present conflicts. It is true that those who are Christians do love life but it is not true that they do fear death. On the contrary: in searching for the strength in the identity of the other they do not fear for their lives. This is a kind of power which has no need for force. On the basis of this power nobody is forced to violence in order to establish a strong identity. With such a position Christians can help to overcome the weaknesses among Europeans. They do not have to fix their identity as a Christian but they can have a plurality of identities and one of them is this Christian identity which has overcome violence. So, the Christian identity of Europe does not depend on having God's name in the European Constitution, it depends on two other capacities: not to respond to violence with a logic of resentment and not to fear death when loving life.

François Bousquet

Recognizing God in Nonviolence: A Reflection on Mark 15:39

It is urgent now, more than ever, that we reflect upon the conflicts and violence that have become unavoidable aspects of the daily reality in which we perceive and seek God. But, the words and concepts of intellectuals often tend to overlook what is actually lived by ordinary people. As for theologians and deeply religious people, they should emphasize the critical strength faith brings to the battle against illusion, ideological manipulation or, more simply, lies. The world is not a dream, good or bad: it has to do with the life and death of each one of us. And, let us not forget that the Christian faith has its own efficacious resources to combat violence and the many masks behind which it hides. One essential element of this is that Christianity does not seek to counter violence with violence, which would do little more than accelerate a vicious downward spiral.

To demonstrate this, let us return to the fundamental event that is at the center of Christian Faith and examine the effects it produced. This event is the life of Christ that was completed when he affronted death. And it produced a sharing of the breath of life, the Holy Spirit, the breath of Jesus and of his Father to overcome violence and to live conflicts differently: "for the Glory of God and the salvation of the world."

Recognizing God in his Nonviolence

Let us take a moment to examine a verse from the New Testament. Mark 15:39 reads: "Upon seeing how he took his last breath, the centurion standing there in front of him cried out: truly, this man was the son of God!"[1]

---

[1] The Greek original reads: Ιδών δέ ὁ κεντυρίων ὁ παρεστηκώς ἐξ ἐναντίας ἀυτοῦ ὅτι οὕτως κράξας ἐξέπνευσεν εἶπεν αληθώς οὗτος ὁ ἄνθρωπος υἱός θεοῦ ἥν.

"*Seeing.*" Nothing can really change events, especially our perceptions of them, without visibility. The problem with violence is that it is perceptible, cruelly perceptible, to those who suffer from it, but is masked by speeches or mass media of those who could benefit from its dissimulation. But, when placed before the death of a martyr, cheating is no longer an option. Then, one sees sharply where injustice leads: to the murder of the innocent.

"*How* he took his last breath." "He" is the Christ and we shall briefly comment "how he took his last breath." In theological reflection on the death of Christ, a Christology "from above" must reflect on the birth, and the death of the Son of God, who becomes fully human: the Word becomes incarnate and has taken the human condition. From this approach emerges a paradox of the object of our Faith: the Eternal enters into time, the Infinite into finitude, and that He who is Life, one day, encounters death. However, Christology "from below" is also necessary since its basis is "the man Jesus," a man indeed different but human like us, a man among others. This second approach allows us to understand that what happened to Jesus, not only his death but also his resurrection, can happen to every human, and thus concerns all of humanity. Yet, one must not forget to consider not only *that* he died, but *how* he died upon the cross. It is the spirit (or Spirit with a capital) according to which (or whom) is lived that which is lived, that (who) makes the difference. The essential element is this. It is upon seeing *how* he took his last breath, without violence even towards those who were killing him, that the crucified Jesus was recognized as the Son of God, God born of God.

The mediocre network of sin leading to the death, in this case the death of the innocent, is complex: one disciple who betrays him, the others who flee, Pilate who washes his hands, powerful leaders who mock him, or the shouting crowd that demands injustice. Even today such are the reasons for which individuals, as well as masses, are injured or put to death. There is always a network of multiple causes: those who betray for their own best interests, those who say nothing and take flight, those who simply wash their hands of the matter, those who are stupid or those who side with the powerful. The list is endless. The end result, however, remains the same: the death of the innocent.

There are, however, New Testament texts that could lead one to imagine that the cross scenario could have played out differently:

"You who have saved others, save yourself ... " (Mk 15:29-31). And Jesus who, by the power of God, overthrows those who seek to harm innocent members of humanity allowing only the "good" to survive. Indeed, one must take the "Wrath of God" seriously. In the Bible, such wrath is mentioned each time humankind is scathed or humiliated because, as Saint Ireneus put it, "the glory of God is the human being fully alive." Wouldn't it be enough then to simply kill those who kill? Yes, but how would such logic come to an end? To use the title of one of Helder Camara's books, would this not simply perpetuate a "spiral of violence?" Another possibility can be seen in the death of Jesus. He dies as a just person, the Just *par excellence*, and now resides with God. But, what is God going to do with this world where vineyard workers murder all those sent by the proprietor, and even his own son (cf. Lk 20:9-16)? Decidedly, little can be done for humanity living in this type of world. In fact, such a world must be destroyed to begin something new. But, that is precisely what did not happen. What did happen then?

Knowing that he is facing an inevitable death, Jesus does not choose to use violence to counter his persecutors or those whose indifference, cowardice or pride cause the death of innocent people still today. On the contrary, he prefers to take death upon himself by refusing to use his divine status as a way out (cf. Ph 2:6) so that others could change and live. It is in and through this that one recognizes in this man God, what comes from God.

"Seeing how *he took his last breath*" (*exepneusen*). Perhaps the French word *expiré* is closer to the original Greek. It is a question of breathing out for the last time (one may prefer *pneuma,* or spirit to the term "breath"). Here, Trinitarian theology perceives the very heart of God: the Son who wishes to do his Father's will (not that there will be blood, even though he does not spare his own blood – in the Bible blood is life – but that people change and live fully). Jesus, the Son of God, gives his breath, the Holy Spirit that is his life, to the Father who in turn gives it back to him through eternal life and resurrection. Christian iconography depicts this idea beautifully in the "throne of grace" representations (the Father is represented on the cross supporting his Son's arms from behind; a dove, symbolizing the breath of life and the love of the Holy Spirit, is passing from the mouth of one to that of the other): there is no distance between the Father and the Son. Upon the cross the Father gives himself entirely. His entrails represent the Son and his breath, the Spirit. He is one, clinging to nothing of his life, giving all so that we may share this life, his life, the eternal life.

"*The Centurion.*" In fact, the centurion is a pagan, or a *goi*. This suggests that the discovery of God is meant for all, not merely a chosen few.

"*Cried out.*" A cry, what good news! The recognition of God's inherent nonviolence ... one merely has to consider the violent images of God that have nourished human fantasies in archaic "religions," for example, since the time of cavemen, or as developed by deficient interpretations of the Scripture.

"*Truly.*" *Truly* means "in reality." Here, we are not dealing with representations or words but rather with acts, and more precisely, the essential act: the essential love that is a gift and that constitutes Jesus, the Son of God, not only as true man but as a man who is true. For us, it is in act that the story of Christ continues, and this is what constitutes our faith.

"*This Man.*" It is not worth pushing the point, but this is an essential element shown by all Christologies "from below." Jesus, a unique man as the Son of God, is one among others, which implies three things. Firstly, it is not humanity in general that is called to be saved, but each and every person individually. Secondly, salvation is for everyone regardless of race, social status or intellectual and physical capacities. And thirdly, it is only from singular truth that the universal can begin to take shape.

"*Was the Son of God.*" At the heart of the Trinitarian revelation of God, upon the cross, are interwoven fraternity and filiation. That which governed the end of Jesus' life governed his whole life. On the one hand, it is the symbol of the vertical relationship with his Father, vertically meaning for us an ever-greater God. On the other, the horizontal image of open arms forever expanding towards brotherhood symbolizes a constantly growing humanity. One must not forget that radical filiation and universal fraternity are joined in the form of a cross which leads us to two elements to contemplate.

The first, concerning God, is that the Covenant resides within his essence; it is not something added on. Beyond the Trinitarian sequence of Easter, Ascension and Pentecost (as our liturgy shows), we have to admit that touching God is the same as touching humankind, touching humankind is the same as touching God. Thus, in God, alongside the Crucified's glorified humanity (and ours), there is the promise of resurrection and life. Hence, the eternal, Trinitarian and Living God became forever linked to that which we are becoming.

The second element to contemplate concerns human nature throughout history as defined by filiation and fraternity. This invites us to envisage all from the cross which represents the *"corps à corps"* of God himself through the human body of his Son along with all of humanity, in particular human beings in need of salvation, not only because they are sinners but just as much so when they are innocent, humiliated, sick, suffering of injustice or lost in death. It is from and through the eyes of the Crucified upon the cross, and not in the clouds, as if we were looking down at history, that the Christian sees all that is: the breath of faith that incarnates charity and vested hope.

The Conversion of Power

A clarifying remark is due. In saying "God's nonviolence," there is no suggestion that the innocent should allow themselves to be crushed without fighting, taking a stand or defending themselves. In fact, one may recognize a certain prophetic role in groups who deal with conflicts nonviolently without arms. Moreover, God's nonviolence is given to us to use in our daily struggle for justice and peace, the end goal being eternal life. And, such ends cannot be reached by avoiding conflict.

However, faith in the Crucified/Resurrected gives us ways of handling conflicts in other ways than with violence. It is theology and spirituality that must emphasize these resources by giving form and visibility to the Good Tidings upon which hope is founded. Indeed, salvation (health, freedom and life, from now until eternity) is for everyone, starting with those left behind; the lost, poor and outcast of this world.

Nonviolence's path toward fraternity is made through a conversion of power. Here, it must be added that the word "power" cannot always be interpreted negatively. Power is, in fact, that which allows us to attain and accomplish being, a notion that is linked to that which is "possible," and that allows for all that is possible to remain a genuine reality and not merely restricted to the imaginary realm. Power, including that attained through money and technology, only becomes blessing or curse according to the way it is used. This distinction is entirely ethical. Concepts such as common good and universal destination of goods must be regulatory. That to which God's radical nonviolence appeals in its central charitable essence (*agapè*, or love of giving) is to use power for the good. This calls for a difficult conversion of power's usage. In this matter, what are faith's resources? Two clarifying remarks are due before answering this question.

Firstly, it is not faith in and by itself (faith upon which theology reflects in culture) that can provide solutions. In fact, simply having faith does not dismiss us from reflection and meditation, two key aspects of our intelligent and thinking nature. No one is free from reflection or analysis simply because they are believers. Aware that God's action is not magic, trusting in God does not rid us of our responsibilities as humans. One may be moved by the depth of the negative expression of the commandment, "You shall not kill": we have not finished realizing (in the double sense of the word: knowing and doing) what life is about: but we know the limits from which the inhumanity starts: "You shall not kill." In the same way, moreover, the prohibition of idolatry means that we have not finished discovering who God is, while at the same time there are grounds for thinking that our concern is not about God, but what prevents us from sharing in his life, his way of being. The first resource is thus confronted by our capacity to analyse, to understand and to use our creativity, in the image of God and his power, to open up new and real possibilities.

Secondly, a criterion and strength are given to us by the crucified who, for Christians, embodies truth in the flesh, the highest form of truth. This truth has three dimensions: knowledge, ethics and faith. Today, knowledge dominates. Objectivity consists in a relationship between knowing subjects and objects of knowledge and this leads to technological mastery. Here, in one way or another, the ideal is that of *adaequatio rei et mentis,* or the relationship between our symbolic representations and reality. The second type of truth, the ethical, is often forgotten. In this case, truth speaks of the relationship between subjects and allows the other in a relationship to really be responsible for his or her own becoming. It is however the third dimension of truth that interests us the most as theologians. Here, the ultimate truth is the very person of Christ himself who was crucified and has been risen from the death, the truth of humanity humiliated and risen, the truth of God as a gift to humankind. In this case, the supreme truth by which all others are judged is the *corps à corps* with human beings, even with those who seem lost, the truth that God himself incarnates in his son.

Indeed, there can be no morality without knowledge, but morality is distinct in itself. Faith cannot do without ethics, but faith is something else. In fact, that which presents faith as the ultimate truth judges all our ethics (aristocratic ethics where the poor have no place, for example). But, ethics must ponder upon the power that knowledge procures.

The concrete and cardinal truth that is the body of the crucified Christ is not only Judgment, the nonviolent light that allows us to discern, or God's gaze upon our ability to convert power: the real truth is promise and already salvation, because God is forever linked with what we are becoming, now and for eternity.

Jamal Khader

Opportunities and Threats for Religions in Conflict and Violence: How (Not) to Use the Name of God

In the early 1970s people asked, "Who takes religion seriously?" At the beginning of the third millennium, many people are taking religion seriously but not always in a positive manner. In speaking of the Middle East, since the beginning of this century, especially after 9/11, one cannot avoid phrases such as "religion," "religious tension," "religious terrorism," etc. Is Islam alone implicated? What about the two other monotheistic religions? We will begin with Islamic fundamentalism, but we will see later that fundamentalism is not exclusively an Islamic phenomenon.

The Holy Land is holy for the three monotheistic religions, Judaism, Christianity and Islam. Believers of each of these religions claim to speak in God's Name; what are the implications of this for a peaceful coexistence in the Land they all call holy? Is their common belief in one God an attribute of unity or dispute?

Muslims regard the Holy Land as God's endowment, in which individuals live and respect its sanctity and protect it for God and for themselves as a gift from God. Christians perceive this land as their own, and for them the Holy Land precedes any other sacred site or place of visitation around the world, because it is the place where Jesus Christ was born, lived, taught, died and rose from the dead in glory. To Jews it is also a Holy land and the land of their faith and roots. It is for this reason of sanctity, in addition to all the international and local political reasons, that there is conflict about this land.

The question is: Did God choose the faithful of any religion to announce their faith and knowledge of God by killing the other children of God? These nations should see what has led them to religious wars: Is it really for the glory of God or for the glory of humankind and their personal interests? This is the reality we are living today. We believe in God, and we reject those who have a faith different than ours.

An analysis of fundamentalism, its roots, history and influence exceeds the aims of this paper. What we will try to do is to have a close look at the role of religion and especially religious fundamentalism in the Middle East, and more specifically the Holy Land and its influence on the Palestinian–Israeli conflict. Theological aspects within the historical context will prevail over other aspects.

Fundamentalism in General

Florien Wineriter, head of the Humanist Institute in New York, offers the following definition:

> Fundamentalism is the affirmation of religious authority as holistic and absolute, admitting of neither criticism nor reduction; it is expressed through the collective demand that specific creedal and ethical dictates derived from Scripture be publicly recognized and legally enforced. The fundamentalists of the three Abrahamic religions feel it is their mission to establish earthly theocracies in preparation for the arrival of a messiah. They use political influence to enact government laws and regulations that will give their beliefs the force of secular law thereby forcing everyone to live according to their moral precepts.[1]

Some common characteristics of fundamentalism include: 1) religious idealism as the basis for personal and communal identity; 2) an understanding of truth as revealed and unified; 3) envisioning themselves as part of a cosmic struggle; 4) the seizure of historical moments and reinterpretation of them in light of a cosmic struggle; 5) the demonization of opposition; 6) selectivity in what parts of their tradition and heritage they stress.[2]

---

[1] In a lecture given by Florien Wineriter on March 25, 2003 to his Humanist Institute class in New York City as a response to B.B. Lawrence, *Defenders of God* (San Francisco: Harper & Row, 1989).

[2] The five ideological characteristics are: fundamentalists are concerned "first" with the erosion of religion and its proper role in society; fundamentalists are selective of their tradition and what part of modernity they accept or choose to react against; they embrace some form of Manicheanism (dualism); fundamentalists stress absolutism and inerrancy in their sources of revelation; they opt for some form of millennialism or

Several writers have tried to study fundamentalism, searching for its common characteristics.[3] Theologically, there are several traits that may lead to fundamentalism, and eventually to violence in the name of God.

1. Each of the three monotheistic religions claims to be the one true religion of God on earth. Each has the right to do so, but if this means in the process that they may fight to prove that the others are wrong, the conclusions are different. The logic of "true or false," "light or darkness," "white or black" tends to divide the world into righteous and evil people; the battle is then set to rid the world of the evil, in the name of God.[4]

2. Exclusiveness is another characteristic. The example of the Holy Land is clear. This land is holy for Jews, Christians and Muslims. To exclude the others seems to be the logic necessary to preserve the holiness of the land.

3. Holy Scriptures represent the core of any religion. The possibility of different interpretations or of a partial selection of texts, coupled with a lack of authority to define the truth of these texts, can pave the way for the manipulation of these texts for political reasons, where someone may look for a pretext or excuse to support his or her ideology.

4. The simplistic approach. As the situation is complex, fundamentalists tend to oversimplify the questions and the answers: "God gave us the land (the Holy Land)" is one of the slogans used to convince people to join the struggle to do "God's will."

5. Finally, pretending to speak in God's name and defending his interests may lead to a legitimization of war; be it in the name of

---

messianism. (See http://religiousmovements.lib.virginia.edu/nrms/fund.html)

[3] For example, H. Lazarus-Yafeh, "Contemporary Fundamentalism: Judaism, Christianity, Islam," in L. J. Silberstein (ed.), *Jewish Fundamentalism in Comparative Perspective: Religion, Ideology, and the Crisis of Modernity* (New York / London: New York University Press, 1993), 42-55.

[4] See R.M. Young, "Fundamentalism and Terrorism," at http://www.humannature.com/ rmyoung-/papers/pap135h.htm.

forthcoming eschatological period, the fulfilment of God's promises of a land, or a war to spread the "true" religion of God.

In the Middle East, religion and politics are mixed. Facing problems and challenges, every believer searches for answers in his or her own faith which is supposed to provide them with answers. If the search for answers is not done dialectically and in common with all the believers, the easiest way is often to address a strong leader who "has all the answers." If these "ready answers" are not questioned, the leader bears the responsibility of leading his or her audience into a one-sided view.

Let us look at the three monotheistic religions that exist in the Middle East, and their fundamentalist approach to the problems facing their believers. Finally, we will ask the question: what is the true meaning of religion in all this and especially the role of our Christian faith.

Islam

The Palestinians' response, after the Arab defeats of 1948 and 1967, was political, secularist, and nationalist. The Palestinian cause was seen as a national disaster, which called for a struggle that could lead to the return of Palestinians to their land and the foundation of a secular and democratic state.[5] All religious arguments were totally absent from their literature.

With the influence of the Muslim Brotherhood in Egypt, and especially after the Iranian Revolution in 1979, the religious dimension became more evident. The Islamic movement began its interpretation of the conflict in religious terms.

---

[5] See the Palestinian National Charter (July 17, 1968) where the only mention of religion is: "The liberation of Palestine, from a spiritual point of view, will provide the Holy Land with an atmosphere of safety and tranquility, which in turn will safeguard the country's religious sanctuaries and guarantee freedom of worship and of visit to all, without discrimination of race, color, language, or religion." Cf. L.S. Kadi (ed.), *Basic Political Documents of the Armed Palestinian Resistance Movement* 12 (Beirut: Palestine Research Centre,1969): 137-41.

Faithful to the Muslim Brotherhood's grassroots method of establishing a Muslim society, the Islamic Resistance Movement (Hamas), founded by Sheikh Ahmed Yasin, initiated a welfare program that was associated with the Muslim Brotherhood, creating a charitable network in the Gaza Strip, consisting of clinics, drug rehabilitation programs, youth clubs, sporting facilities, and Quran classes.

Hamas and the Islamic Jihad interpreted the Palestinian tragedy in religious terms. It had happened "because the people had neglected their religion"; "Palestinians would only shake off Israeli rule when they return to Islam."[6] They were fighting a battle for the future of the entire *ummah*. Islamic Jihad was interested an in armed struggle against Israel.

Hamas believes that "There is no solution to the Palestinian problem except by Jihad." "Palestine is a *waqf* (religious endowment) land. It is a *sharia* (Islamic judicial system) ruling that any land acquired by the Muslims by force is proclaimed Islamic endowment for the Muslims. It is an eternal Islamic heritage."[7]

A central feature of classical Islam is the total, comprehensive integration of state and religion. The Hamas Covenant (1988) states that

> The Islamic Resistance Movement is one of the wings of Muslim Brotherhood in Palestine. Muslim Brotherhood Movement is a universal organization. It is characterized by its deep understanding, accurate comprehension and its complete embrace of all Islamic concepts of all aspects of life, culture, creed, politics, economics, education, society, etc ....[8]

---

[6] Beverley Milton-Edwards, *Islamic Politics in Palestine* (London and New York: Taurus Academic Studies, 1996), 184-85.

[7] "The Covenant of the Islamic Resistance Movement (HIRM) (Article Eleven)": The Islamic Resistance Movement believes that the land of Palestine is an Islamic *Waqf* consecrated for future Muslim generations until Judgment Day. Neither it nor any part of it be squandered or given up. The law governing the land of Palestine is to be in accordance with the Islamic Sharia (law) and the same goes for any country the Muslims have conquered by force, because during the times of (Islamic) conquests, the Muslims consecrated these lands to Muslim generations until the day of Judgment.

[8] *The Covenant of the Islamic Resistance Movement*, art. 2.

It aims at "the [re]birth of the Islamic message, of the righteous ancestor, for Allah is its target, the Prophet is its example and the Quran is its constitution, Jihad is its path and death for the sake of Allah is the loftiest of its wishes."[9]

Hamas deplores the loss of Islamic values. Their fight is in the name of God. Their objectives are "the fighting against the false, defeating it and vanquishing it so that justice could prevail, homelands be retrieved and from its mosques would the voice of the *mu'azen* emerge declaring the establishment of the state of Islam, so that people and things would return each to their right places and Allah is our helper."[10]

From this perspective, there is no solution to the Palestinian question except through Jihad, the individual duty of every Muslim, Hamas thus considers the "initiatives, and peaceful solutions and international conferences, in contradiction to its principles," they are considered "a waste of time and vain endeavors."[11] The link between religion and nationalism is strong; such that

> abusing any part of Palestine is abuse directed against part of religion. Nationalism of the Islamic Resistance Movement is part of its religion .... Hamas does not consider these conferences capable of realizing the demands, restoring the rights or doing justice to the oppressed. These [peace] conferences are only ways of setting the infidels in the land of the Muslims as arbitrators.[12]

Hamas considers the Palestinian problem to be a religious one, which should be dealt with on this basis.

> Jihad is not confined to the carrying of arms and the confrontation of the enemy. The effective word, the good article, the useful book, support and solidarity – together with the presence of sincere

---

[9] *The Covenant of the Islamic Resistance Movement*, art. 5.

[10] *The Covenant of the Islamic Resistance Movement*, art. 9.

[11] *The Covenant of the Islamic Resistance Movement*, art. 13.

[12] *The Covenant of the Islamic Resistance Movement*.

purpose for the hoisting of Allah's banner higher and higher – all these are elements of the Jihad for Allah's sake.[13]

Finally, Hamas asks that the Arab and Islamic peoples support Hamas, "as Allah wants them to, extending to it more and more funds till Allah's purpose is achieved." And when will this "purpose" be achieved? The same covenant predicts that there will be a "constant struggle till the Day of Judgment in the Holy Land."[14]

As we can see, Hamas, as part of the Islamic fundamentalism in Palestine, has its own reading of the Quran, and it is convinced it is doing God's will. To defend the holiness of the land and God's rights, Hamas is ready to fight "till the Day of Judgment," till the eschatological battle. Hamas is nourished by uncertainty, poverty, religious feelings, and the absence of any future and just solution to the Palestinian problem. Hamas is typical of fundamentalism.

Islamic fundamentalism has inspired not only Hamas but a wide range of the Palestinian population: suicide bombers come from the Fatah movement, from the Popular Front for the Liberation of Palestine (PFLP), a Marxist-inspired movement, as well as from Hamas. What used to be a national and a territorial problem has taken on an impressive religious dimension.

Judaism

Jewish fundamentalism is no different from Islamic fundamentalism. The argument is simple: "God gave us this land, it is a Holy Land (Eretz Israel); it is ours and only ours"; "if the State of Israel was viewed as the unfolding of a messianic scenario, then the miraculous victory of the 1967 War was an essential stage in that process. The territories belong to the Jewish people (i.e., the State of Israel) by Divine decree and they may not be handed over to foreign hands."[15]

---

[13] *The Covenant of the Islamic Resistance Movement*, art. 30.

[14] *The Covenant of the Islamic Resistance Movement*, art. 34.

[15] D.E. Wagner, *Anxious for Armageddon* (Ontario: Herald Press, 1994), 62-68.

A clear example of Jewish fundamentalism is the *Gush Emunim* movement. The Israeli occupation of the West Bank in the 1967 War aroused the passionate determination in many Israelis to ensure that these territories should be part of the state of Israel permanently. Future members of Gush Emunim – whose founders first formulated the settlement ideology[16] – became active in establishing Jewish settlements in the occupied territories. However, not until after the 1973 War did they feel the need to organize politically. In the gloomy public mood occasioned by the first territorial concessions in the Sinai Peninsula (required by the disengagement agreement with Egypt), the founders of Gush Emunim were determined to organize in order to oppose further territorial concessions and to promote the extension of Israeli sovereignty over the occupied territories.

All of Gush Emunim's spiritual authorities and many of its leaders were educated by Avraham Yitzhak ha-Cohen Kook, the first Ashkenazi chief rabbi of Israel. Kook believed that the era of redemption for the Jewish people had already begun with the rise of modern Zionism and the growing Zionist enterprise in Palestine.[17] Israel's victory in the 1967 War transformed the status of Kook's theology. Suddenly it became clear to his students that they were indeed living in the messianic age. Ordinary reality assumed a sacred status; every event possessed theological meaning and was part of the meta-historical process of redemption.[18] Although shared by many religious authorities, this view was most effectively expounded by Kook's son, Rabbi Zvi Yehuda Kook, an influential Rabbi in modern Jewish thought. The younger Kook defined the State of Israel as the halachic Kingdom of Israel, and the Kingdom of Israel as the Kingdom of Heaven on earth. The belief that they were living in the messianic age and that redemption was at hand has operational consequences for Gush members.

---

[16] E. Sprinzak, *Gush Emumin: The Politics of Zionist Fundamentalism in Israel* (The American Jewish Committee, Institute of Human Relations, 1986); cf. "Gush Emunim: The First Decade" (Hebrew), in *Nekuda* 69 (February 2, 1984): 5-7.

[17] Cf. Z. Yaron, *The Teaching of Rav Kook* (Hebrew 3rd ed.) (Jerusalem: Jewish Agency 1979), 270-73.

[18] Z. Raanan, *Gush Emunim* (Hebrew) (Tel Aviv: Sifriyat Poalim, 1980), 64-67.

Almost all the biblical rules regarding the Kingdom of Israel are literally applicable in the messianic age.[19] Gush Emunim recognizes a selective interpretation of the Jewish religious law as its sole authority. Their aim is to create a "halachic Jewish state,"[20] a theocracy where the only law is religious in nature and all obligations and rights are defined in ancient religious terms. Their "Land of Israel" is not a strip of land with territorial boundaries; it is a spiritual and theological concept which must be realized.

To understand *Gush Emunim*, it is necessary to see how they manage to meld politics and religion. They define themselves as a group of devoted religious believers for whom the concept of compromise is practically foreign. They know Truth, and of course Truth cannot be compromised or abandoned in any manner. According to the fundamentalists of *Gush Emunim*, the Land of Israel – every grain of its soil – is holy. Thus no individual can escape holiness and every place upon which a Jewish foot is set is holy.

Since 1967, the issue of Israel's borders has assumed an unprecedented seriousness. The proponents of the messianic idea only have one consideration in mind: the biblical covenant made by God with Abraham. They soon discovered that the territory so promised was not confined to the area taken by the Israeli army in the 1967 War but extended to the Euphrates on the northeast and – according to one school of biblical interpretation – to the Nile on the southwest.[21] While no unanimity on the operational meaning of the biblical map has been

---

[19] Cf. Yaron, *The Teaching of Rav Kook*, 270-73.

[20] Halacha is the name of the system of Jewish religious law that, according to the Orthodox tradition, is based on the divine revelation to Moses at Sinai, and has been handed down, developed and interpreted by the sages from generation to generation. Halachic principles and rules apply to all aspects of human conduct.

[21] Gen. 15-18. About the different borders indicated in the Bible and interpreted by the religious Zionism, see A. Marchadour and D. Neuhaus, "Vers le pays que je te ferai voir," in *La Terre, la Bible et l'histoire* (Paris: Bayard 2006), 23-71. In the Bible, different borders were indicated; see for example Gen. 15:18-21; Deut. 34:1-4; Joshua 1: 1-6. See also J.M. Henshaw, "Israel's Grand Design: Leaders Crave Area from Egypt to Iraq," at http://www.jerusalemites.org/articles/english/apr2003/9.htm.

reached, not a single fundamentalist authority is ready to alienate a square inch for either peace or security. Some even favor further territorial annexations.

Rabbi Israel Ariel is a typical fundamentalist. In an interview, when asked about current political constraints and diplomatic limitations, the rabbi replied that Joshua had far worse political constraints and limitations. When pressed further about potential casualties and national losses, the fundamentalist rabbi referred to a biblical ruling that in a holy war no question about casualties is legitimate until one fifth of the nation is extinct.[22]

In 1979 the Rabbinate ruled that no part of the Holy Land could be alienated even in the context of a peace treaty. "According to our holy Torah and unequivocal and decisive halachic rulings there exists a severe prohibition to pass to foreigners the ownership of any piece of the land of Israel since it was made sacred by Abraham's Covenant."[23]

What role do the *Gush Emunim* fundamentalists accord to the Palestinian Arabs in the age of Jewish redemption? What rights, if any, should they retain in the Holy Land of Israel? For years *Gush Emunim* spokesmen enumerated "three alternatives" to be presented to Arabs: acknowledge the legitimacy of the Zionist doctrine (*Gush Emunim*'s version); obey the laws of the state without formal recognition of Zionism and in return receive the rights of resident aliens (with no political rights); or immigrate to Arab countries.[24] It is possible to identify three positions on the status of non-Jews in Israel in this fundamentalist school: limitation of rights, denial of rights, and – in the most extreme case – extermination. Each position is anchored in an authoritative interpretation of Scripture. The first stems from the conviction that the notion of universal human rights is a foreign ideal that has no meaning in the context of the Holy Land.[25] In the Bible, non-Jewish inhabitants of Palestine were accorded the status of resident

---

[22] Interview with Rabbi Ariel, *Ha'aretz* (January 31, 1985), 20.

[23] See U. Tal, "Foundations of Political Messianism," at http://www.geocitiescom/ala- basters_archive/messianic_ trend.html.

[24] E. Sprinzak, "Gush Emunim: The Iceberg Model of Political Extremism," (Hebrew), in *Mimshal Veyahasim Beinleumiim* 17 (1981): 32.

[25] See Tal, "Foundations."

aliens, enjoying some privileges but never obtaining rights equal to those of the Jews. One consequence of this view is that in times of war no distinction should be made between enemy soldiers and civilians since both are of the category of people who do not belong in the land.

A minority have proposed extermination, using the biblical precedent of the Amalekites, a people so cruel that God commanded the Israelites to slay them without mercy (1 Samuel 15:23). In 1980, Rabbi Israel Hess argued that the Palestinians were to Jews what darkness was to light, and that they deserved the same fate as the Amalekites.[26] In the same year, Gush settler Haim Tzuria wrote that hatred was "natural and healthy":

> In each generation we have those who rise up to wipe us out, therefore each generation has its own Amalek. The Amalekism of our generation expresses itself in the extremely deep hatred of the Arabs to our national renaissance in the land of our forefathers.[27]

None of these views has so far been ruled out as erroneous by Israel's Chief Rabbinate, the highest official religious authority.

Rabbi Kook's followers only concentrated on the more aggressive biblical passages, in which God commanded the Israelites to drive out the indigenous people of the Promised Land, to make no treaty with them, to destroy their sacred symbols, and even to exterminate them.[28] They interpreted the belief that the Jews were God's chosen people to mean that they were not bound by the laws obligatory for other nations, but were unique, holy, and set apart. God's command to conquer the land, argued Rabbi Shlomo Aviner, was more important than "the human and moral considerations of the national rights of the gentiles to our land."[29] Their reading of the Bible is selective.

---

[26] *Bat Kol* (February 26, 1980).

[27] See E. Sprinzak, "The Politics, Institutions and Culture of Gush Emunim," in Laurence J. Silberstein (ed.), *Jewish Fundamentalism in Comparative Perspective: Religion, Ideology, and the Crisis of Modernity* (New York and London, 1993), 127-28.

[28] Ex. 23:23-33; Josh. 6:17-21; 8:20-29; 11:21-25.

[29] I.S. Lustick, *For the Land and the Lord: Jewish Fundamentalism in Israel* (New York, 1988), 75-76.

Despite their small number, Gush members can rely, in times of need, upon a large pool of reinforcements from the religious educational system, in addition to its political resources. Despite their extreme positions on settlement issues, Gush activists are always welcome in high political circles. Fully backed by the National Religious Party, they could be sure that no decisive military action would be taken against them for fear of a general government crisis. They also enjoyed the support of many Israeli politicians, such as Menachem Begin, Yizhaq Shamir and Ariel Sharon.[30] In 1978, its official settlement organization was recognized by the World Zionist Organization.[31]

The Kookist rabbis were especially incensed by the Oslo Accords: "By signing away the sacred land, the government had committed a criminal act."[32] Some saw Rabin (a former Israeli prime minister) as one who actively threatens the life of Jews. Yigal Amir, a former student of a religious school, said that his study of Jewish law had persuaded him that Rabin was an enemy of the Jewish people; he had a duty to kill him, which he did.[33]

Members of Gush Emunim argue that

> what appears to be confiscation of Arab-owned land for subsequent settlement by Jews is in reality not an act of stealing but one of sanctification. From their perspective the land is redeemed by being transferred from the satanic to the divine sphere .... The Jewish fundamentalists believe that God gave all of the Land of Israel to the Jews and that Arabs living in Israel are viewed as thieves.[34]

---

[30] Cf. G. Goldberg and E.B. Zadok, "Regionalism and Territorial Cleavage in Formation: Jewish Settlement in the Administered Territories" (Hebrew) in *Mimshal Veyahasim Beinleumiim* 21 (1983): 84-90.

[31] E. Sprinzak, "Gush Emunim: The Iceberg Model of Political Extremism," 41.

[32] S.C. Heilman, "Guides of the Faithful: Contemporary Religious Zionist Rabbis." in Scott Appleby (ed.), *Spokesmen for the Despised: Fundamentalist Leaders of the Middle East* (Chicago: University of Chicago Press, 1997), 354.

[33] K. Armstrong, *A Battle for God* (London: HarperCollins, 2000), 353.

[34] See http://www.israelshamir.net/Hebrew/Heb10.htm.

The concept of holiness includes the land and people. When the concept of holiness is applied to a specific group, this group becomes superior. So the concepts of "promised land" and "chosen people" may imply that the possession of the land is exclusive to one religion "by divine law" ("This land was given to us by God," they argue); as such, Israel is interpreted to be the historical realization of the biblical aspiration of the return to the "promised land" and Jewish blood is seen as more valuable than other people's blood.

Someone once said: "When the Jew is humiliated, God is shamed! When the Jew is attacked – it is an assault upon the Name of God!"[35] Someone recently wrote: "Since the Jews are a God-called, covenantal people, whose very existence as a people expresses God to the world, then those who fight against them and persecute them, fight against God."[36]

What is important for us is to see the implications of these ideas on the conflict of the Middle East. The question is: "Is Israel a state like any other state, regulated by international law? Or should it be treated differently because it is the realization of divine promises?"[37]

The results of such beliefs are disastrous for the Palestinians and for the possibilities of peace in the Holy Land. Palestinians are dispossessed of their land, they are not recognized as citizens with equal rights because the state is "Jewish," the settlements are built on their land in the name of "returning to biblical sites," refugees are denied the right to return home to what has become Israel or even to the Occupied Territories (because they represent a demographic danger to the Jewish identity of the state of Israel). In their struggle to obtain their legitimate rights, Palestinians are faced with theological arguments about the divine law. Those who most oppose peace are the religious parties, and those in favor of a compromise are secular Jews. What role does religion have to build peace? In the name of God, human beings are humiliated and basic human rights are denied.

---

[35] E. Sprinzak, "Three Models of Religious Violence: The Case of Jewish Fundamentalism in Israel," in M.E. Marty and R.S. Appleby (eds.), *Fundamentalism and the State* (Chicago / London: University of Chicago Press, 1993), 480; Armstrong, *A Battle for God*, 350.

[36] Sprinzak, "Three Models of Religious Violence."

[37] Sprinzak, "Three Models of Religious Violence."

Jewish fundamentalism played a role in Israeli politics and public opinion. As of yet, Israel does not recognize the Palestinian people as a nation with rights; nor that the West Bank and Gaza Strip (occupied in 1967) belong to Palestine and as such are occupied. They consider it as part of Eretz Israel. At best, some of it can be given (not restituted) to Palestinians to solve the demographic problem and in order not to be accused of dominating another people.

Christianity

Christian Zionism is the Christian version of fundamentalism. Although some may argue that Christian Zionism is an American phenomenon, while true, the special interest of Christian Zionism concerns the Holy Land which makes it a Middle Eastern phenomenon.

Let us first take account of the main axioms of Zionism: 1) Zionism argues that the Jews are a people like all other peoples – "the people of Israel," constituting a "nation"; 2) Zionism furthermore argues that there is a Jewish Land – "the land of Israel" – for the Jewish people – "the people of Israel";[38] 3) in the Jewish land, the Jewish people must establish a Jewish sovereign state; 4) this is, according to Zionism, the solution to the problem of Jewish survival in a world that will always be hostile to them. These basic axioms of Zionism say nothing about the other (Muslim and Christian Palestinians) inhabitants of the Land. Some early Zionists were shocked to discover that Palestine was not "a land with no people for a people with no land."[39]

With regard to the relationship between religion and state, even secular Zionists tend to regard the Bible (Old Testament) as a historical document that legitimates Jewish sovereignty in the Land. In conclusion, it is important to distinguish between Judaism and Zionism. Judaism is a millennia-old religious, cultural and historical tradition. Zionism is a modern political ideology, formulated within the context

---

[38] Although some early Zionists (including the founding father of political Zionism, Theodor Herzl) were even willing to consider Jewish colonization of Uganda in Africa or parts of Argentina, this was seen as temporary until Jewish settlement of Palestine could be carried through.

[39] Wagner, *Anxious for Armageddon*, 92.

of nineteenth-century Europe and as a response to the particular plight of the Jewish people within this modern context.

After the Second World War, Western Christians have been progressively discovering the Jewish roots of their faith, increasing their sympathy for Jews and Jewish political claims. This is particularly true of the Catholic, Protestant and Evangelical Churches. Zionism is interpreted to be in accordance with what the Bible says, particularly the Old Testament that posits the Jewish people in the Land promised to them by God. Reading the Bible would seem to predispose the reader to accept Zionism as both seem to speak about Palestine as a land given to the Jews by God. The strong biblical formation of some British and American politicians has been a decisive factor in their support of Zionist aspirations and the state of Israel.

Christian Zionism is based upon three fundamental pillars.[40] 1) There is a first a biblical view of the world and the attempt to read contemporary events within a biblical framework. 2) Then there is the eschatological question: When will Jesus return? Christian Zionists strongly promote the idea that we are living in the end of times and that Christ's return is imminent. World events are seen as playing out this end-of-time scenario. 3) The focus on the Jewish people and the State of Israel: Christian Zionism holds that the promises to the church for the end of time, regarding the universal recognition of Jesus Christ as Lord and Savior, must be preceded by the fulfilment of the Old Testament promises to Israel. These promises include the return of the Jews to their homeland, the establishment of a Jewish state and the building of the Third Temple. This will ultimately provoke the war at the end of time that must precede the Second Coming of Christ. Jews should return to the Holy Land in order to hasten the return of Jesus Christ. God will then use Israel as a divine instrument in the punishment of the unbelievers. These ideas grew in popularity within Christian evangelical circles, particularly in the USA after the establishment of the state of Israel and even more so after the 1967 war and the Israeli conquest and occupation of the biblical heartland of Judaea and Samaria.

---

40 N. Ateek *et al.* (eds.), *Challenging Christian Zionism: Theology, Politics, and the Israel-Palestine Conflict* (London: Melisende, 2005), 86-87.

The fundamentalist reading of Old Testament history and prophecy passages focuses on the themes of election, people and land. The biblical text is understood without any historical context or critical distance and the events described in the Bible are applied to present realities. An unbroken continuity is seen between the Jewish commonwealth in Palestine before 70AD and the emergence of the State of Israel in 1948. The Land has been promised to the Jews and this promise is as valid today as it was in the days of Abraham. God's plan for redemption works through Israel. It was only because Israel refused Jesus Christ that the Church was founded, this vision being founded on a reading of Romans 9-11. According to Christian Zionism, the time of the pagans (the time of the Church of the Gentiles) is coming to an end as predicted by Jesus in Luke 21:24. The events of 1948 (the establishment of the State of Israel) and 1967 (the extension of Jewish sovereignty over the Old City of Jerusalem) seem to point to the approaching end.

Particular eschatological passages in the Old Testament[41] and in the New Testament[42] are used to foretell in very precise terms the triumph of "God's people" in cataclysmic events. This is understood as beginning to be fulfilled in our present times.

Christian Zionists tend not only to know the details of these events but also the timetable for their realization. 1948 and 1967 were important turning points as the eschatological clock started ticking to mark the beginning of the end. In the time of tribulation[43] that precedes the Second Coming of Christ, Israel will fight the wars of the Lord. This will culminate in the battle of Armageddon.[44] After Christ returns, the thousand year (millennial) rule of Christ will begin that will culminate in the ultimate defeat of Satan and his emissaries. This time chart is full of violence, war and destruction. In this war scenario, Islam and Muslims play the role of the powers of darkness.[45] Israel will confront Islam and bring it to its knees. Muslims have two options according to the Christian Zionist view: they can either convert to

---

[41] Especially the prophets – Ez. 37-38, Daniel and Zach. 12-14.

[42] Luke 21:21-24, 1Thess. 4-5, Revelation.

[43] Cf. Mark 13, Revelation 12-19.

[44] Revelation 19.

[45] Before Islam, it was Communism that played this diabolical role.

Christianity, accepting the Christian Zionist view or they can die in the cataclysmic events of the end of time. Christian Arabs, in fact, have the same option as the Muslims.[46]

Christian Zionism's fusion of religion with politics guarantees Israeli interests. A scriptural foundation of this political behavior is God's word to Abraham that God "will bless those that bless you and curse those that curse you."[47] However, it is important to note that, although Christian Zionism is seemingly pro-Jewish, it is not in fact. In the end, Jews have the same ultimate choice as Muslims: they must confess Jesus Christ or be swallowed up in the eschatological catastrophes.

The alliance between the religious elements in the Jewish Israeli right wing and the Christian Zionists is particularly strong. However, the alliance is a tense and fragile one. Right-wing Jewish Zionists focus on their present needs (in the present situation of war they need the support of the Christian Zionists who constitute an important political lobby in the USA), whereas Christian Zionists focus on the apocalyptic future (the Jews will be believers in Christ). Religious Jews are profoundly uncomfortable with the proselytizing of Christian Zionists and Christian Zionists are profoundly uncomfortable with the anti-Christian attitudes of right-wing religious Jews. Moments of tension have emerged on various issues.[48] However, shared interests include: opposition to any territorial compromise in negotiations with the Palestinians, support for the colonization of all Palestinian territories, insistence on the unity of Jerusalem under Israeli sovereignty, encouraging Jewish immigration to Israel, encouraging Palestinian Arabs to leave Palestine and hostility towards Islam and Arab nationalism.

In addition to the alliance between Christian Zionism and religious Jewish Zionism, important figures in the US administration have been susceptible to this ideological configuration. American evangeli-

---

[46] See http://www.cc-vw.org/articles/czdefine1.html.

[47] Genesis 12:2.

[48] In Israel today there are a few thousand Jews who believe in Jesus and resist definition as Christians, calling themselves "Messianic Jews." They meet in over 90 congregations and insist on their Jewish identity. Many of them are Christian Zionists and some are hard-liners when it comes to the Israeli-Palestinian conflict.

cals have thrown themselves into the political arena and many of them share basic Christian Zionist beliefs. Some of these have served as important advisors to the American presidents, particularly in the times of Presidents Reagan, Bush Senior, and George W. Bush. This ideological configuration is also strongly promoted in the evangelical media, a vast network of television stations that presents the evangelical agenda to American and worldwide viewers. Christian Zionism has a sophisticated and successful grasp of the importance of media and political activism. Needless to say, in the light of the American military engagement in Afghanistan, in Iraq, and the declaration of a war on terrorism (often synonymous with radical Islam), the Christian Zionist ideology has had an even greater voice. As a French intellectual put it, with some irony: "les fondamentalistes veulent faire la volonté de Dieu, que Dieu le veuille ou pas."[49]

Fundamentalism, and Christian Zionism as a form of it, deforms the very essence of religion. Christian Zionism has tragic effects on the Christians of the Arab World and their Churches. The common people are not always able to distinguish between these sectarian groups and Christianity. At the very least, they are embarrassing the Christian Churches, especially in the Holy Land. It is known that these people organize arrogant, triumphalistic and provocative manifestations in the Old City of Jerusalem on the occasion of Sukkot (Feast of Tabernacles) and other Jewish festivities under the protection of the Israeli police and soldiers. Christian Zionism has a strong proselytizing movement within the Christian community in the Holy Land. In this way, they are fragmenting the Christian community, which is already very fragmented, and thus limiting the credibility of its witness; they affect negatively their reading the Bible (mainly the relation between the Old and New Testament), their dialogue with Muslims and the possibility of a positive and dialogic understanding of Judaism.

As far as Christian Zionism is concerned, we have to say that this ideology is not merely an ideology of a limited sector in the world. It has indeed become a major force in the contemporary international arena. In addition to their growing numbers, Christian Zionists benefit from the alliance with the new right wing in the United States and

---

[49] R. Khoury, "Effects of Christian Zionism on Religion, Christian Local Churches and Peace Research," in N. Ateek *et al.*, *Challenging Christian Zionism*, 210-34.

many extremist Zionist organizations. They are a fundamental part of the American administration presently in power in the White House, which makes these groups a danger for peace in the world in general and in the Holy Land in particular. To this propagandistic and political support, they add their financial support to building new settlements in the Palestinian Territories, as is the case, to give only an example, with a settlement south of Jerusalem, built up with the financing of these Christian Zionists in Holland.

Christian Zionism is a mixture of religious fundamentalism, apocalyptic visions, messianic interpretations, political ideology and societal projects. Actually, and in this turning point of our history, the different religions try to overcome these sad side effects of religions, developing a concept of religion, which truly honors God. They try to put the transcendent principles at the service of humankind and formulate aspirations for reconciliation, peace, togetherness, development and comprehensive progress (material, human, ethical, spiritual ...). The different religions are trying to get back to their very deep and positive roots in order to offer to humankind an alternative to destruction and death.

Conclusion

Every religious fundamentalist makes the same claim. The way that the fundamentalists justify the exercise of their influence and power in society is that God is on his side, and needs his efforts to see that God's work is done. This isn't the only basic appeal in fundamentalism. Another appeal, equally damaging, is the notion that one is one of "God's chosen." Such an idea is an outright appeal to vanity and egoism. Here the unspoken implication is that if one is one of God's chosen, the other *is not,* and that the former is somehow, therefore, better and superior.

Fundamentalism is a danger in our world and a threat to peace and a just settlement of the Middle East crisis. Its system of ideas is not limited to small numbers of fundamentalists; it influences the comprehension of religion for large masses. Through its faith and total integrity to its roots, whether Muslim, Jewish or Christian, society must shape a new vision of God in whom it believes for itself. In other words, society needs a new vision of God, along with a new vision of all the children of God who are different from us.

Our reality in the Holy Land is one of suffering, humiliation and fear. It is in the logic of people, and not in the logic of God to respond to violence with violence and to violation with violation. Humanity's inability to take revenge has filled their hearts with hatred, along with anticipation of the right moment to take that revenge. A person who believes in God is capable of more than hatred and revenge. He or she has the spiritual power that enables him or her to be victorious and to put an end to all this situation of injustice. We can believe in God as the source of love and peace through our faith in God. We can avoid the path of killing or hatred that spoils the purity of religion and that is born inside the spirit of humanity.

So what is the role of religion in all this? Can the existing religions in the Holy Land contribute to peace and justice? If religion is one of the causes of the conflict, it is simply because believers empty religion from its divine message, reduce it to mere human dimension, sociological or national, and hence instead of leading to God, and helping human beings rise above in order to reach the love of God to all his creatures, they make God absent and they take away his love and bounty from their hearts. By so doing, they see in others, who are different, people who are to be the object of proselytism, or even enemies, or just strangers to be ignored and abandoned to their fate. Instead of being the imitators of God in His bounty towards all His creatures, fundamentalists force upon God Almighty their human patterns of aggressiveness, hatred and death. With this, they firmly believe that they are the true and sole defenders of God on earth.

A basic true religious vision should be this: God is the Creator of all persons and of all peoples. The dignity of each person is God-given. We are all equal in this dignity. From this we have the equality of persons and peoples in their rights and duties as well as the necessity to recognize and respect the rights of others and not to hinder the fulfillment of their duties nor the demand for their rights. Every person and every people have the right and the duty to defend their rights when violated and to enjoy complete freedom in exercising their duties and in defending their rights. Every person and every people must be aided in this pursuit of justice, because justice guarantees peace for all. Without justice, that is, whenever rights are being violated, the way of peace remains closed. Another principle in our basic vision is:

only the ways of peace can lead to peace. Through violence a war or a battle may be won. But peace will only be the fruit of peace.

In the East, religion penetrates and influences all actions both private and public. Everything is placed under the name of God. Everything begins and ends in the name of God. War begins in the name of God and peace agreements as well. That is why the voice and directives of religious leaders can have a decisive influence on the faithful of one side as well as the other. They can incite the people to war and to violence, or invite them to peace.

Hendrik M. Vroom

Why Are We So Inclined to Evil?
Religious Views on the Sources of Evil

Introduction

Some of the main questions that arose after September 11, 2001 and March 11, 2004 (not to mention all the other horrible events that occurred across the world) and the American president's call for a "War Against Evil" are: What is evil? Is this one kind of evil? Does evil have one form with many roots or does it have one root with many forms? Is there only one way to combat evil or do we need several different strategies for to combat evil or at least do some damage control? These questions are as unanswerable as they are important. Take simply the suggestion of a final solution, *Endlösung* – rhetoric that suggests that any weapon may be used against evil – and we soon become, willy-nilly, participants in the discussion of whether a world without evil could exist and whether, therefore, evil is not a necessary component of our existence. Without evil, so goes the old argument, we could neither be free nor responsible. We have thus been given the privilege of developing "our" own character which cannot be divorced from the various evils that are logically necessary conditions which open a space within which we can act and do things whether right or wrong. Thus, "for a man to bear his suffering cheerfully there has to be suffering for him to bear." There have to be acts that irritate for another to be tolerant of them. Likewise it is often said, acts of forgiveness, courage, self-sacrifice, compassion, overcoming temptation, etc., can be performed only if there are evils of various kinds.[1]

A perfect world would be boring; in order to be happy we need to be challenged, we need to suffer a little – otherwise we'll fall asleep. Life must be dangerous: we care about safety because we might die if we were to fall from great heights; we work hard because we would die if we did not eat; we take showers so that we don't contract dis-

---

[1] Thus Richard Swinburne as summarized in V. Brümmer, "Moral Sensitivity and the Free Will Defence," in *Neue Zeitschrift für Systematische Theologie und Religionsphilosophie* 29 (1987: 86-99 (89f.).

eases, and so forth. Evil motivates us. We need evil; otherwise we would not be who we are. The argument is clear enough: evil is God's tool in his education of humankind. The question that is left aside in this approach, however, is how human beings would survive in heaven, where all evil has been removed and only good lives on, a perpetual game of checkers, Bach's fugues without end, and the Beatles in a post-yellow submarine world – because even the bad memories of evil have been healed, that is, taken away (otherwise we could not be fully happy). All evils silenced forever and the world matured to adulthood – tediousness indeed.[2] In the end this argument, sometimes incorporated into Christian thought, forgets the confession of that the creation is good (And the Lord saw that it was good (Gen. 1)) and, as an inevitable corollary, the eternal healing of evil. According to this argument, if evil is gone, human life is as meaningless as the life of fishermen in heaven who discover that the sea has disappeared (Rev. 21:1). Thus, if evil makes life meaningful, a permanently happy life is meaningless.

These arguments about the necessity of evil for human maturity are also too simple because they forget about the sheer imbalance with which humans are struck by evil – the sometimes unbearable suffering and sheer meaninglessness of evil that blows like the wind: nobody knows from whence it comes or where it will strike. As Lance Morrow shows in his book on evil, some forms of evil are meaningless, random, with no clear point to them. What is the root of evil – of senseless evil and of its milder forms in daily life? Does evil only have one source or does the water come from all sides? Can the battle against evil succeed or is evil omnipresent and invincible? How do different religious traditions explain the depth of evil?

Beyond Good and Evil

The most sophisticated solution to evil of which I know – in Zen Buddhism – is the one that declares that true life as it should be and

---

[2] See B. Williams, "The Makropolis Case: The Tedium of Immortality," in B. Williams, *Problems of the Self: Philosophical Papers 1956-1972* (Cambridge: Cambridge University Press, 1973), 72-93.

can be realized if we learn to loosen our grip on our lives and the things around us is lays beyond good and evil. Although we will explain this position shortly, it is very difficult to properly express exactly what is at stake here. Briefly, the argument in Zen thought goes as follows: suffering is evil and brings further evil; the root of evil is egocentrism; egocentrism is inevitable in human development. We learn to be who we are: ourselves; people take care of us, and we start thinking that we are important, not just to our parents and friends, but to ourselves as well. This idea feeds our need to be respected, to receive an equal share and the will to survive. The result is bondage to ourselves: we are captives in our own world; this bondage lies below the surface of everyday life and is the very cause of the contrast between good and evil. However, evil is not the real problem; the real problem is the *distinction* itself between good and evil. *The root of evil is the distinction between good and evil itself, and the cause of that distinction.* This distinction makes it impossible to be open to life as it is.

This is a difficult message for self-conscious beings. As Pure Land (*jodo*) Buddhism says, we need a *bodhisattva* in his great compassion to look upon us and help us free ourselves from our bondage to ourselves. Think of Cannon's gentleness and grace. The fight against ourselves can be hard; we could use some help yet, as we all know, a gentle practitioner can clean dirty wounds. The real helpers are not always as kind as Cannon, but powerful and auspicious, like the *boddhisatva Acalanãtha*, who binds us with ropes and can violently, with his sword, slash our ego. The attachment to our ego is the root of suffering; suffering is not taking things as they come but judging between good and evil and seeing the sun rise if the sun rises and set if it sets. If, and only if, we do not have an ego, things just happen, without that inner voice that is pleased by some and disappointed by other events. We have to realize that we do not have a substantial, inner self that suffers or enjoys but are a part and parcel of reality as a whole, which works in us as it does in other phenomena. In our upbringing and education we have learnt to be an ego and we need many lives to overcome this inculturation process. The real war against evil is the struggle in our own hearts: whoever conquers him or herself is much stronger than whoever conquers a city. However close such a Buddhist idea may be to the Christian one and to the Muslim confession that the great *jihad* is a struggle with oneself, the major difference between Zen and theistic religions is that the root cause of all evil (and good) lies in the very idea of *self*: we are mistaken about our "selves" and interpret what happens as good and evil because we use an illusionary measuring stick: We are bound by the idea that we have (and are) a self and can lose our health, possessions, honor, and friends – precisely for this reason we suffer and are not free to live life as it is. Because there is only one root cause of evil, there is only one solution as well: overcome this idea of a self or a soul, immerse ourselves in true reality and take everything as it comes and goes. We are empty; we are phenomena; let us not think that we are more worthwhile than anything else. Everything is just as it is and we should drop the distinction between good and evil.[3]

This is neither the place to explain the depth dimensions of this approach nor can I convey the feeling that is bound up with this Zen insight into real life, but let me try one more time. Suppose, on a Saturday afternoon, you are walking anonymously on a crowded sidewalk in Amsterdam or Hong Kong, among thousands of people you can hide your identity as easily as in a lonely forest and then you realize that you are just doing what everyone was doing: they have free time, just as you do; they want to walk and see the marketplace, just as you do; they have worked the rest of the week, just as you have; they have been lucky in having had good parents and friends or unlucky in having had bad parents and friends. And so within a few moments everything around you and in your self becomes relative and is taken up into one big reality in which things are connected and related to one another by many threads. Slowly you become part of the crowd and discover more commonality and fellowship and loose part of your feeling of particularity – and of being good or bad! We all are part of the whole of existence. The world is as it is. Its forms appear and disappear. These forms are emptiness, they are as simple as they appear and disappear; ultimately there is no substance. There is no evil; there is no good. There is what is: form is emptiness and emptiness is form

---

[3] See M. Abe, "The Problem of Evil in Christianity and Buddhism," in P. Ingram and F.J. Streng (eds.), *Buddhist-Christian Dialogue: Mutual Renewal and Transformation* (Honolulu: University of Hawaii Press, 1986), 90-107; M. Abe, "Kenotic God and Dynamic Sunyata," in J.B. Cobb and C. Ives (eds.), *The Emptying God: A Buddhist-Jewish-Christian Conversation* (Maryknoll: Orbis, 1990), 3-65; and my "Boven goed en kwaad uit? Ethiek in het denken van de Kyoto-filosofie," in *Tijdschrift voor theologie* 42 (2002): 35-49.

– as the Heart Sutra says.[4] If we realize that, we reach tranquility, compassion and wisdom as shown in the face of the great Buddha of Kamakura.

This is a more radical solution to the problem of evil than the doctrine that the world needs evil because we would otherwise be bored, and would not learn to overcome difficulties. On the religious level we say: there is no evil, there is no good; there is no good life but just life as it is. In practical life we advise people to live in a certain way and not in another, because some ways of life are more selfish than other ways of life. Attached people are not free but bound by a great many things. Since they are not free they need rules and moral codes instead of acting spontaneously. Life should ultimately be lived as it comes and goes. Everything appears in Being: it comes and it goes – even god and the gods, as Heidegger stated.[5]

The World is Necessarily Evil

The opposite analysis of the root of evil is that in a sense it is not we who are the problem but that we are imprisoned in an imperfect world that never will be and can never be perfect. Worldly existence is not permanent and not perfect and will produce a great deal of suffering, ignorance, bad decisions and new problems "for ever and ever." The root cause is that the world is finite and transitory. Only the center of our selves (of our soul, atman or self) can be made perfect and reach its goal – not by buying and selling or by technicians but by purifying ourselves. The only way out of this tricky world is to do the right thing and not remain imprisoned by the temptations of the world. We do not have to be enlightened and live a detached life in this world but must

---

[4] "Heart Sutra," in e.g. Edward Conze (transl. and ed.), *Buddhist Wisdom Books: The Diamond and the Heart Sutra* (London: Unwin, 1988), 103-36.

[5] M. Heidegger, "Brief über den Humanismus," in *Wegmarken* (Frankfurt a.M.: Klostermann, 1967), 19: "The appearance of beings and how god, the gods, history and nature appear in the open place (*Lichtung*) of Being, whether they are present or not, is not decided by human beings. This rests in the happening of Being (*Geschick des Seins*)."

be liberated from the world. We do not have to learn to be in the world without being of the world but to *leave* the world. Such a view is representative of Hindu thought; in its neo-Platonic clothing it has been very influential in European history as well. The Hindu idea is that, on the deepest level of their existence, human beings are one with *brahman* but exist on earth in earthly forms in which they can never be fully happy: matter always brings limitations and limitations render conflicts, accidents, illnesses and pains. The only way to become truly free from evil is to be liberated from earthly existence so that the soul can return to the divine. These basic ideas can be interpreted in various ways: *bhakti* movements invoke the help of divine grace; other traditions employ meditation (and stepping out of the chain of karma). Nevertheless, the root of evil is two-sided: a broken union with the divine and being caught in finite, earthly, imperfect existence. Evil now has a metaphysical status: being human is being imperfect. Good is becoming one with the divine (again).

With the exception of *sadhus*, the holy men who have freed themselves of their worldly ties, nobody can live with such a bifurcation of supernatural good and natural evil, because we need some practical direction in life and feel that some acts are better than others. Thus, another moral "system" is needed to tell us what is better and what is worse in this imperfect existence. Morality cannot now rest on individual autonomy: on the contrary, it should point out how we should live and do what we should do – whether we want to or not. So the world order, *dharma*, tells what we should do in our lives – and not just how to take care of ourselves.[6] The only self-development that is legitimate and wise is the development of the self in which the self becomes free from the illusionary self and one with the divine. What we have to do is to take care that we fit into the order of this world, that we live our lives within the total order and thus prevent ourselves from acquiring bad karma. We, therefore, have to loosen the ties in which we are imprisoned in the imperfect earthly world, until we are liberated enough in a future life to merge with the divine. Although

---

[6] On *dharma* (and *rita*), see M. Biardeau, *Hinduism: The Anthropology of a Civilization*, transl. R. Nice (Delhi: Oxford University Press, 1989), 41. For the classical Hindu texts cf. Radhakrishnan, Sarvepalli and C.A. Moore (eds.). *A Sourcebook in Indian Philosophy* (Princeton: Princeton University Press, 1973), 3-223. 349-572.

many everyday worries are more or less the same for everyone – food, health, income and work, family life, relations etc. – in this view the whole framework in which they have their meaning is different. Very clearly that has been the case in the caste system and now we can see why this is much more persistent than people have thought and why new laws do not easily change the structure of society. From a secularized perspective wealth is often considered good but *brahmins* (the best reincarnation) can be very poor. Ideas of the world order differ, ideas about the roots of evil differ, and the ways to overcome evil differ as well.

On Cross-Cultural Hermeneutics

Let us stop for a moment to reflect on method and cross-cultural hermeneutics. It cannot be stressed enough that multiculturalism does not say – as many (or most!) scholars in Western philosophy seem to think – that the same categories are filled with different content. In this case we would all have the same ideas of what is good and evil and differ only in our preferences. All differences in relation to good and evil are variations on the basis of a common understanding if these concepts. On the contrary, categories differ and the same terms translated into English (and not into Japanese, Hindi, Arabic, Hebrew, etc.) do not have the same meaning. It takes imagination to realize that the "same" categories have different meanings. The role of ethics differs from culture to culture, from religion to religion, and from worldview to worldview. The reason for this is that the web of ideas in which ethics has its place differs. There is much more tension between religions and cultures than secularized Westerners would like to admit – their ideology of neutrality, a common humaneness and their idea that Western individualism is the measure for the whole world hinders them from seeing the otherness of other cultures. "We" tend to think that everyone distinguishes between good and evil, inquires into the source of evil, and asks how "we" can solve our problems. But people in other cultures and especially in some Asian religious traditions have other ways of experiencing the world and other value systems, other views of death and life, and even another understanding of human valuations of what happens as good or as evil: some reject the distinction between good and evil on the deeper level; they think it is an attachment that we should overcome, but other cultures speak of what does and does not fit with non-duality, avoiding the duality of good/evil and say that we have to learn to see things as they really are (different from our attached false images of good and evil) – and we interpret their distinctions as variations of our duality of good and evil. Different traditions can have different views of "evil" and the roots of "evil" vary considerably, just as the paths for overcoming "evil" do. Most will not say that we should start thinking for ourselves, as Immanuel Kant's well-known explanation of Enlightenment says.[7]

On the concrete level of everyday life the situation looks different because, to a large extent, people cope with the same problems: food and shortage, poverty and wealth, health and illness, raising children, the climate etc. For that reason there are many commonalities – which accounts for the fact that after a few weeks in a hotel in a foreign culture people conclude that everywhere in the world people are human, struggle with the same problems and are much more similar than those anthropologists and philosophers who admire difference like to suggest. Unfortunately, this misunderstanding has occasioned many problems in the world: the *neglect of the otherness* of other cultures is one of the biggest causes of conflicts and evil in the world. It has cost a great many people their lives – disrespect for otherness is one of the most serious causes of conflict and death in this world. Otherness is not just a humane and political issue but an intellectual challenge as well: the study of cultural and religious differences is not simply a must for our global culture but an intellectual challenge that is much more difficult to deal with than people imagine. In continuity with its colonial past "the West" tends to presuppose more "sameness" than there actually is – from the universality of natural laws and technology it derives the "sameness" of cultural and religious traditions in global culture.

---

[7] "Enlightenment" means quite different things in the Kantian and the Buddhist traditions.

Evil in Islam

Let us look at the Muslim view of evil. Here worldly life is not evil in itself, because God has created human life intentionally and therefore it makes sense; evil is doing what one should not do. Evil is not directly that which overcomes us because God reigns and what God does is right. Thus illnesses, hunger, pains, and disasters are not clearly evil but punishments or temptations in which our faithfulness is tested.[8]

What is the root cause of the evil that we commit? The answer is simple (and I will start with some formulations that are slightly superficial): the cause of all evil (and therefore the cause of many of the disasters that overcome us) is that we do not live as God says we should. Disobedience is the root of all sin. For example, if we offend somebody, the sin is not just that the other has been hurt, the deeper issue is that we do not live as God wants us to live. An atheist could object and say that we are not wronging God – we are wronging the other and our act is wrong in itself. I think a Muslim would answer that this is so only on the surface because there are no wrong acts as such. First, acts are good or bad if and only if one places them in a larger framework. Second, the real question is that of the perspective from which the deed is done. Thus, people do something wrong because they have not accepted the moral order and does not really see themselves as creatures in God's world; if they did, they would act properly. If we internalize the idea that God declared life is good and so has commanded us to live according to His will. So the source of evil is that we do not accept the world as it is but create our own world and impose our own standards. Therefore the root cause of evil is that we do not follow God's will but our own and we do not see that it is truly foolish not to follow God's will and to do things in our own stupid ways, because God knows everything that we do and will judge us the moment we close our eyes. We can never escape His judgments therefore it is not simply disobedience – as we can be disobedient to

---

[8] For this I draw especially on the master's thesis by one of our students, Annemiek Spronk, Faculty of Theology, Vrije Universiteit, 27, 8 (2004); She gives a survey of Koranic teaching on evil, the various words, the main sins, and some well-known stories from the oldest traditions, the *hadieth*.

one another – but all wrongdoing rests on a wrong judgment of the situation in which we live. Disobedience stems from a lack of insight, both of God and ourselves.

I think that we should understand the Muslim position in this way: the root of all evil is unbelief; there is no true insight into life and no obedience. True insight into life is belief and real belief is right conduct; trust God, know his intentions and do what is right. See that his laws are good – all that *is* is good. I think that it is superficial to say that evil is doing what God has forbidden. On a deeper level the point "unbelief is the cause of evil" is that we do not live according to how things are but in one way or another live for ourselves. In offending our neighbor, we disobey God; if we learn to live with God, we will not offend anybody.

Evil in Christianity

I will not delve too deeply into Christian views of evil, but traditionally there is a great deal in common with Islam: if one does not live according to the will of God, one is a sinner. The point is that God has ordered the world properly, so that discord is neglect of the order of life itself – an order that can be seen by everybody who opens his or her eyes and heart and listens to one's conscience (Romans 2:15). In the past, under the influence of neo-Platonism, Christianity related bodily existence as such with evil. According to Augustine, after the Fall from Paradise we were unable to do any good on our own. Evil was hereditary and inherent to human life.[9] We could not obey God, even though we should have. The only way out was through the grace of God and the forgiveness of sins through Christ. Otherwise, we would be punished after death – and there were concrete and alarming images of the Last Judgment and Hell. In our age the historical reality of both Paradise and the Fall has lost its plausibility and the idea of Hell has lost its attraction. Many of us cannot accept the idea that our world was ever perfect or that the evil people suffer would be a pun-

---

[9] Because the *anima generalis* fell in Adam; see e.g. A. Adam, *Lehrbuch der Dogmengeschichte* I (Gütersloh: Gütersloher Verlagshaus / Gert Mohn, 1965), 268.

ishment or a test. Many Christians are not as optimistic as some others who think that we could live properly if we only tried harder. With the apostle Paul, the Reformation concluded that we are justified by grace only, even though we remain sinners in many respects. Human persons are *simul iustus ac peccator*: justified and sinful at the same time. Some would say that this view of sin and evil is more pessimistic than that of Islam and humanism. However, from the perspective of the Reformation it is more realistic and in another way more optimistic as well, because people can live in the certitude of being accepted by God in grace without having to be perfect. Sins will be forgiven. The Cross and resurrection characterize the Christian idea of God and humankind – however it has often been belied by crusades, the slave trade, and numerous small silly mistakes in our private lives.

On one point, the structure of Christian theology comes close to that of Mahayana Buddhism. We *are* already no-self; our real existence has always been so – we just have to see it, open our eyes and see things as they are. This is the Buddhist version. The Christian one is that we should open our eyes and see creation and ourselves as part of it and listen to the message that we are children of God to whom God offers forgiveness even though we will remain imperfect our whole lives. Among the deep differences here is a structural similarity: form is emptiness and emptiness is form/*simul iustus ac peccator*: a sinner is righteous and the righteous person is a sinner – and we see immediately how the concept of good and evil in each tradition differs from the other.

Concluding Remarks

Let me make two concluding remarks. The first concerns the roots of evil. As we have seen we have to distinguish between the evil that we do and the evil that we suffer. Is there one root of evil? I think that on the abstract level there is. The common view in the classic religions seems to be that the root of the evil that we do has its origin in that we do not fit in well with life "as it really is" – to use the well-known Buddhist expression. In *Buddhism* it is called *shunyata*, emptiness, but we think that we have to care for ourselves and our loved ones first: attachment to self and ignorance of real reality. *Hinduism* sees it as a matter of worldly existence. We are attracted to it and become attached, but it is *maya* and not ultimate reality. We thus reinvent ourselves, make up our own world and do not live according to *rita*, the nature and laws of the true reality to which we have become blind. The *theist* position is that the evil we do comes forth from our blindness to creation and the Creator; we do not see ourselves as creatures and members of the larger whole of existence. This world may not be perfect, but we could do more if we would accept our limitations, be less selfish and trust God more.

Structurally these views do converge, but they differ on the level of content. They offer different insights into the nature of the world, humankind and the divine. However, there is another level: practical life with its concrete evil conduct and misconduct. Here we find the "same" phenomena of evil: selfishness, lies, conflict, etc. The moral codes of the practical religions overlap in many ways. Paul can say that greed (money) is the root of all evil and the Buddha that thirst is its root and a hasty student will conclude that their teachings are the same. If we explore the classical scriptures of all religions and cultures, we will find that they indicate a great many "roots" of evil, but that the most important and deepest one is egocentrism – related as it is to egoism, attachment and ignorance. However, as we have seen in the above, the ways to overcome attachment and egocentrism differ as much as the various goals of life do, and so do the interpretations of the evil that we suffer: a test, punishment or the consequence of a material and imperfect world and body.

In this way we can explain the commonalities between the various religions. We conclude that on a practical level they agree with respect to a great deal with what concerns misconduct although their "ways out" differ according to their views of the real world and the healing of egocentrism: be still and take things as they really are and be free to accept everything and then one will be free to act wisely and with compassion. Another possibility is that we should free ourselves from earthly existence and the burden of all these imperfect lives by living out our karmas, or we should serve God and be obedient and He will judge us after our deaths and we will live forever. These are different paradigms for seeing and living life.

My second concluding point is this question: How do we choose between these views? My answer is: believe what is plausible, which does not mean that which is intellectually coherent. It means that a worldview offers insights that correspond to our experiences. The main point is not whether I can understand everything but: are those insights true to life? That configuration of insights that covers most parts of our lives will be true. It is clear enough that we cannot judge these questions without taking sides but the kind of questions on which we have to reflect and discuss are these: Is it true that this earthly life as such is insufficient and not worth living and that we should try to be liberated from it? Is it true that we can follow the ethical rules on our own, without any help? Do we not always – if we look at ourselves critically enough – fall short of being fully just, merciful and loving? Or can we live properly if we try harder? These and many more such questions are at stake when we compare views of the sources of evil, and especially the roots of evil in our own lives. This is not the place to formulate my own answers to these questions, but in the rising global culture nobody can escape posing these questions.

PART III

ENVIRONMENTAL AND ECOLOGICAL CHALLENGES

Peter Tom Jones and Roger Jacobs

Globalization, Ecology and Sustainability: How Sustainable is Sustainable Development?

The pen is mightier than the sword. Whoever can succeed in creating hegemonic terminology and its allied thought perception, not only determines, to a large extent, how people look at a complex reality, but also obscures the perspective of policymakers and individuals whose goal it is to envisage solutions in order to alter this reality. This is equally true in the socio-ecological debate. During the last two decades, a gargantuan shift in paradigms has taken place: while in the seventies and the eighties the concept of "limits to growth" dominated the environmental debate, this mutated into the more ambiguous term "sustainable development." We contend that its current, hegemonic meaning, raises a smokescreen around the real issues concerning the global socio-ecological question. It is our aim in this missive to provide an alternative framework that attempts to unite ecology and justice harmoniously, building on innovative concepts such as "ecological sustainability," "ecological debt" and "environmental (in)justice."

Limits to Growth

Commissioned by the Club of Rome, scientists embarked on a course of plotting, with the help of a computer model, a number of projections concerning the future of the ecosystem earth. Their findings were published in the landmark report *Limits to Growth* in 1972. They concluded that – if the trends in growth of global population, industrialization, pollution, food production and depletion of the natural resources continued – the limits of growth would be reached before the year 2100 with the collapse of the world system as an inevitable result. In contradiction to the caricature that is being made of it today, the report was far from being a doomsday prophecy. In point of fact, rather than making "predictions," it put forward "projections" for possible futures situations, based upon selected scenarios. The conclusions of this highly influential document caused an uproar in the environmental debate. Presumably for the first time in history, blind faith in progress was questioned from a scientific point of view. The report clearly highlighted the biophysical limits of the planet Earth, both as a source of renewable and non-renewable resources and as a sink for emission and waste streams.

Although the *Limits to Growth* report accentuated the potential exhaustion of non-renewable resources, we have since learned that the overburdening of the waste absorption capacity of Earth's ecosystems (e.g. the CO_2 absorption capacity of the oceans and the terrestrial biosphere) and their limited regenerative capacity actually constitute more acute problems. Scientific literature demonstrates that since the mid eighties the total impact of the global population on the environment is overshooting the ecological carrying capacity of planet Earth. Currently, this ecological deficit is estimated – roughly, albeit conservatively – to be in the vicinity of 20%.[1] Furthermore, the wealthiest 20% of the global population lay claim to around 80% of global consumption. Thus, clearly the limits to biophysical growth have already been surpassed though it is not clear how long this global ecological overshoot can be maintained. Nevertheless, Ecosystem Earth has already been compromised which can be seen by indicators such as the Living Planet Index which has declined by 40% since 1970.[2] From a scientific point of view, Ecosystem Earth is currently residing in a *no-analogue state*,[3] a term that indicates that the magnitude, spatial scale and pace of human-induced changes are unprecedented in the history of this planet. This signifies that, as the earth system is being pushed beyond its natural operating domain, we are treading on *terra incognita*.

---

[1] J. Loh and M. Wackernagel (eds.), *Living Planet Report 2004* (Gland: WWF, 2004); M. Wackernagel *et al.*, "Tracking the Ecological Overshoot of the Human Economy," in *PNAS*, 99/14 (2002): 9266-971.

[2] Loh and Wackernagel (eds.), *Living Planet Report 2004*.

[3] Cf. W. Steffen *et al.*, *Global Change and the Earth System* (Berlin: Springer-Verlag 2004).

Towards the Genesis of Sustainable Development

Nevertheless, in recent decades the perception of finiteness (the unsustainability of endless growth) has been changed. A new ideology of "sustainable development" has replaced the former, and the mind boggles as to how this was so swiftly achieved in political and economical circles. In the early eighties, the UN commissioned a new body on environmental and development matters. In 1987, under the presidency of the Norwegian politician Gro Harlem Brundtland, this *World Commission on Environment and Development* published its final report *Our Common Future*. Even today, whenever talking about sustainable development, one still refers to the canonical definition put forward by the Brundtland Commission: a development that meets the needs of the present without compromising the ability of future generations to meet their own needs. The *United Nations Conference on Environment and Development* (UNCED) that took place in Rio De Janeiro in 1992 can be considered as the second milestone in the consolidation of the term sustainable development. Although this conference did look at both the environmental crisis and the call for global justice, it did not dare to face the tricky issue of the relationship between these two questions. As a result, both the problem of the unrelenting economic race in the North and the unconditional mimicry of this model in the South were not subjected to a much needed microscopic investigation.

Whereas in the past the term "sustainability" referred to the biologically sustainable use of renewable "resources," such as forests or fish populations, it had now transmuted into an adjective being suffixed by the world "development." However, the waters have been muddied around the content of development, as this can mean almost anything from the construction of exotic hotel resorts in pristine natural environments for prosperous segments of the population to elementary water supplies for the 1 billion souls who don't have easy access to this blue gold; or from intercontinental "ecotourist" flights to pristine islands such as the Seychelles to elementary mobility for the majority of the world populations who don't own cars or jet around the world. In a nutshell – is development to be measured in terms of an increase in Gross National Product or does it concern the qualitative improvement of the life of the millions of have-nots on this planet? Unfortunately the former has gained the upper hand, as accurately highlighted by Herman Daly and Kenneth Townsend:

The Earth ecosystem develops (evolves), but does not grow. Its subsystem, the economy, must eventually stop growing, but can continue to develop. The term sustainable development therefore makes sense for the economy, but only if it is understood as "development without growth," i.e. qualitative improvement of a physical economic base that is maintained in a steady state by a throughput of matter-energy that is within the regenerative and assimilative capacities of the ecosystem. Currently the term sustainable development is used as a synonym for the oxymoronic sustainable growth... a culture dependent on exponential growth for its economic stability.[4]

The Revival of the Development Discourse

Because of the vagueness of the concept "development" no questions were asked in Rio about the fact that, from an ecological point of view, the "North" is "overdeveloped." Given that it is biophysically impossible to replicate the consumption patterns of the Northern consumer class to the entire world population, this was an unforgivable omission. Immanuel Kant would have described this situation as by definition "undemocratic" as the resource consumption of the rich can only be sustained by appropriating carrying capacity from other parts of the world and, unfortunately, from future generations. Nevertheless, according to the hegemonic economic gospel a country can't be overdeveloped; it is either developed or underdeveloped, the barometer of this reasoning to be expressed in GNP figures. We hear echoes of Harry Truman's inaugural address to Congress in 1949 when he crammed the immeasurable heritage of the Southern Hemisphere into one single category: the underdeveloped countries that need a helping hand.

What Truman and his proponents did not take into consideration was that development-as-growth is a race without an end. In *Ecofeminism* (1993) Maria Mies and Vandana Shiva argue that the development-as-growth ideology justifies itself as a project that relieves pov-

---

[4] H. Daly and K. Townsend, *Valuing the Earth: Economics, Ecology, Ethics* (Cambridge MA: MIT Press, 1993), 267.

erty. Poverty was the problem; economic growth the solution, the alpha and omega of society. The North was put forward as the reference model to be attained as soon as possible by the countries in the South, referred to by the concept of "catching-up development." Precisely because the synergistic interaction between the ecological and the global justice crisis was not seriously taken into account during the Earth Summit in Rio, the global economic race and the Western development model, with its accompanying consumerist lifestyle, were not fundamentally questioned. The growth fetishists felt strengthened in their global grasp for power: "sustainable development" became the new buzzword. Environmental problems in the South were (and are still being) presented as a result of insufficient capital, obsolete technology, lack of expertise and slackening growth figures. The solution, i.e. the growth-oriented development paradigm, is predetermined by the actual definition of the problem.

What was ignored was that local elites and the upper middle classes of these countries mopped up the benefits of any kind of high growth figures in the South. Although growth was supposed to relieve poverty, in reality the development age resulted in a dual polarization, both between and within countries. Since the onset of neo-liberal globalization, this trend has of course been substantiated, to the detriment of the world's have-nots. This dual polarization goes hand in hand with the formation of a "transnational consumer class." According to the Worldwatch Institute, 362 million Chinese and Indians currently enjoy the same affluence level, with the associated environmental impact, as the "average" European, North American and Japanese consumer.[5] Clearly, the divide between North and South is no longer geographic. A high level of consumption (water, fossil fuels, meat, materials, etc.) is no longer a strictly Western affair. The true divide runs between the global, integrated transnational consumer class and the large group of "local poor," the redundant, the unwanted and the dehumanized, those who don't count in the global supermarket because of their lack of spending power.

---

[5] *State of the World 2004* (New York / London: Worldwatch Institute, 2004); N. Myers and J. Kent, "New Consumers: The Influence of Affluence on the Environment," in *PNAS* 100/8 (2003): 4963-68.

Insufficient Attention for Intragenerational Solidarity

If sustainable development is perceived as "sustainable economic growth," the issue of justice with regard to relations between the "North" and the "South" fades into oblivion. In Western countries, ecology is often looked at too one-dimensionally as being a question of justice for *future generations;* this can also be seen in the classical Brundtland definition of sustainable development, which refers to the "needs of future generations."[6] Implicitly, this means that the injustice in the present division of the ecological pie remains unattended. To put things differently: *intergenerational* solidarity is clearly mentioned, but *intragenerational* solidarity does not receive the attention it is entitled to. Although an eye to the future is of course crucial important, this vision can come at the expense of the attention that is badly needed for intragenerational justice. This is the reason why proponents of ecological justice highlight the fact that it is equally important to account for the way in which *today's* pressure on the environment and the associated risks are being divided between "North" and "South," between poor and rich. In *The Environmentalism of the Poor* (2002), Joan Martinez-Alier speaks of "ecological distribution conflicts" which arise over the use of the available environmental space. As this space is biophysically limited, subsistence needs often directly compete with luxury wants. A typical example of this conflict can be found in the "mangrove versus shrimp" debate. Due to a growing worldwide demand for shrimps, mangrove forests in the South are increasingly sacrificed for commercial shrimp farming, with all the associated ecological shadow costs. This includes a decreased coastal defence against cyclones and tidal waves, a connection which is not often made by Western consumers enjoying the taste of shrimp-based dishes. Who has the advantage and who has the disadvantage in the exploitation of natural resources? Who wins and who loses?

The disregard for intragenerational solidarity becomes blatantly evident in, for example, the discussions on the dangers of global warming. While Western environmental scientists point correctly to

---

[6] Note, however, that in other parts of the Brundtland report, clear attention is given to the needs of the present, poor generations. Nevertheless, in the famous Brundtland definition of sustainable development this is not sufficiently highlighted.

the potential catastrophic effects of abrupt climate changes within decades (e.g. shutdown of the North Atlantic thermohaline circulation, the collapse of the West Antarctic ice sheet etc.), they often forget to focus on the fact that global warming is already leading to a number of slow, insidious consequences, especially for the poorest in the world. Even though it is precisely the industrialized world that is responsible for the major part of the emissions of greenhouse gases, most of the victims will fall, especially initially, in the countries of the South. Despite the fact that the effects of climate change will be worse in that part of the world, people with little purchasing power are less able to protect themselves from the consequences of floods, hurricanes, contagious diseases, drought etc. For communities living on the periphery of the global economy, social and ecological problems often go hand in hand. For the people whose livelihood is directly related to their access to forests, land, pastures or oceans, the fate and health of these ecosystems is evidently of vital importance. When the ecosystems they are dependent on are degraded or hijacked for cash crop production, their subsistence rights (food, health, shelter etc.) are undermined. The environment is not so much a luxury of the rich as a necessity of the poor.[7]

The Contest Perspective

In *Planet Dialectics* (1999), Wolfgang Sachs correctly states that the term sustainable development, in the hegemonic meaning of the word, is essentially a term of repression. Although continuous growth is something that needs to be absolutely maintained, it is silently accepted that this will remain geographically as well as demographically limited. Sachs refers to the scope of sustainable development as a *contest perspective*, where the blame for the degradation of the environment is being attributed to the "poor" in the "South." Their "explosive birth rate" serves as a convenient explanation for the two most acute problems facing the Western world: environmental insecurity and mi-

---

[7] J. Martinez-Alier, *The Environmentalism of the Poor* (Cheltenham / Northhampton: Edward Elgar Publishing, 2002).

gration. Once more this view overlooks the fact that the Western population is in itself almost overstreching the total ecological carrying capacity of the planet: overconsumption and overdevelopment should be considered as being part of the root causes of the contemporary socio-ecological crisis. Although the globalization process has clearly led to a situation where many of the environmental burdens caused by exuberant consumption levels in the "North" are shifted to the "South" and the future generations, it is now evident that the separation line, both in space as in time, between winners and losers, is no longer absolute. The first signs that the globalized rich are (and will be) increasingly exposed to the less pleasant side of a world characterized by inequality and lack of sustainability are: terrorist attacks, flares of violence, war, migration, exhaustion of essential resources, extreme weather phenomena etc. If the international community does not succeed in constructing *another* type of globalization, the multiple dividing line between "North" and "South" will hit back like a boomerang against the transnational consumer class.

Other, and better, definitions of sustainable development are therefore necessary. At the core of the term, in its uncorrupted meaning, are two concerns which will significantly define the 21st century: the growing gap between "North" and "South" as well as the continuous pollution, depletion and degradation of the global ecosystems on which humanity is ultimately dependent for its existence. The challenge lies in finding a way to address both problems at the same time, without falling into the biophysical trap of "sustainable economic growth." According to Wolfgang Sachs, one can distinguish, besides the dominant contest discourse described earlier, two other visions on sustainable development. While the *astronaut's perspective* recognizes biophysical limits to growth and tries to create a global framework to solve both the crisis of justice as that of the environment, the *home perspective* pleads for structural adjustments in the "North" (far-reaching moderation), so that space can be created for global justice (a redistribution between "North" and "South"). In what follows, we propose a thoughtful synthesis of these two visions.

The Astronaut's Perspective

This perspective is based on the scientific assessment that planet Earth is one integrated, non-growing, materially closed ecosystem.[8] Due to the accelerating development of scientific ecology, significant progress has been made during the last decades in setting up new observation techniques to map the condition of the globe. Sachs uses the image of the astronaut who observes, from space, the blue, fragile planet earth against the cold and dark background of the universe. The concern is no more or no less than saving the Earth. This perspective therefore focuses on the major, life threatening, global environmental problems. From the astronaut's perspective, sustainable development is being interpreted as a problem of global management. Especially in scientific journals such as *Nature* and *Science*, the necessity of monitoring and managing is often being emphasized. It is the task of experts and scientists to bring the planetary environmental impacts of humans in harmony with the ecological carrying capacity of the earth. This "ecological sustainability" forces humanity to respect the biophysical limits imposed by the finiteness of the global environmental space, referring to Mathis Wackernagel's definition of sustainability as "living within the regenerative capacity of the biosphere."[9]

This view clearly differs from the contest perspective as it recognizes the necessity for a new balance between "North" and "South." The unity of humankind is based on a shared dependence, not only with regard to biophysical sources and sinks but also concerning crucial life support systems such as a stable climate and a protective ozone layer. By analogy with the reconstruction of Europe after the Second World War, environmental scientists call for a *Global Marshall Plan*: a union of all interested parties on the planet to deliver common efforts to limit population growth, design eco-efficient technologies, install fairer trade rules etc.

Several criticisms have been advanced towards this vision of sustainable development. On the one hand, it goes without saying that it is somewhat of a conundrum to define completely the carrying capac-

---

[8] For a scientific description of this so called "Earth System Analysis," Cf. H. John Schellnhuber, "Earth System Analysis and the Second Copernican Revolution," in *Nature* 402 (1999): C19-23.

[9] M. Wackernagel, *et al.*, "Tracking the Ecological Overshoot."

ity of the earth quantitatively and thus set safe limits for the exploitation of nature. As a result of the complexity of ecosystems, the mutual dependence of system segments, the existence of hard-to-calculate non-linear feedback mechanisms and the irreversibility of several system evolutions, it is a momentous task to determine the exact position of crucial thresholds, never mind managing and controlling them.[10] In opposition to the rise of the science of *ecology*, Wolfgang Sachs states that the rapid development of ecological *science*, which places the management framework on a platform, has given green light to the technocratic recuperation of the struggle of the environmental movement for the recognition of growth limits.[11] Sachs presents this poetically as follows:

> Satellite pictures scanning the globe's vegetative cover, computer graphs running interaction curves through time, threshold levels held up as worldwide norms are the language of global ecology. It constructs a reality that contains mountains of data, but no people .... They provide knowledge that is faceless and placeless, an abstraction that carries a considerable cost: it consigns the realities of culture, power and virtue to oblivion. It offers data, but no context; it shows diagrams, but no actors; it gives calculations, but no notions of morality, it seeks stability, but disregards beauty.[12]

In our opinion, Sachs is too one-sided in this respect, as will be shown in the next paragraph. Nevertheless, there is another fundamental criticism on the astronaut's perspective. Some authors have suggested that this perspective is fundamentally anthropocentric: the natural world is seen in a purely utilitarian way. One asks: what can nature do for us? In that sense the term "natural capital" – which is central in the astronaut's perspective – is a huge misconception, as if nature has asked to be abstracted in economic terms. Once again it becomes clear that language in itself can already be repressive. In this vision ecosystems are considered as material resources created for consumption by

---

[10] For a scientific description of these new insights, cf. M. Scheffer *et al.*, "Catastrophic Shifts in Ecosystems," in *Nature* 413 (2001): 591-96.

[11] W. Sachs, *Planet Dialectics: Explorations in Environment and Development* (London / New York: Zed Books, 1999), 62.

[12] Sachs, *Planet Dialectics*, 44.

humans. The unbridled materialism of Western culture is being forgiven, as long as it respects the carrying capacity of the Earth.

Sustainable Development and the Home Perspective

From the home perspective, sustainable (Western) development is considered as a *contradictio in terminis*. The central problem today is the absolute overdevelopment of the North, which owes a major ecological debt to the South. A fundamental position of the home perspective implies that, given the real biophysical limits to growth, the crisis of justice can no longer be resolved through the classic Keynesian growth strategies pursued in the sixties. According to this vision, the crisis of justice could be "solved" by enlarging the economic pie. Rather than (re)distributing the existing pie more fairly, the left as well as the right pleaded for enlarging the pie through economic growth, so that everyone would be able to achieve a larger piece. Likewise, the Brundtland report (1987) called for the augmentation of the World Economic Product by a factor of five or ten, so that the "poor" would also be able to attain Western levels of affluence. Unfortunately, this vision is outdated today. The economic pie cannot grow endlessly in size. Therefore the home perspective states that we have to abandon this classic growth strategy. Instead of more economic growth, a radical redistribution of the *existing* economic pie on a global scale is necessary. The struggle against poverty is simultaneously a struggle against excessive wealth.

Through the home perspective the more radical parts of the Western global justice movement meet the local movements and organizations of the South (personified by charismatic figures such as Vandana Shiva and Walden Bello). On the global scale they call for fair trade relations between North and South, for the abolition of the financial debt of the third world or for technological transfers from North to South, as a compensation for its ecological debt. The Western development model is being considered as part of the problem. Adherents of the home perspective plead for local, endogenous development paths as an alternative to export oriented growth strategies. This development paradigm contains concepts like economic deglobalization, relocalization and decentralization of a restorative economy, decommodification, etc.[13]

In the home perspective. the biophysical limits are evidently recognized. Rather than looking at these limits as confinements, they are considered as challenges that encourage us to rediscover the art of living. Limits are thus being fashioned into opportunities so that a new, less materialistic and less anthropocentric culture can endure. This does not call for the idealization of small-scale traditional societies, or for the restoration of old provincialism and the indulgence in splendid isolation of a village mentality. We do, however, require nothing less than a new paradigm of civilization, in which human development can step into a direction which respects life in the broadest sense. The Brazilian liberation theologian Leonardo Boff pleads in his *A Etica Da Vida* (2000) for a new *cosmovision*, beyond the classical, modern and reductionist world view.

Searching for the Synthesis

The criticisms that the home perspective infringes on the astronaut's perspective are, according to us, only to a certain extent correct. In its unalloyed form, the home perspective suffers from shortcomings too. Given the seriousness and the nature of the current environmental crisis, some kind of global eco-management is indispensable. Global environmental problems such as climate change demand far-reaching, global cooperation, monitoring and coordination, regardless of the way the problem came into being in the first place. Besides, as a result of the rise of ecological sciences, there are also many positive things to mention. It is from ecoscience that we have gained the current insights with respect to the unpredictability of the functioning of dynamic ecosystems. Recent developments have shown that, given the omnipresence of non-linearity and a multitude of critical threshold values ("tipping points"[14]), the precautionary principle is still absent.

---

[13] See for example W. Bello, *Deglobalization: Ideas for a New World Economy* (London / New York, 2002).

[14] See, for example, G. Walker, "The Tipping Point of the Iceberg," *Nature* 441 (2006): 802-05.

This principle is extremely relevant in light of the climate issue. Even though there is still considerable uncertainty about the position of certain critical threshold values and the inherent non-linear reactions in the ecosphere-climate system, it is better, given the possibility of catastrophic outcomes, to be on the safe side and ensure that the climate system is not challenged so to react violently and abruptly. The European Council, in keeping with this precautionary approach and presumably influenced by the recognition of multiple threshold values, has adopted a long-term policy goal of limiting the global average temperature increase to 2°C above preindustrial temperatures.[15] In a growing number of studies, this tipping point is designed as a temperature limit above which "dangerous climate impacts" may occur. In order to avoid such "dangerous anthropogenic interference with the climate system," leading environmental scientists have, therefore, called for effective measures to be undertaken today without hesitation or delay (such as a reduction in CO_2 emissions of at least 60%).

There is another reason why the home perspective offers insufficient guarantees for sustainability. Local events and excessive ways of life can have detrimental consequences in other parts of the world. This often leads to the ironic result that people in the most isolated parts of the world are being exposed to the risks and dangers that have been caused in the center of the global economy. For instance, scientists were baffled when they encountered the highest PCB concentrations ever measured in the milk of Inuit women in northern Canada. PCBs (polychlorinated biphenyls) interfere with the functioning of our hormones and can cause serious health risks. In the meantime we have learned that "persistent organic pollutants" (such as PCBs) are capable of travelling distances of thousands of kilometres through the air currents in the direction of the polar regions. Through this process PCBs can accumulate in the ecosystems at the North and South Poles, especially in the fat tissue of mammals like polar bears and whales, as they are close to the apex of the food chain. The research showed that PCBs had also "bioaccumulated" in the breast glands of the Inuit women. A similar example is that of the hole in the ozone layer, which

---

[15] Nevertheless, the 2°C "tipping point" remains a relatively arbitrary threshold value. See also S. Schneider and M.D. Mastrandrea, "Probabilistic Assessment of 'Dangerous' Climate Change and Emission Pathways," in *PNAS* 102/44 (2005): 15728-35.

was caused by the massive use of CFCs (chlorofluorocarbons) almost exclusively in the industrialized world. Yet the (seasonal) hole in the ozone layer was situated close to the south pole, in the exact region where no CFCs were being applied. Global warming is another famous example. The slum dweller in La Paz, the fisherman in Senegal, and the shepherd in Ethiopia are in no way responsible for global warming, yet they are the first and most likely victims. These examples illustrate immediately why we are obliged in one way or another to bring the reach of our responsibility into accordance with the reach of the effects we create. The astronaut's perspective remains, therefore, sorely needed and must be combined with the best elements of the home perspective.

John D'Arcy May

Whose Universality?
Which Interdependence?
Human Rights, Social Responsibility
and Ecological Integrity

The West has inherited an unresolved controversy from Europe's Middle Ages concerning the status of so-called "universals." Are intelligible ideas "real" in their own right, whether or not they are instantiated in observable reality (*universale ante rem,* Plato's classical "idealist" position)? Or are they simply "names" which have no reality apart from empirical instances to which they are conventionally applied (*universale post rem,* the skeptical view of "nominalists" such as Roscellin, Abaelard and William of Ockham)? As in so many other such vexed questions, the "critical realism" of St Thomas Aquinas forged a synthesis deriving from Aristotle: we know all that we know through the senses, which attain only the singularity of really existing particular things, but knowledge itself consists in the intellect's grasp of the essences of things, their universal forms which have a separate existence only in the mind (*universale in re*).

Esoteric as this epistemological excursus may seem, its consequences are in fact enormous when we transpose them to the validity of ethical principles in a multicultural world of global intercultural communication. The moral force of ethical principles, on which the stability of "ethical globalization" (Mary Robinson) and our nascent world order depends, is premised on their supposed universality: if they are valid *at* all, they are valid *for* all. But who is to define and determine universal validity? The religions? Despite their claims to universal truth, the new global context reveals them all to be culturally particular to an almost obsessive degree, each disqualifying its universal claims by the vehemence with which it defends them against those of others. Then surely the United Nations' *Universal Declaration of Human Rights* (10 December 1948) settles the matter? But substantial cultural blocs such as the Africans and the Muslims have formulated their own charters of human rights, precisely because they hold that the UN Declaration is *not* universal but a product of Western Christian individualism.[1] Critics with a Nietzschean sense of the hollowness of all pretensions to universality, such as Michel Foucault, Frantz Fanon or Edward Said, have shown how "universal truth" is usually *somebody's* truth imposed on others and proclaimed universally valid so that it can serve as an instrument of power. Yet it remains equally incontrovertible that unless agreement can be reached on the universal validity of at least some determinate rights, there is little hope of achieving the "globalization of ethics" which many would see as the necessary basis for an international civil society.[2] And there are further questions: Is the concept of "having rights" the appropriate category if ethics are to become not just notionally universal but truly global? How do social responsibilities correlate with rights? Is there a place in such conceptions for the earth itself and all the non-human life it contains?

In order to broach these questions I wish to reexamine the way the universality of ethics was formulated for European modernity by taking a fresh look at it through African eyes (1). I shall then suggest ways of expanding the scope of ethical validity beyond "rights" and the human to embrace communal and ecological dimensions of ethics (2).

---

[1] The "Banjul Charter" or "African Charter of Human and Peoples' Rights," adopted in 1981 by the (then) Organisation of African Unity, stresses social integration as constitutive of the human, the rights of peoples as well as those of individuals, and duties towards the family, the state and the international community. For a discussion of this and other examples, especially the Islamic Declaration of Human Rights, in the context of the theoretical debate about universalism and relativism, see D. O'Sullivan, "The History of Human Rights across the Regions: Universalism vs. Cultural Relativism," in *The International Journal of Human Rights* 2/3 (1998): 22-48, and "Is the Declaration of Human Rights Universal?" in *IJHR* 4/1 (2000): 25-53.

[2] On the prospects for this see R. Falk, *Predatory Globalization: A Critique* (Cambridge: Polity Press, 1999), chap. 11, and *Religion and Humane Global Governance* (New York: Palgrave, 2001).

Whose Universality? Kant through African Eyes

Immanuel Kant (1724-1804) was revered in his native Königsberg and throughout Europe as a man of integrity whose vision of a world society based on freedom and reason was far ahead of his time. His little tract *On Perpetual Peace* (1795)[3] drew conclusions from his great *Critiques*, in which he had mapped out the boundaries of reason in the spheres of scientific theory, aesthetic judgment and practical morality, for the ordering of a future world society. Wishing to address intelligent readers rather than academic specialists, people perplexed by the constant state of war in which Europe and in its colonies found themselves, Kant modeled his exposition on a peace treaty, with preliminary and principal articles followed by codicils and appendices. Though some of his thinking – especially his jaundiced view of democracy as "despotism of the people" – is colored by his time, his main theses are as pertinent today as they must have been then.

Well knowing that perpetual peace is unattainable, Kant nevertheless posits it as a normative idea, striving towards which is a categorical imperative of moral reason. War as an institution should be abolished, for before the tribunal of reason it is stripped of all legitimacy, whereas the securing of peace by a treaty between peoples becomes an immediate duty.[4] This, in turn, presupposes that relations between peoples be treated on the same moral basis as relations between persons, that is, as requiring understanding of and trust in the other. Peace is not simply a ceasefire; it must be created and institutionalized, and the only way to do this is by a truly representative form of government characterized by freedom, which for Kant was a republican constitution.[5] A federalism of free states, hitherto known only in

---

[3] I am using the Reclam edition, *Zum ewigen Frieden: Ein philosophischer Entwurf* (Stuttgart, 1973), edited with an introduction by T. Valentiner.

[4] Cf. *Zum ewigen Frieden*, 33: "… die Vernunft vom Throne der höchsten moralisch gesetzgebenden Gewalt herab, den Krieg als Rechtsgang schlechterdings verdammt, den Friedenszustand dagegen zur unmittelbaren Pflicht macht, welcher doch, ohne einen Vertrag der Völker unter sich, nicht gestiftet oder gesichert werden kann …."

[5] Kant distinguishes between a representative form of *governance* (*Regierungsart*) and forms of *dominance* (*Form der* Beherrschung [*for-*

Europe, would be the guarantee of universal hospitality and world citizenship, what we might call "global civil rights," so that no stranger, arriving in the territory of another people, would be treated with animosity.⁶ Kant goes out of his way to remind his readers that European imperialism tramples on these principles at every turn, ignoring the sovereignty of foreign countries such as India, China and Japan and despising their cultures. But "the denial of rights in any *one* place on earth is felt in *all* places."⁷ While nature itself appears to have used the human proclivity to wage war to displace peoples and distribute them widely over the face of the earth, it also teaches that civility, not strife, is to their greatest advantage, and as the power of money is by far the greatest impulse to wage war, so the spirit of trade between free peoples is the greatest guarantee of perpetual peace. Politics and morality, in the end, are compatible.

The boldness of this vision is matched by its enduring relevance, and equally astonishing is the degree to which Kant seems to have been informed about international relations, economic affairs and the cultural peculiarities of distant peoples, as a close reading of his footnotes reveals. He could never be tempted away from his native city because Königsberg, as a vibrant seaport with a vast hinterland, gave him unparalleled opportunities to inform himself about the wider world by reading and listening to travelers' tales and conversing with men of affairs from a variety of countries, without necessitating the inconvenience of travel.⁸ Though his second- and third-hand sources

---

    ma imperii]), among which he counts democracy. Cf. *Zum ewigen Frieden*, 27-28.

6   Kant's terms are *Weltbürgerrecht* and *Hospitalität*, *Frieden*, 35-36.

7   Kant sees human community as so far developed that "Rechtsverletzung an *einem* Platz der Erde an *allen* gefühlt wird ...." Cf. *Zum ewigen Frieden*, 39.

8   See E. Chukwudi Eze, "The Color of Reason: The Idea of 'Race' in Kant's Anthropology," in E. Chukwudi Eze (ed.), *Postcolonial African Philosophy: A Critical Reader* (Cambridge, MA / Oxford: Blackwell, 1997), 103-40. The Minister of Education made a special exception to permit Kant to lecture from his own notes of these conversations, there being no textbook on matters cultural and anthropological available at the time!

may have been quite unreliable, Kant spent much more of his time as a researcher and university lecturer trying to establish the relationship between what he called "Anthropology" and "Physical Geography" than he did on his critical philosophy, pioneering the introduction of these subjects into the university curriculum.[9] Some of this material found its way into his works on ethics and metaphysics, and it has even been suggested that the *Critiques* themselves are Kant's attempt to formulate a universal grounding of human nature, revealed in all its variety in the course of his anthropological studies, by a "transcendental deduction" of its defining characteristics. On closer inspection, however, certain aspects of Kant's enterprise turn out to be quite alarming.

For Kant, anthropology and physical geography were intimately related as the internal and external, psychological and bodily dimensions of the one human nature. As a person, indeed, the human being is a free individual and is as such above nature; but the human is embodied in ways determined by the physical environment, which result in the differences between the races, and these in turn are correlated with skin color.[10] Kant had no moral difficulty in developing a full-blown, transcendentally grounded theory of race, drawing on the taxonomies proposed by contemporaries such as Carl von Linné (1707-1778) and Georges-Louis Leclerc, Comte de Buffon (1708-1788), but in the spirit of a notorious comment by David Hume (1711-1776) that negroes and other colored races are "naturally inferior to the whites" because they have invariably proved incapable of higher cultural achievements.[11]

Deeply impressed by his reading of Rousseau, Kant held that there is a universally fixed "human nature" underlying all the observable differences, but there is nevertheless a profound difference between the "pure state of nature" (*l'homme naturel*) and the "state of human nature" (*l'homme de l'homme*). In the latter sense, human nature inexorably brings forth language and society, and here an equally profound ambiguity in Rousseau comes to light: civilization corrupts

---

[9] Eze, "The Color of Reason," 104.

[10] Eze, "The Color of Reason," 105-06.

[11] See the texts in E.C. Eze (ed.), *Race and the Enlightenment: A Reader* (Cambridge, MA / Oxford: Blackwell, 1997), including Hume's footnote, 33.

"nature" (as in *The Origin of Inequality*), yet the creation of civil society is the outcome of "making oneself" as a moral process (*The Social Contract*).[12] Kant was not interested in the romantic cliché of the "noble savage"; "Rather, Kant found in Rousseau a 'restorer of the rights of humanity' – but a humanity defined as social, civilized and moral."[13] This, it transpires, applies almost exclusively to white Europeans, not to the black, yellow and red races into which Kant classified the rest of humanity. The one human genus, Kant speculated, contained "seeds" (*Keime*) and "predispositions" (*Anlagen*) which are triggered by different climatic and geographical conditions to produce very different varieties of humanity with widely divergent feelings for the "sublime" and the "beautiful."[14]

It is here that we reach the morally ambivalent core of Kant's enterprise, for he is not only proposing that "talent" is correlated with skin color, but also that the resulting *Klassenunterschiede* ("species differences" in Kant's terminology) are transcendentally grounded and therefore universal. This amounts to nothing less than what Emmanuel Chukwudi Eze calls a "depth-structure of humanity," adding:

> Whether this "depth-structure" of humanity is understood as already given or as potential, it is obvious that the notion derives from Kant's appropriation and reinterpretation of Rousseau, for whom there is a "hidden" nature of "man" which lies beyond the causal laws of (physical) nature, not merely as an abstract proposition of science, but as a pragmatically realizable moral universal character

so that the transcendentally grounded structures of feeling are given the objectivity of scientific description "by conferring on them a quality of permanence and universality."[15] At the same time, this transcendentally grounded *theory* of "race" is perfectly consonant with the

---

[12] Eze, "The Color of Reason," 108-12; Kant's project of integrating the scientific knowledge of causes and the pragmatic character of moral knowledge is clearly at work, 107.

[13] Eze, "The Color of Reason," 112.

[14] See the texts in Eze, *Race*, 42, 55.

[15] Eze, "The Color of Reason," 118-22.

theory of civilization which informs Kant's vision of perpetual peace and which he shares with Rousseau:

> ... the ever continuing and growing activity and culture which are thereby set in motion, and whose highest possible expression can only be the product of a political constitution based on concepts of human right, and consequently the achievement of human beings themselves.[16]

For Kant, as interpreted by the African philosophers Eze and Serequeberhan, "'race' as an a priori idea is founded on *nature*," which is as much as to say that his "universal" principles are undermined by his pseudoscientific Eurocentric racial prejudices.[17] Granted that for Kant "human nature" is teleological, an essence that is not static but ethical and for that very reason "transcendental, universal, transcultural and ahistorical," there are nevertheless fixed racial essences that determine "talent," which amounts to nothing less than a biological essentialism.[18]

In Kant's defense it is only fair to remind ourselves that his views are perfectly in tune with those of eighteenth century contemporaries from Jefferson to Cuvier, from the French *Encyclopédie* to the *Encyclopaedia Brittanica*, whose scientific interest was to explain why some races became black, when the obvious norm for humans was the beauty of the white Caucasian.[19] The same set of prejudices underlies the confident pronouncements of Hegel about "peoples without history" (*geschichtslose Völker*) in other continents:

---

[16] From Kant's review of Herder's *Philosophy of History*, which he criticizes for the unreliability of its data (somewhat ironically in view of Kant's own sources!) and its lack of internal organization based on a transcendental principle of universality, Eze, *Race*, 68, 70.

[17] Eze, "The Color of Reason," 124-25, and, in the same volume, T. Serequeberhan, "The Critique of Eurocentrism and the Practice of African Philosophy," 141-61, an attempt to unmask and deconstruct the Kantian "pre-text" of racial prejudice inherited by Hegel and Marx.

[18] Eze, "The Color of Reason," 126.

[19] Texts in Eze, *Race*.

> The characteristic feature of the Negroes is that their consciousness has not yet reached an awareness of any substantial objectivity – for example, of God or the law – in which the will of man could participate and in which he could become aware of his own being. The African, in his undifferentiated and concentrated unity, has not yet succeeded in making this distinction between himself as an individual and his essential universality, so that he knows nothing of an absolute being which is other and higher than his own self.[20]

Having no knowledge of evil, the individual in the natural state of innocence can have no knowledge of the good, nor any notion of a Supreme Being or of justice, no "ethical relationships of an essentially universal content" or "inner universality":

> Where this universal quality is weak or remote, the political union cannot be that of a state governed by free rational laws ... for the state is based on rational universality, which is a law of freedom.[21]

Quite apart from Hegel's patent lack of evidence for such assertions, the form in which he casts them disqualifies Africans, Asians and other "colored" peoples from ever attaining the plane of universality, thus once again undermining the putative universality of the theory itself.

Such, then, was the context of origin of the modern ideal of universality in both science and ethics. Though there were those such as James Beattie and Johann Gottfried von Herder who tried to view European pretensions through the eyes of the blacks, it was hard to pull this off in a scientific environment in which the main problem was to explain blackness as some kind of physiological aberration triggered by climatic and geographical conditions. A century later, the Japanese philosopher Tetsuro Watsuji, who was to have an unseemly part in legitimating Japanese nationalism, was on his way to Germany to study these very thinkers, and as he passed through the different climatic zones of the China Sea, the Arabian Peninsula and the Mediterranean, he speculated on the ways in which they shape the national

---

[20] From Hegel's *Philosophy of History*, in Eze, *Race*, 127.

[21] Hegel in Eze, *Race*, 137.

characters of the peoples who inhabit them.[22] It seems that Europe was not the only place in which such essentialism went hand in hand with delusions of racial superiority *proposed as universal truth* and backed up by transcendental or phenomenological groundings. But of what? The human sciences have not yet reached the stage of objectivity where their findings can be regarded as devoid of all prejudice or distortion, and they now build this subjectivity and contextuality of viewpoint into their own methodologies. No one, not even the purportedly "neutral" Western scientist, can reassure us that we have a comprehensive account of the "human," unaffected by the "pre-texts" (Serequeberhan) and "prejudgments" (Gadamer) of racial prejudice. This being so, attempts to state "universal" principles as the basis of morality run the risk of *reinforcing* racism, inequality and oppression, just as Kant ended by "transcendentally grounding" his own European prejudices. By the same token, "equality," which supposedly mediates the objectively universal principle to the particular ethical judgment, is an abstraction, not an empirical description: it is obvious that human beings vary greatly in every respect and are profoundly different from the other animals with whom they share so much in common, yet our constitutions proclaim the equality of all and ecological ethics suggests equivalences between human and non-human life. Equality, too, is a normative idea and an abstract postulate, to be aimed at rather than verified empirically. Yet without agreement on the universal validity of at least a core set of ethical principles, it seems that there can be neither a viable ethic nor a stable civil society, both locally and globally.[23] Kant, it will be remembered, often referred to "duty" and "nature" in the course of formulating his idea of world peace, and he premised it on a "treaty" or formalized agreement based on under-

---

[22] See W. Tetsuro, *Fûdo: Wind und Erde. Der Zusammenhang von Klima und Kultur,* Darmstadt: Primus Verlag 1992, and my comments in J.D. May, *Transcendence and Violence: The Encounter of Buddhist, Christian and Primal Traditions* (New York / London: Continuum, 2003), 105-06, also 75.

[23] Though it may have been too abstract in conception and somewhat premature in the way it was proposed, Hans Küng's *Global Responsibility: In Search of a New World Ethic* (London: SCM, 1990), was a clarion call to moralists to awaken from their dogmatic slumbers and take multireligious and intercultural universality seriously.

standing and trust. This may provide some clues to the next steps in our investigation.

Which Interdependence? Cultural Constructions of the Human

Kant and his peers were unable to concede that non-European "colored" forms of humanity share the "dignity" of their white European counterparts, though they do possess a certain "value." It is therefore apparent that, if there is to be any "universal" formulation of human rights, Kant's own categorical imperative must be reasserted against his racial prejudices: *each* individual human life is a unique world constituted by consciousness and an originating source of free acts; it is therefore an end in itself and must never be misused as a means to other people's ends. The concept of "human rights" is *one* way of acknowledging this unique moral status of human dignity, in that rights accrue to the individual person simply by virtue of his or her being rational, autonomous and free. The notion that this principle applies, or applies fully, only to Europeans is a grotesque distortion which lies at the root of the pseudoscientific theories of racial inequality that blighted the twentieth century (Nazism, Apartheid, white supremacy etc.). Yet conceptions of what it is that makes the human uniquely valuable are very differently constructed in different cultural and religions traditions.[24] Conceptions of universality, as we have seen, may themselves be culturally determined. They are necessary generalizations which allow us to state that whatever is understood to be moral applies to *all* human beings *everywhere*, without exception. The moral impulse, however, is always particular; it arises prototypically in the face-to-face situation, not *because* it can be generalized, as Kant thought, but *prior* to all generalization in the primordial realization that the presence of the other is the ethical imperative not to kill, as Levinas has shown.

---

[24] For examples see L. Hogan and J.D. May, "Constructing the Human: Dignity in Interreligious Dialogue," in *Concilium*, 2 (2003): 78-89; J.D. May, "Universalität oder Partikularität der Menschenrechte? Eine interreligiöse Perspektive," in J. Jans (ed.), *Für die Freiheit verantwortlich: Festschrift für Karl-Wilhelm Merks* (Fribourg / Freiburg: Academic Press / Verlag Herder, 2004), 148-61.

My suggestion, then, is that "universality" is not available *a priori* but remains implicit in the intersubjectivity of human interaction until it is "realized" through shared practice and the negotiation of meanings, and this applies *per analogiam* to encounters between peoples with their different religions and cultures.[25] Rights language, this seems to imply, though a powerful instrument for the implementation of justice, will not measure up to the demands of universality until its Western conceptual presuppositions are complemented by the metaphors, stories and ideas supplied by other cultures, even if these consist in generalizable "oral folk wisdom" rather than in explicitly universalized ethical systems. Once this begins to happen, and in the light of growing ecological awareness, we begin to realize that the concept of rights has to be complemented by the concept of duties and expanded to include nature itself, not only all sentient beings but species as well, within the scope of justice. Care for cultures and ecologies is then seen to form part of one overarching ethical purpose. Abstract universality turns out to be premature unless it is interwoven with interdependence. It is this thesis that I wish to develop in what follows.

Though it is undoubtedly oversimplified, the schema below sets out the terms in which I wish to discuss the problem of universality. The diagram merely illustrates the three sets of mediations which I believe have to be carried out if universality is to be realized as interdependence. It is not meant to imply that "individual rights" are an exclusively Western notion, along the lines suggested by Kant and Hegel, whereas less developed cultures have to be content with "reciprocal duties," while "ecological care" is confined to uncivilized indigenous peoples. In Thai Buddhism, for example, the "dhammic democracy" proposed by Phra Prayudh Payutto argues for individual freedoms, both political and economic, whereas the "dhammic socialism" of Buddhadâsa Bhikkhu extols the ethical value of community

---

[25] For further development of this *analogia relationis* see J.D. May, "Verantwortung *Coram Deo*? Europa zwischen säkularer und interreligiöser Ethik," Karl-Wilhelm Merks, (ed.), *Verantwortung – Ende oder Wandlungen einer Vorstellung? Orte und Funktionen der Ethik in unserer Gesellschaft* (Münster / Hamburg / London: LIT Verlag, 2001), 193-207; Karl-Wilhem Merks, *Transcendence and Violence*, 125-136.

responsibility.[26] Nor is the relationship between rights and duties necessarily complementary. While it is self-evident that, once rights are established, either as claims to something that is due or as freedoms from something that is unjust, these entail duties on the part of others, the inverse inference does not necessarily hold: it is not so evident that duties, obligations and responsibilities aimed at maintaining community harmony and social cooperation entail rights on the part of those to whom these duties are owed. It has been argued, for instance, that there is not even an "embryonic" concept of rights in traditional Buddhism and that the social relevance of Buddhist compassion stands out all the more clearly in consequence.[27] Compassion is far more fundamental than rights, and it only becomes necessary to insist on rights when the practice of compassion declines.[28]

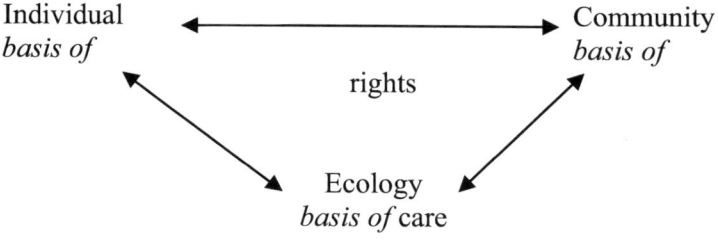

---

[26] See S. King, "From Is to Ought: Natural Law in Buddhadasa Bhikkhu and Phra Prayudh Payutto," *Journal of Religious Ethics* 30 (2002): 275-93, 288-90, and S. Hongladarom, "Buddhism and Human Rights in the Thoughts of Sulak Sivaraksa and Phra Dhammapidok (Prayudh Payutto)," in D. Keown et al. (eds.), *Buddhism and Human Rights* (Richmond, Surrey: Curzon, 1998), 97-109.

[27] See the discussion in Keown *et al., Buddhism and Human Rights*, between D. Keown, "Are There Human Rights in Buddhism?" 15-41, and C. Ihara, "Why There Are No Rights in Buddhism: A Reply to D. Keown," 43-51, where Keown distinguishes between claim-rights and liberty-rights (19) and suggests that the term "due" comes closest to Buddhist terms which conflate rights and duties, while Ihara rejects the notion that duties invariably entail corresponding rights (45) and suggests that Buddhism would be better off without the concept of rights (51, n. 21).

[28] This case is argued in the same volume by J. Garfield, "Human Rights and Compassion," Keown *et al., Buddhism and Human Rights*, 111-40.

The role of ecology in different human rights discourses complicates matters still further. The potent combination of population growth and technological advancement is sufficient indication of both the human rights issues (family limitation, abortion) and the environmental devastation involved in, say, providing every family in China with an automobile and an air conditioner. But in my view the ecological dimension could be even more fundamental in bringing about the mediations outlined in the diagram above. Buddhism, conceived entirely within the worldview defined by *karman-samsâra*, the endless cycle of rebirth according to the residue of deeds in previous lives, sees human life as an integral part of this perpetual flux of life forms. Its relationship with the rest of sentient nature is thus one of constant "recycling" until radical release (*moksha*) is achieved in *nirvâna*. For this reason the ancient Indian unwillingness to harm any sentient being (*ahimsâ*) is an integral part of Buddhist ethics. This does not mean that Buddhism has a ready-made ecological ethic for today, but it is a promising starting point.

Christianity, on the other hand, was so preoccupied with human sin and redemption that it reduced nature to the exemplar of "natural law" as it applied to humans and lost sight of care for creation as an ethical goal, so that the idea that nature could have "rights" or that ecology could be a matter of justice now seems incomprehensible.[29] This is as much an indication of the limitations of rights language in expressing a universal ethic as it is of Christianity's tendency to be individualistic and anthropocentric. To take another example, when the "primal" traditions of indigenous peoples, oral cultures without scriptures and philosophies but with close bonds to land and nature, are affected by "progress," "development" and "globalization," we observe in a modern context how the universality of rights language is undermined in a way analogous to the difficulties we discovered in the great

---

[29] See R. Frazier Nash, *The Rights of Nature: A History of Environmental Ethics* (Madison: University of Wisconsin Press, 1989), 17: "After the decline of Greece and Rome and the advent of Christianity, nature did not fare well in Western ethics;" J.A. Nash, *Loving Nature: Ecological Integrity and Christian Responsibility* (Nashville: Abingdon Press, 1991); and my discussion in J.D. May, *After Pluralism: Towards an Interreligious Ethic* (Münster / Hamburg / London: LIT Verlag, 2000), 133-37, 139-44. Most of us are capable of carrying on an extended discussion of "religion and violence" without even mentioning animals!

thinkers of the Enlightenment. It is precisely the "universality" of Western norms that is invoked to justify such interventions.

Human rights language is undeniably Western, unable to conceal its origins in the legal categories inherited from Greece and Rome.[30] So conceived, it is an abstract universal which is logically independent of the myths and doctrines in which the various religions seek to found the unique worth of human nature. The concept of human rights, though at home in the Western liberal context of individual autonomy and political freedoms, is nevertheless communicable to cultures that construct the human differently, and this communicability across cultures is a clue to the type of universality we are looking for. The Dalai Lama, for example, has no problem endorsing human rights as a means of obtaining justice while insisting on the priority of wisdom and compassion, and, though they initially resisted human rights as "liberal," neither do the popes in their social teaching.[31] The question is: in what categories and under what conditions is an "ethical universal" such as human rights communicable across cultures? Certainly not those of the assumed superiority of Western ideas and values and their imposition on others by force, as has happened often enough in the colonial and missionary past of Western Christianity. The recognition of differences in the mythical attempts to provide human dignity with a foundation does not imply that the various "stories" are functionally equivalent and may be substituted for one another or combined at will to reinforce an account of the human that is already given *a priori*, as the Enlightenment thinkers tended to presuppose. It is the human itself that is differently constructed, and the Western construct is one among others.

It is at this point that we need to reflect further on the role of generalization in arriving at the universal. By grasping what different things have in common – what the Medievals would have called "abstracting the forms of their essences" – we are able to make comparisons and construct classifications (species, genera etc.). This capacity of the intellect, most strongly developed in literate cultures but present

---

[30] See R. Panikkar, "Is the Notion of Human Rights a Western Concept?" *Invisible Har-mony: Essays on Contemplation and Responsibility* (Minneapolis: Fortress Press, 1995), 109-33.

[31] See the essays by Garfield and Strain in Keown *et al.*, *Buddhism and Human Rights*.

in all, is the main instrument by which the sciences, but also ethics, formulate laws which are said to obtain generally ("across the genera") or universally. This happens, however, in markedly different ways and in a variety of media according to cultural and religious context.

"Truth," whether it is defined as correspondence, coherence or consensus, is attributed to propositions that have this quality of holding good "in general"; even a statement about a singular instance carries the presupposition that, if the same set of circumstances occurred again, it would still be true. It is thus tempting to develop comparison and classification across cultural, ethical and religious systems with the help of cognitive science, mathematics and chaos theory to the point where any symbolic expression whatsoever, whether in nuclear physics or religious ritual, can ultimately be correlated with any other.[32] On the verge of being implicated all over again in the medieval controversy about universals, we realize that this project, to have any relevance to ethics, presupposes that *absolute* generalization is both possible and meaningful, a prospect that may well fire the enthusiasm of mathematicians or computer programmers but seems to lead us further and further away from the kind of *pragmatic* generalization required by law and medicine as well as ethics and religion.

Ethical obligation transcends both the concrete and the general: the pre-ontological ethic of Levinas, deriving from a phenomenology of encounter with the other – particularly the unexpected and unwanted stranger – in whose face (*visage*) the "infinite" is disclosed as the always immediate and unique occasion of ethical commitment, can never be reduced to the "totality" of a general system based on abstraction. Something similar can be said of religious conceptions of the "transcendent": they are in no sense abstract generalizations but unique singularities, embodied in the symbolic languages of particular cultural traditions. It is this that makes it so difficult for the religions to communicate with one another about the things that matter most to

---

[32] At this point I am relying on my notes of the remarkable Charles Strong lecture given at the 2003 annual conference of the Australian Association for the Study of Religions at Griffith University in Brisbane by Professor Wayne Hudson. Hudson, for whom German idealism is realism pure and simple, presented his thesis as a "non-Hegelian phenomenology of mind," though another participant called it "neo-modernism."

them, but it is not a failure of abstraction or generalization: rather, it is a limitation intrinsic to any symbolic expression of the kinds of "absolute" convictions found in faith and ethics.[33]

This makes the discussion of the universality of rights even more complicated in ways that were foreshadowed by Kant's appropriation of Rousseau and foreseen by Ernst Troeltsch as he tried to come to grips with the "absoluteness" of religions:[34] inasmuch as they are normative, ethical principles and religious doctrines display an *a priori* necessity that transcends the contingency of their historical origins; but these norms are nonetheless the products of historical processes. They are human constructions, and as such they can be transformed and redefined in new cultural contexts and historical situations. Traditions that forget that they are "earthed" in concrete cultures and in nature as mediated by culture run the risk of becoming absolutistic, and they bequeath a legacy of petrified rites and institutions whose status as expressions of an original identity is no longer reflected upon and whose universal validity is taken for granted. Absolute generalization, then, is not the kind of universality we are looking for and is at the opposite pole to the kind of interdependence that is the key to a global ethic.

Conclusion: Universality as Interdependence

The transition from an *absolute* universality, posited *a priori* on the model of the Medieval universals and either grounded in reason or derived from divine authority, to the *pragmatic* universality of meanings negotiated across cultures until agreement is found, will not be an easy one. Tempting, as it is to imagine oneself in possession of the former, all too often, as we have seen, such claims to universality are prema-

---

[33] For an interesting experiment in the power of theological reasoning to provide a basis for communication between traditions, see Frank X. Clooney, *Hindu God, Christian God: How Reason Helps Break Down the Boundaries between Religions* (Oxford / New York: Oxford University Press, 2001).

[34] See E. Troeltsch, *The Absoluteness of Christianity and the History of Religions* (London: SCM, 1972).

ture and are a function either of unwarranted feelings of superiority, or of actual domination, or both. Ethical principles based on such claims, however noble they may be in themselves, are thus undermined by the moral ambiguity of their contexts of origin and application, and their cultural particularity is exposed.

This becomes painfully obvious in acute practical situations such as conflict mediation, especially when the conflict is religiously motivated. The arrival of professional mediators with generalized methods of conflict resolution can easily make the conflict worse, because the alleged universality of such methods simply reinforces the threat to the parties' identity by an alien "other," which is at the root of the conflict in the first place: their fear of "cultural annihilation by assimilation."[35] Only when outside mediators have the humility to listen and the patience to identify the problem-solving potential indigenous to the traditions involved is there any hope that the parties will discover their own "prosocial values" and bring them to bear on the conflict.[36] Indeed, "... the real challenge may be to discover the interpersonal values most highly prized by a culture and how an enemy at some early stage of the relationship violated those values, thus intentionally or unintentionally striking at the heart of the relationship."[37]

> Universal commitments, such as human rights, may play a crucial role in achieving international consensus on basic civic values .... But this may not be a sufficient common denominator for people who are defining their religiosity in opposition to universal, secular values.[38]

---

[35] This thesis is impressively developed on the basis of experience in the Middle East and elsewhere by M. Gopin, *Between Eden and Armageddon: The Future of World Religions, Violence, and Peacemaking* (Oxford: Oxford University Press, 2000), 175; and *Holy War, Holy Peace: How Religion Can Bring Peace to the Middle East* (Oxford: Oxford University Press, 2002).

[36] Gopin, *Between Eden and Armageddon*, 59; see also chap. 7 and *Holy War*, 131-32.

[37] Gopin, *Between Eden and Armageddon*, 84.

[38] Gopin, *Between Eden and Armageddon*, 199.

In all such situations there is tension between "the need to integrate and merge versus the need to be unique,"[39] and it is futile to try to preempt this by imposing "universal" principles and methods. "The only response to exclusivity is not absolute universality and the blurring of all boundaries ... In this conclusion, I am clearly parting company with Kant's absolute universalism in terms of the construction of moral standards."[40] This is precisely the conclusion that our own reflections have reached by another route.

My proposal is that the mutual recognition of interdependence places the need for universality in a new context, signified by the "inter-" in terms like intersubjective, intercultural and interreligious. "Equality," in such a context, takes full account of irreducible human differences while insisting on the mutual respect which transcends them. "Rights" are defined in order to counteract the manifest inequalities introduced by domination and exploitation, particularly of individuals by states but also of one people by another. "Pluralism" can no longer be misused to disguise the restriction of rights and the values underlying them to exclusive groups, particularly where these are racially defined. The "human," finally, is no longer seen in a dualistic antagonism to the natural world but as an integral part of "nature," which in turn is recognized as having something analogous to rights because of its intrinsic value.

This new context is a process, not a given; it must be continually constructed as radically different meanings and interests are subordinated to the pragmatic imperative of interdependence, the realization that others, though alien and possibly threatening, have their own reasons for being and doing as they are, and that we who are different can nevertheless have need of what other cultures have to offer. This applies to our relationship with nature as well and to the reciprocity of ecologies and the cultures that sustain them. The codification of abstract rights is a necessary part of establishing justice, but in this wider context of interdependence it becomes apparent that love and wisdom, care and compassion, duty and obligation are more fundamental still. Kant might have formulated things this way if his dawning awareness of the diversity of humanity and the earth itself had not been distorted by his commitment to reason and freedom as absolute values realized

---

[39] Gopin, *Between Eden and Armageddon*, 203.

[40] Gopin, *Holy War*, 106, 107.

only by Europeans. Both his vision and ours are idealistic, but perhaps the experience of the intervening centuries has taught us to be more pragmatic in our idealism.

PART IV

GENDER

Gabriela Di Renzo

Latin-American Theologies Developed by Women

Introduction

Women have been completely erased from the planet; they have been excluded in the processes of comprehension, interpretation, and explanation of humanity's past and present, as well as in the future orientations for our civilizations. To become aware of this, it is enough to look at the struggle women have had to engage in to receive an education and minimal rights as citizens. In Latin America we have to add marginalization, oppression and the extreme poverty of women to this list. In this context, the goal of this conference is to make us more aware and sensitive to the challenges of this reality both yesterday and today, in the theological development of Latin-American women and from the perspective of this reality that concerns us and affects both our lives and thinking.

On this subject, I would like to provide, first, an introduction on the relationship between contextual theologies and feminism; secondly, I would like to discuss the intersection between gender and poverty (the starting point of this entire issue); thirdly, I will develop some of the most significant theologies which respond to the situation of women in Latin America. We will end by drawing some conclusions.

Contextual Theologies and Feminism

Around the 1980s "feminist theology" found its way into Latin America and diverse theologies developed by women came about. These theologies are characterized by a combination of the tendencies of theologies "in the context" of the poor and of the challenges that arose as a result of the aspirations of women. This is theology done in the subjective genitive because it focuses not only upon women and their experiences as objects of study but also upon women as theological subjects.

Latin-American theology done by women has been influenced, on the one hand, by a contextual theological tradition of liberation and, on the other hand, by the awakening of Latin-American women theologians to feminist theology and to the increasing feminist movement. Along this intersection and the degree of feminist consciousness and politics, various currents of thought appeared that can be grouped as "feminist theology of liberation," or "theologies from the perspective of women." We have to emphasize that the relationship between liberation and the situation of women had already been suggested since the mid-1970s by several American and European theologians advocating a liberation theology from a feminist perspective, and a feminist theology as a critical theology of liberation.

It is presently obvious that the widespread poverty of the third world and the different development projects aimed at improving the situation, affect men and women differently. The relationship between the contextual theologies that are developed as a response to situations of poverty and injustice, and the feminist theologies that originate in women's experiences, is that, in the former, we consider the liberation of the poor and, in the second, we take as our starting point sexual discrimination, and as a result, the liberation of women. The point shared by both theologies is that both assume the challenge of a concrete form of discrimination, whether social, gender-based or ethnical. Their overlap grows when the poor subjects, in addition, are women.

If we take into account that liberation theology wants to be an interpretation of the world of the poor and assumes, in full consciousness, as its horizon of reflection, the interests, dreams and struggles of the oppressed, then, it should also favor the self-expression of women. If it doesn't do so, liberation theology risks transforming itself into mere rhetoric by distancing itself from certain oppressed faces. The theological contribution of the work of women has been to perceive, here, an ideological oversight that neglects the sexist aspects of society, of the church, and of theology.

Poverty and Gender

Since the intersection of poverty and gender, the concept of the feminization of poverty was born. This concept arose in the Unites States of America parallel to the increase of poverty in families in which the woman was the sole economic source. It appeared between the 1960s and the mid-1970s, yet, it was really in the 1980s that this concept was taken into consideration by women intellectuals in other countries. Since the *Summit on the Economical Development of Rural Women* (Geneva 1992) the repercussions of poverty on women have officially become known as the feminization of poverty.

The statistics gathered in Africa show a dramatic reality; of the 400 million poorest people, 260 million are women; illiteracy among adult women in impoverished areas is greater than 80%. In Latin America, the feminization of poverty is increasing with the rise of the number of women who are alone to support their family. They must, at the same time, work and take care of their children. In our country, we can speak of three situations, among others, of poor women: 1) The women who are *jefas de hogar*; 2) segregation of work along gender lines; 3) the situation of women in poor rural areas.

In speaking of the women who are *jefas de hogar*, the sociologist Rosa Geldstein claims that the situation of women who are "the principal economic source" is due to the increase in their participation in the working world and the rising deterioration of the work of men. In Latin America, and Argentina is not an exception, the family alone takes on the primary responsibility for the tasks and duties related to reproduction and the caring for members of the family. This is due equally to the socially accepted cultural values as to the shortage in government sponsored social services. Because of this fact, Argentinean women have the sole responsibility for all household chores, which represents for women who also have remunerated work, a double work load. With regard to gender segregation at work, in Argentina, as in the majority of the world, work are differentiated along gender lines. Whereas men find their place in a vast array of activities, women tend to concentrate mostly in the health service sector, education and domestic areas. The reasons are twofold: economic and cultural.

Economically, women accept lower paid positions where lower qualifications are needed (because they have been less capacitated and because they are almost always subordinate to men). Culturally, they are expected to take on roles similar to that of being a mother (teaching, nursing, cleaning). The same author indicates that during those periods when the numbers of women in the workforce increased, the gender segmentation of the work market also increased. Finally, with regard to the women living in poverty in rural areas, this poverty appears to follow a precarious work market for all: men, women, and their families.

In these vulnerable social groups, women have a very limited scope of work from which to choose, not only for socioeconomic reasons but also because of gender reasons. For example, in the case of the citrus workers at San Miguel de Tucuman (in the northeastern Argentina), 90% of the woman surveyed were temporarily employed, 60% did not receive any social security benefits, 40% enjoyed only limited social security benefits, and 70% had an informal working relationship without any social contract.

This situation presents a challenge for our theology. It deals with gender discrimination that, in addition to poverty, renders the situation of many women much worse. I will now briefly present the feminist theology of liberation and theology from the perspectives of women.

The More Significant Theological Approaches

Feminist theology of liberation. The earliest representative authors from our countries who considered their preoccupation with women as part of their Christian commitment situated their reflections within the matrix of liberation theology. This is the case for Maria Pilar Aquino, who in her first book, *Nuestro Clamor por la Vida* (1992), ("Our Cry For Life") develops the theme of women as the subject of theological reflection. I will present the basic elements of feminist theology of liberation, of which she is considered to be one of the main representatives.

This theology originates from a theological discourse that proposes to discern the actual experience that women have of God with the help of analytic categories furnished by the critical gender theories. The importance of gender theories is that these create the primary foundation upon which we can develop all social construction of human relations which has as its point of reference the social condition. As a result, the feminist conceptual framework offers the theoretical tools for criticism of the social and ideological systems that limit the equitable inclusion of women into the social, cultural, and educational framework. Latin-American feminist theology tries to explain the connection between God's world, characterized by the abundance of salvation, grace and integrity for life, and the world of women, characterized by lack, inhumanity, and violence.

In this sense, we see this theology as a critical reflection on the experience that women have of God in the practices that attempt to transform the causes that lead to poverty and violence against women as a social group. It is therefore a matter of moving towards new social relations based on justice and integrity of life for women and also for all human beings. This theology is characterized by the search for new paradigms in the domain of gender studies, allowing for interpretation, explication, and action with regard to the aspects that characterize women's experiences, such as daily life, wisdom, ethnic and social conditions, sexuality, power and violence, health and politics. Maria Pilar Aquino indicates that this theology acquires the status of fundamental theology because it brings about three important developments in theology: 1) it delegitimizes theologies considered universal and normative, 2) it reconstructs and rehabilitates the emancipatory contribution of women that preceded us in history, and 3) it recuperates the emancipatory force of the Jewish, Christian, as well as the continental and Caribbean aboriginal traditions.

The inclusion of daily life as a fundamental factor in the reflection on faith is one of the greatest contributions of the Latin-American feminist theology. Whether public or private, daily life represents one of the principles forces behind this theology. It highlights the social division of work along gender lines, which represents gender stereotypes that affirm masculine superiority and sexuality. The incorporation of these elements, previously left aside in liberation theology, finds itself, at this moment, tightly tied to the urgent need of a new historical and theological subject internal to the popular subject: women. The compromises, practices, and reflections of women will bring a great richness to liberation theology by enlarging its horizon, its method and content.

The particularity of the gendered subject, within the historical subject, refers to the oppression of women as women in their social class, in their families, as part of a "couple," and in society in general. These questions have remained invisible within movements that are critical of the social structures now in place. That feminist liberation theology presents women as a new historical subject means that this is not a discussion about women, as if they were an object of reflection, or a discussion for women as if they were passive and submissive subjects waiting for others to define their destiny. It is also not a matter of an elaborate discussion by women as if they were unable of expressing the wisdom and justification of the faith. It is not a matter of speaking in the name of women but of conceiving them as the subject of their own proper theoretical elaboration, of their own conscience and their own reality.

Another representative author and the first to associate herself with this theology is the Brazilian theologian Ivonne Gebara. Based on her option for liberation theology and in contact with the feminist, European, and American theology, Gebara expresses that in the theological task of women we perceive a capacity to look at life as a place of experience that is at the same time oppression and liberation, happiness and despair. This is a perception that includes that which is plural, that which is different, other. Her theological work is also of growing importance for what she calls eco-feminism. This is a way of interpreting how women and nature have suffered male domination in the framework of a hierarchical, patriarchal system that needs to be criticized.

At the epistemological level, eco-feminism offers a critique of the patriarchal epistemology that is indebted to the Western androcentric tradition and biased by the exaltation of the actions and thoughts of male figures. This theologian tries to open a perspective towards the fundamental aspects of life that have been totally excluded from the cognitive domain. This change in perspective implies a central revalorization of relationally or interdependence of human beings, between each other and with the cosmos. This interdependence has the particular properties of affectivity and inclusively.

Theology from the Perspective of Women. Apart from the feminist line of liberation theology, other approaches are presented from within theologies done by women. They can be grouped together as theologies from the perspective of women. This is the case for the thought of Maria Teresa Porcile (Uruguay) and Ada Maria Isasi-Di (Cuba) among others.

Let's begin with Maria Teresa Porcile who is considered to be a pioneer because of her original work. Her thought is neither expressly framed by feminism nor by liberation theology but through dialogue with both of these. Porcile's work presents research towards an anthropology that is specifically feminine, keeping in mind the dignity and equality that all created beings share, by valuing and by integrating the different ways of life of human beings. The author aims to trace the contribution that women can offer church and society.

In response to her question – what do all women have in common? – she speaks of the body. She refers to a woman's body as a sexual body. This is the primary identity of the female being: the feminine body that implies a certain way of being in the world, of situating oneself, that is a way of being and of being perceived. A woman's body has particular biological conditions. It is because of these that women have often been attributed, as if by nature, with the condition of dependency, inferiority and passivity. It is on this point that the author recovers the essence of the feminine.

The female body is one that has the capacity to shelter and nourish life, that gives life at the risk of losing its own, that is capable of suffering violence but not of exercising it. These are characteristics that give women a particular character and that enrich all human beings. Maria Teresa Porcile affirms that the maternal breast of a woman is the first home for all human beings, whether male or female. The challenge is to reflect from the position of the female body, which contains within itself time and space, place and cycles of life. The body is also able to trigger social and theological consequences that the author develops.

From this understanding, Porcile makes several suggestions for the mission of Christian women in accordance with an anthropology of space based on the dimensions of corporeality. The author focuses her concerns mainly from an ecclesiological perspective that extends towards the social dimension. She highlights two aspects: the mission of women and the feminine mission of the church as a whole. These could be extended to include the role of women in society, to their institutions, and to their organizations, and to the feminine dimension of these. According to Porcile, the great feminine task of our time is that of unfolding the convergence between that which is concrete in women and that which is metaphorical in the female being of the Church. If women know anthropologically and existentially what this language means, they can, and this is fundamental, bring their particular being to the entire church so as to feminize it, so as to make it hospitable.

In this way, based on the concrete experiences of women, one can think about and examine the meaning of ecclesial space and, consequently, of social space. This theologian recognizes that a church that has a feminine identity presupposes a different feminine manner of conceiving, exercising, and completing its mission. As a vulnerable, open, habitable, interior space, the church's mission will be to be sensitive to the others, in their suffering and in their search; to be open to the others in their necessity, to welcome the others with their richness and differences. It is more of a mission of protection than one of conquest.

Let us now turn to the thought of Ada Maria Isasi-Diaz. This theologian received her first call to fight for peace and justice during an experience with the poor from Lima, Peru. She believes that theology lacked a vital element, one which became the central axis of her theological work, being the forum of the voices of Hispanic women. This concerns the Latin women living in the United States who suffer permanent oppression as well as discrimination and poverty. For Isasi-Dias, the practices and basic convictions of these women are part of God's permanent revelation and, consequently, they are the carriers of a voice that has to be considered in all theological reflection. She calls this development *mujerista theology*. For her, the *mujeristas* are making a preferential option for themselves and for their Latin sisters, knowing that their struggle for liberation has to begin with a deep analysis to know in what ways sexism, ethnic prejudice and classicism combine and reinforce one another to oppress them.

Isasi Diaz considers that the source of *mujerista* theology is the lived experience of Hispanic women. This brings her to explore the social sciences with the goal of finding methods that are not objectionable to those who are Hispanic, to their experiences and to their reality. The methods she uses are ethnomethodology, ethnography, and meta-ethnography.

With regard to the first, ethno methodology: one starts from a critique of the social sciences because these do not represent real people with their own histories and biographies. This method is precisely a theory on daily life whose principles are that we, as people, have and make use of practical reason; that daily life is reflective, contextual, descriptive, and non-explicative and, finally, that social interaction can be documented.

The second method, ethnography, consists of a prolonged interaction with the population to be discovered of which the investigating theologians are themselves members. Finally, meta-ethnography consists of holistic interpretations of the given information by the two other methods. This theologian found, from within these methods, three axes to be considered: 1) The voices of specific Hispanic women represent all Hispanic women. 2) There is a dialogue between researchers in *mujerista* theology and the voice of Hispanic women that they include in their work. 3) In compiling these Hispanic voices one tries to make them understand themselves in their daily struggle for survival.

The author specifies that *mujerista* theology has been developed as a liberating praxis. She affirms that praxis is understood as reflective action based upon a critical analysis of the historical reality from the perspective of an option and a commitment for the liberation of Latin women. In defining praxis as reflective action, she distinguishes it from action as it is currently understood and emphasizes that in praxis action and reflection are inseparable.

This praxis, the daily struggle for survival, is not only the *locus theologicus*, but it is also the theological place from which *mujersita* theology functions.

Conclusion

We can appreciate that these feminist theologies developed by women are based upon the fact that that which is masculine has represented all of humanity and that the other half has been completely forgotten. In this way, the discussion is biased and doesn't allow us to appreciate reality correctly. In so far as men think that their experiences, their perspectives, and their ideas represent all human experience and all human thought, the description of reality is also false. This represents a challenge for our theological endeavor. That what was considered to be universal theology excluded women and their points of view and there is no reason why one of the sexes has the right to monopolize the truth about God or about people.

Evidently these theologies are aware of the radical restructuring of the thought and analysis that we deduce from reality. A reality that shows that humanity is composed of men and women. In other words, we have been telling only one half of the story. Therefore, these theological approaches give priority to the other half, to women, to their contributions to the world, to their participation in constructing, developing society and civilization.

We, female theologians, we are optimists patiently waiting for the old ways of speaking to become new ones that can speak of God in a manner that is inclusively human, male and female.

Veerle Draulans

Human Dignity Violated by Increasing Aggression: A Gender Analysis

In spite of the tropical heat that killed more than 10, 000 people in the summer of 2003, a great part of France was shocked by the news that Bertrand Cantat, the 39-year old singer of the rock group Noir Désir and a comrade of the antiglobalist José Bové, had beaten his girlfriend, the famous movie star Marie Trintignant, to death in a hotel room in Vilnius, Lithuania. A social reality that is mostly kept behind closed doors and not openly discussed all of a sudden appears on the front pages of newspapers, which publish figures about and testimonies of women who have been victims of partner violence.[1] Partner violence confronts us with a specific form of violence against women, because it is tangled up with many different factors and feelings, such as the desire for intimacy, jealousy and psychiatric pathologies. Different factors and feelings lead to violence against women in the context of war or in human trade, such as contaminating the enemy with one's own ethnic blood or to demonstrate through rape the weakness of men who do not seem to be capable of protecting women and children. Or there is a desire to pursue maximum profit through extreme exploitation in human trade. However different the situations are, the consequences of all these forms of violence against women are no less destructive than the personal and social lives of women.

In this article I will look systematically at these three distinct forms of violence against women: 1) violence against women in a situation of war and conflict betweens peoples and nations, 2) human trade as a form of violence and, last but not least, 3) partner violence. I

---

[1] See for example the editorial "Femmes battues," in *Le Monde*, 9 August 2003, 9; "Les chiffres de la violence conjugale," in *Le Monde*, 9 August 2003, 1; "Six femmes meurent chaque mois sous les coups de leurs conjoints," in *Le Monde*, 9 August 2003, 5; the cover: Marie Trintignant, "La tragédie des femmes battues," in *Le Point*, 8 August 2003, with different articles with reference to this fact of manslaughter.

will try to develop this subject from a gender-specific approach, which I will elaborate upon in my introductory remarks.

Gender: A Vague Concept?

As a concept "gender" has developed and grown to be a common and generally accepted term after the 1995 Peking Conference. However, it is still a very vague concept, especially when people find themselves outside the familiar circle of women movements and women or gender studies. Even then, the origin and meaning of this term in the context of women and gender studies is not very clear.[2]

The term "gender" is derived from the Latin *genus*, which refers to a human race, breed of animal or sort of plant. In Latin we can also find the word *sexus* which just means "sex." In English, people differentiate between the terms "gender" and "sex." Other European languages do not make a strong terminological distinciton and therefore they find it fairly difficult to translate this term "gender" in a proper way. Due to this difficulty, the English word "gender" is borrowed and used as such in French, German and Italian etc.

Yet even with this explanation, it is not clear what this gender-specific approach can contribute to an analysis in the framework of women's studies or gender studies. To start with, people usually refer to a study made by the British sociologist Ann Oakley in 1972, in which she systematically promoted the terminological difference between "sex" and "gender" in order to show the difference between the biological attribute "sex" and the cultural attribute "gender."[3] As I will point out later in this article, this distinction is passed on in the views about men, women and violence. Since then this concept has been fur-

---

[2] V. Draulans, "Wetenschapsbeoefening: genderblind of genderbewust?" in *Onze Alma Mater – Leuvense Perspectieven*, 55/3 (2001): 279-305; V. Draulens "Jongens en wetenschap? Jongens en (harde) wetenschap, meisjes en (zachte) communicatie: wetenschapskritiek vanuit genderperspectief," in *Tijdschrift voor Sociologie* 24/2-3 (2003): 139-64.

[3] A. Oakley, *Sex, Gender and Society* (London: Maurice Temple Smith, 1972).

ther refined. I prefer to use the definition given by the historian Joan W. Scott, who refers to the two dimensions of the gender concept, namely a social relational component and one that refers to power relations.[4]

The social relational component refers to the reciprocity in the concept of gender: shifting patterns in experiencing motherhood and the fact of being a woman do have consequences in experiencing fatherhood and the fact of being a man. Nowadays, we often hear people using the term "gender" as a synonym for "women," without paying much attention to the relational or the power relational dimensions. Therefore, I find it very important in a debate "starting from gender perspective" that we clearly clarify how we use the concept "gender." For me, "gender" focuses explicitly on the reciprocal relationship between the culturally attributed notions of masculinity and femininity and the way in which power relations play a role in these relations. For example, young fathers in Scandinavian countries have come together in discussion groups in many places to reflect on the consequences of the participation of women in the labor market and the division of roles in families for the way in which they experience fatherhood. Another example of this reciprocity can be observed in Brazil: youths and men derive their status from sexual activity and financial independence. Yet a large number of young people are unable to find work. This means that they can forget about the possibility of acquiring status in society and making money through a position in the labor market. Therefore, they look for alternatives to show off their personal status and power and try to get involved in sexual activities, often with many girls at the same time, in order to have a firm basis for their masculinity. Girls are often very vulnerable in these circumstances because the same culture expects them not to be sexually active before their marriage. Girls are mostly suspected of promiscuous behavior, especially when the people around them realize that they are looking for information on sexuality before their marriage.[5] This fact

---

[4] J.W. Scott, "Gender: A Useful Category of Historical Analysis," in J.W. Scott (ed.), *Feminism and History* (Oxford / New York: Oxford University Press, 1996), 152-80. Published earlier in *American Historical Review* 91/5 (1986): 1053-75.

[5] N. Sadik (ed),. *Samen leven in aparte werelden: Mannen en vrouwen in een tijd van verandering. Wereld bevolkingsrapport 2000* (New York: UNFPA – United Nations Population Fund, 2001), 21.

also illustrates the impact of socioeconomic factors on gender relations.

Anyone who attentively tries to verify how the terms "sex" and "gender" are used in the literarture, is soon confronted with the inconsistent use of language. In many enquiries, the respondents are expected to indicate, next to their age, the important research variable "sex." The research results are then often defined in terms of a "gender analysis," whereas the actual answers and findings are based on the biological factor "sex." The opposite is also true: obviously clear biological accounts regarding "sex" also often have a deeper gender explanation. We can illustrate this by the following example: it is stated that in certain regions of Africa there is a difference between the weight of baby boys and baby girls at birth. A naive researcher can interpret this detail as based on biological sex: baby boys weigh more than baby girls. An accurate analysis, however, teaches us that this difference in body weight is caused by a culturally fixed gender difference and by the patterns of food distribution: when food is scarce, women try to feed their husbands first, followed by their sons, their daughters and if there is anything left at all, then the mothers. In other words, something that can apparently be viewed as a difference in the biological factor of "sex" actually follows from culturally determined "gender" differences.

A Culture of Dichotomies

An important moment in gender analysis is to raise the question regarding the influence and role of social dichotomies. People quite easily associate "masculinity" and "femininity" with a number of categories such as: transcendent - immanent, public - private, objective - subjective, see - touch, power - love, impersonal - personal, autonomy - heteronomy, rationality - emotionality, intellectual life - daily life, spirit - body, culture - nature, active - passive, known - unknown, disciplined - undisciplined, superior - inferior, etc. Such dichotomies play a strong role in the discourse about war and peace. Gender analysis, among other things, intends to throw light on the ways in which such dichotomies influence thinking patterns.

Gender symbolism is often subtle, and thus many people are oblivious to its presence. Let us look, for example, at the opening ceremony of the Olympic Games in Sydney, where Kathy Freeman, an Australian top athlete was asked to light the Olympic fire. She is an aboriginal, and the Australian government wanted this gesture to be a sign of its reconciliation with the aboriginal community. But it was not as simple as that. Her bodily features attracted the attention of the media and were the basis for much gossip. At the same time, they also referred to the seductiveness of the "unknown" and the "exotic," which she (her body) radiated. Another example, a more familiar one, is the famous photograph of the Vietnamese girl running away from the napalm bombs. We see a number of stereotypes converging in that photo: the horror of war and childlike innocence, as well as the gender dimension of the Asian girl and her nakedness, over against the pilot of the North American air fleet, a man who was dropping the bombs and who stayed out of the visual field.

A clear example of this dichotomous thought is the belief that women are intrinsically more peace-loving than men. This belief is of recent origin and it has emerged as a result of the industrialization which brought about sweeping changes in society. Labor became something that occurs outdoors. Partly in protest to the grimy, hard, and competitive work situations, ordinary people fostered the ideal of placing women in the home, where she could experience the safety of the private sphere with enough room for expressing and experiencing her emotions and where she also took care of the upbringing of the children. The belief that women are peaceful and peace-loving is a part of this ideal picture. Women were either inherently peace-loving or became so due to their life experiences or because of their feelings as mothers. Pacifist women's liberation before, during and after the First World War often referred to such arguments. As a matter of fact, there was a great deal of discussion among women at that times, about the desirability of pacifism. Clara Zetkin and Rosa Luxemburg, for example, held that armed violence could be considered legitimate, especially as a form of protest against imperialists.

This debate did not subside during the second wave of feminism. Equality thinkers who emphasize equal rights and equal opportunities for men and women in all areas of social life were asked to give valid arguments either for or against the possibility of women joining the armed forces. On one hand, there were arguments about employment for women and the emancipation of women; on the other, there was the experience of the specific organizational culture within the armed forces, which had developed at the mercy of divisions and dichotomies and, thus, women become either victims of sexism or were expected to adapt to the explicitly masculine work culture.

Another feminist trend in the 1970s and 1980s emphasized the differences between men and women. People combined feminism, anti-militarism, and ecological awareness. This question marked the starting point of the analysis: Where can we discover exploitation in society? The male-female relation is one element, the first world – third world is another, the human being – nature is yet another and all these relationships are characterized by domination and exploitation. From this standpoint people came to the conclusion that women, based on a victimized or exploited perspective, are more peace-loving and ecologically conscious than men.[6]

"Are women inherently more peace-loving than men?" "Are men inherently fighters and oriented towards war?" Essentialism, i.e. the reduction to a specific static male or female nature, comes nearer in such judgments and fixates people. Gender analysis shows us that such judgments can confuse biological sex with gender that is attributed culturally. It would be as if every man is a fighter, as if there are no internal differences between groups of women and men, as if men can never be victims of war and aggression and women would never choose the side of the aggressor. The insight that males can also be victims of male violence has paved the way for a specific theoretical accent, stressing that differences (sometimes major ones) can exist among groups of women and also among groups of men. This has led to a terminological difference between patriarchy and kyriarchy in the formulation of feministic theories.[7] Patriarchy is seen as a strong collective term that did not sufficiently take into account the power differences between men. Men can also be victims of exploitation within an economic system. A man who is or has been a victim of the exploitation brought about by economic systems can himself be an exploiter in his familial and sexual relationships. The emphasis on the differences in power and the diversity among women was taken up and put forward for discussion especially by women from the non-Western world. This was then developed further as a continuing point of inter-

---

[6] See, for example, the ideas of the North American theologian Rosemary Radford Ruether and the way in which this theme is worked out in so-called "ecofeminism."

[7] See, for example, E. Schüssler-Fiorenza.

est for study, reflection, formation and action. African-American women who wanted to find out the real-life situation of female slaves were shocked to hear the disturbing stories about the power, might, and hardness of their white female masters. The middle class ideal of the "peace-loving mother" was apparently something that was directed inwards, that is, toward their own white families. This white, female power was prompted not only by racist considerations but also by their anxiety (or fear) that the white masters and husbands would have sexual adventures with some of the female slaves.[8] From this we can see again the complexity of power, in relation to racism and sexual exploitation. This example also illustrates the one-sidedness of the focus on women as victims. An analysis of women offenders is always a painful affair in feministic theory formation.

Finally, I would like to look at the current developments that we, in my opinion, need to follow closely and critically. From another point of view, especially the neo-Darwinian and certain trends in the evolutionary psychology, the essentialist views on being "man" and "woman" are once again being accepted. The causes of aggression are being sought in chromosomes or in the functioning of hormones in our bodies. It is a scientific hypothesis that (masculine) aggression can be related to the hormone testosterone. We do not really need to doubt the hypothesis as such, but some of the conclusions that are related to it, such as the notion that some men cannot resist their urge to rape because it is their reproductive strategy to impregnate a large number of partners in an environment where women choose their partners is to be questioned.[9] In such perceptions, people change offenders into vic-

---

[8] See, for example, the publications of the African-American feminist writer Bell Hooks. The African-American womanist theologian Delores S. Williams develops her analysis of the experiences of African-American women with reference to the story of Hagar (Gen. 16:1-16 and Gen 21:9-21), in which comparable experiences (child of the male master, pride and anger of the female mistress ...) are related. Cf. D.S. Williams, *Sisters in the Wilderness: The Challenge of Womanist God-Talk*, (New York: Orbis Books, 1996).

[9] "Geboren om te verkrachten?" in *De Morgen* (17 March, 2000): 33. R. Thornhill and C. Palmer, *A Natural History of Rape* (Cambridge, MA.: MIT, 2000), give references to the whole controversy in trend-setting magazines like *Nature*.

tims of their own biological nature ("Born to Rape") and run the risk of losing sight of the real victims.

Facing Complexity

The subject of "war and peace" demands an analysis that will take into account economic, political, scientific and military aspects. We need a gender approach within all these aspects, but the difficulty is to continue to see the coherence of the gender dimension within all these complex factors. For example: Do people realize that the weapon industry is a feminized sector? It is easily forgotten that the enforcement of equal salaries for men and women in Belgium was obtained by the pioneering efforts of the female workers at the well-known weapons factory FN in Herstal who organized a strike. The demand of 3500 female workers there for equal pay for equal work gained fame even beyond our borders. Their campaign was an important impetus in the process of emancipation. A trade union, ACV/CSC, established a department for women and after a few months, the other important trade union, ABVV, published a charter under the title: "The Rights of the Working Woman."[10]

Facing Diversity: Women and Men as Categories Do Not Exist

In the 1960s and 1970s, feminist theory emphasized that which united women under the slogan "we, women, victims of patriarchy." Yet the consciousness that there are differences between women developed slowly and steadily. Women (and men) differ from each other with regard to class, economic position, race, age, ideology, culture and sexual disposition. I have already referred to the example about the cru-

---

[10] R. Van Mechelen, *De meerderheid, een minderheid: De vrouwenbeweging in Vlaanderen. Feiten, herinneringen en bedenkingen omtrent de tweede golf* (Leuven: Van Halewijck, 1996), 16; D. Keymolen *et al.*, *Stap voor stap: Geschiedenis van de vrouwenemancipatie in België* (Brussels: Kabinet van de Staatssecretaris voor Maatschappelijke Emancipatie Amsterdam-Eindhoven, 1991), 85-86.

elty of many white women towards their female African-American slaves.

These differences characterize the cooperation and coexistence between people. If we analyze what really happens in contemporary conflict areas, then it is certainly necessary to take these differences into account. Do we sometimes not make hasty judgments from our Western perspective, in conformity with Western patterns of thought concerning emancipation and individual freedom? An effort to transform the situation of women in other cultural contexts requires real collaboration with local partners, such as the local women's organizations that guide the process of making conscientious projects on the basis of the acquaintance with their own culture. The consciousness of the differences is ultimately the reason that leads to certain fundamental questions, which can also yield an ethical debate. We can think, for example, of the tension between universalism and cultural relativism concerning the proper answer to the various existing practices of genital mutilation.

Does the media portray this diversity among women sufficiently? Are we not confronted with the stereotypes of freedom and helplessness in the media about women in war-afflicted areas and in countries that are reconstructing and recovering from all kinds of problems? The old, furrowed woman with the headscarf, sitting among the scattered chickens and looking at the debris of her house; the young woman in a refugee camp in the African Great Lakes region breastfeeding a baby; women dressed in black who shout their support for Saddam Hussein – how critical do we dare to be with regard to the media coverage (especially television) about war? In the 1980s, in order to obtain images of women guerrillas in the Nicaraguan and Salvadoran struggle for independence, one needed to have recourse to solidarity committees or liberation films.

Diversity among Women in War Situations

In the play *The Trojan Women*, the necessity to acknowledge the diversity and specificity of the experiences of women in conflict analysis is nicely worked out. Troy has fallen after the Greek siege that lasted for ten years – the trick of the horse having been successful. The Trojan women see the burning city – some of them are raped, others have lost their husbands and sons, and the Greeks are plundering the city. The sad fate, which they already expect, awaits the women: becoming slaves to the Greeks and even bearing them sons. Pain, sorrow, fury and hatred can be clearly felt in their words. Yet some of the women, Cassandra, Andromache, Hecuba, and Helen react very differently to the same situation: one fosters feelings of revenge and success, the others those of passion for life or the desire to embrace death.

Although it is a classical drama, it can still be linked to the present situation in conflict stricken areas and shows us that women can be more vulnerable than men. Furthermore, different women cope with the same situation in many different ways. Women do not react as a homogenous group, and we cannot talk of a universal feminine experience in the context of conflicts.[11] At the same time, the above-mentioned excerpt strikingly illustrates the fact that conflicts between people usually affect women in their sexuality and in their intimate relationships as mothers, daughters, partners and so on. The discourse of nationalism and militarism limits women to the relationships found in the private familial sphere.

The Gendered Discourse of Nationalism and Militarism

During an exhibition in Rome at the beginning of 2003 I saw a poster from the First World War. It was a drawing of a woman with a teenage daughter and an infant beside an open window, looking at a group of soldiers marching away. At the top of the poster was displayed in big letters: "Women of Britain say – GO!"

Gender plays a specific role in nationalistic discourse, where men play the first violin.[12] Women are fastened and fixed to their procreative function and to their task as protectress and guardian of those tra-

---

[11] I am grateful to Maria Vanden Eynde for this inspiring suggestion. Euripides, *Trojaanse vrouwen*, Inleiding bij de vertaling van Herman Altena, zoals opgevoerd door Het Zuidelijk Toneel (Amsterdam-Eindhoven: Uitgeverij International Theatre & Film Books, 1997).

[12] A. Kovacs, *De impact van nationalistische conflicten op de emancipatie van vrouwen* (Leuven: Unpublished thesis, 1999).

ditions that should be passed on through education. Women contribute to the group identity in a symbolic manner. It is expected of women that they sacrifice their sons for the nation and that they should be mothers not only for their children but also for the whole nation. In this ideology, we can place the picture of the mother who grieves over her own son killed in the war and at the same time exhorts other mothers to support their sons in their fight for the nation (or the ethnic minorities). This discourse focuses on unselfish motherhood as well as on their willingness to make sacrifice.

Women play much less of a role in military discourse, since it is about a closed masculine world into which women are not easily allowed. Heroism and fraternity are linked to masculinity – take for example the popular television serial *Band of Brothers*. In it women are called to represent the weaker sex that has to be protected. In military discourse, men become real "men" through a hard and strongly disciplined training.

Sexual politics is given an important meaning in this whole context. Purity and cultural authenticity are absolutely necessary to defend or to perpetuate the group borders. The Israeli government, for example, uses a double politics with regard to contraception concerning the Jewish and Palestinian women: the government wants to stimulate the growth of the Jewish population (through financial incentives, for example) and makes it very difficult for Jewish women to have access to contraceptives. Contraceptives are, however very accessible to Palestinian women, while the financial allowances for newborn babies are more limited. Nevertheless, Palestinian women have many children, which they sometimes define as a form of protest.[13]

In addition to this, rape should be considered to be a particular weapon during war. In the context of war, rape implies visibility, because through rape the whole family as well as the whole population is afflicted. By raping and victimizing the woman, the rapist wants to strike at the male population and confront them with their weakness and to show them that they are incapable of protecting the women of their own ethnic group. Thus, in the context of war, rape can be considered to be much more than just a criminal action against an individual woman. It is a weapon that is used to afflict the whole commu-

---

[13] Kovacs, *De impact van nationalistische conflicten.*

nity, since systematic rape also occurs when the possibility of sexual satisfaction through prostitution is available.

Can we speak in terms of increasing violence against women as a weapon of war? The United Nations considered this increase in violence as very alarming, so much so that they have expanded the definition of war crimes at a conference of the International Court of Justice in 1998 to include an article on gender rights. Rape, sexual slavery, forced prostitution, forced pregnancy, forced sterilization and other forms of sexual violence are considered to be serious violations of the Geneva Convention.[14] The investigation and training center INSTRAW (United Nations International Research and Training Institute for the Advancement of Women), pays special attention to the theme of "gender aspects of war and peace."[15]

Violence Against Women Beyond the Context of War

As Sadik clearly spells states:

> Violence against women includes rape, mutilation of female genital organs, sexual violence, forced pregnancy, sterilization and abortion, forcing or prohibiting the use of contraceptives, crimes of honor, woman trafficking and violence associated with dowries. Throughout the world, one out of three women are beaten, forced to have sex or abused in one way or another, mostly by an acquaintance, for example a husband or another male member of the family. Half of adult women are beaten at some time in their life or are victims of physical maltreatment by an intimate partner. One out of four women is abused during pregnancy .... According to the United Nations World Population Report of 2000 an estimated number of four million girls are purchased and sold yearly, whether for marriage, prostitution or slavery.[16]

---

[14] Sadik, *Samen leven in aparte werelden*, 6.

[15] See http://www.un-instraw.org/en/index.html.

[16] Sadik, *Samen leven in aparte werelden*, 6.

The figures in this report are shocking: women are five times more prone to be afflicted by sexually transmitted diseases than men; one out of three women in the United States ends up with a sexually transmitted disease after rape; a Nigerian hospital stated that 16% of its STD patients were younger than five years old; 900 children under the age of 12 were treated for STDs at a health center in Zimbabwe in 1990; the number of women in Africa infected with HIV exceeds that of men by 2 million; a rough estimate shows that the genitals of about 130 million women have been mutilated and about 2 million girls and young women run the same risk every year.[17] Other sources report that about 59% of Japanese women have become victims of violence at home; half of the victims of murder in Russia are women who are killed by their own male partner; 80% of women in Pakistan have to face violence in their own homes; about 5000 brides meet with death every year either through murder or suicide since the dowry was thought to be insufficient.[18]

Throughout the world, women are vulnerable to different forms of gender violence during the different phases of their lives. Even before the birth of a child, there can be efforts to harm the mother, such as forced pregnancy, beatings and injuries during (or because of) the pregnancy or selective abortion. A baby girl can be killed just because she is a girl and have less access to food and medical care just because she is a girl. In certain cultures girls undergo genital mutilation as babies. Girls can become victims of incest, sexual abuse and child prostitution. During their adolescence, girls run the risk of becoming victims of violence during a night out or from forced sex, forced prostitution or unwanted sexual intimidation at work. In their reproductive phase, women can be confronted with partner violence, maltreatment or murder because of dowry problems, partner murder, psychological abuse, rape and unwanted sexual intimidation at work. It is also mostly women who are victims in cases of ill treatment or violence against elderly people.[19]

---

[17] Sadik, *Samen leven in aparte werelden*, 4-5, 30.

[18] For gender violence statistics, based based on United Nations reports, see: http://www. learningpartnership.org/facts/gender.html (8/10/2002).

[19] Sadik, *Samen leven in aparte werelden*, 33. As a specific source, this report refers to: L. Heise, *Violence Against Women: the Hidden Health Burden* (Washington D.C.: The World Bank, 1994).

In the framework of this contribution, it is impossible to analyze every issue deeply and specifically. By means of this article I would like to illustrate that every issue at the microlevel (the anonymity of partner violence) and at the macrolevel (the laxity of the courts in punishing human trade, for example and conflicts and cultural practices such as genital mutilation) of the society can and must be discussed from a gender-specific approach. In the following section I will analyze the issues of women trafficking and partner violence.

Women Trafficking

We need to differentiate between what can be called "voluntary" migration, by which women migrate for economic reasons (to look for work in the labor market, such as Polish women in Belgium) and women trafficking in which women are bought against their will.

As we have already mentioned, four million girls and women are traded every year, purchased and sold for the purpose of forced labor and prostitution. Human trade can be described as the recruiting and transporting of people with the purpose of acquiring profit.[20] After arms trade and drug trafficking, human trade has developed into the third major criminal activity leading to huge profits.[21] Almost all states are involved in human trade, whether as the country of departure, country of transit, or as destination country and employment. The smuggling of human beings and payment for illegal transportation also constitute part of human trade.

The greatly increasing mobility and new facilities provided by the Internet have helped in this trafficking. At the foundation of this phenomenon there is poverty and unemployment on the one hand and consumerism (such sex tourism) and exploitation on the other. Human trade is characterized by compulsion, fraud and exploitation: women are then seen as "goods" with which people can trade. We have

---

[20] See D.H. Handy, *Human Trafficking: The Enslavement of Women and Girls for Profit. An Analysis and Critique of International Legal Responses* (Leuven: Unpublished manuscript for Complementary Studies in Applied Ethics, 2003).

[21] Estimates are about 7 million dollars annually.

enough examples from the Southeast Asian rural areas where girls and women are traded with the participation of their own families. Traffickers recruit girls with the false promise that the family will receive a sum of money equal to the value of a full yearly salary in exchange for one of their daughters, who would be employed as a cook or domestic helper. The risk that their actual work will be something else is very real. Most families consent to it on condition that the salary that the girl would earn is transferred to the family. Other reports inform us of cases in which girls are used as guarantees for urgent medical help or for a dowry. Once this has been agreed, a bitter fate awaits most of the girls and women: loss of their autonomy, their official documents (passports) are taken away, brutal treatment, (sexual) exploitation and bad wages. For the most part, they are unaware of the legal procedures or they are not able to acquire the required resident permits and so on. The fact that many of them do not speak the language of the country where they have landed up puts them into a more vulnerable position. Human trade is not a priority in the juridical administration of most countries where migrants arrive and, furthermore, most of the women do not have any confidence in the police, especially when they are confronted with the insolent attitude of the male police officers.

Being a "nanny" is a widespread phenomenon in the United States of America: according to a rough estimate, about 50,000 to 75,000 (young) women are traded to the USA every year to be employed as domestic help in what are often called well-earning "double income" families. Sixteen-hour days in exchange for minimum wages are no exception in these cases. Such a situation leads to specific problems: the emotional and affective relationship that these women build up with the children in the families where they are employed makes it still more difficult for them to make the decision to leave. The "nanny" phenomenon in USA has led to a furious debate about the topic of "double income couples: a nightmare for feminism."[22]

---

[22] See, for example, "Tweeverdieners zijn de nachtmerrie van het feminisme: Voor J.C. Tronto stopt emancipatie niet bij de vrouwen," in *De Morgen* (18 July, 2003), 9; J.C. Tronto, "The 'Nanny' Question in Feminism," in *Hypatia* 17/2 (2002): 34-51.

Partner Violence: As Much a Cause of Death as Cancer for Women between 15 and 44

As I have already stated in the introduction, France was shaken in August 2003 by the news of the death of Marie Trintignant. The victim and the culprit were known to the public. She was 41 years old, unconventional and for many a symbol of the emancipated woman, a mother of four children from three different relationships. He was also married, 39 years old, leader of the rock music band Noir Désir, fighting for the rights of Chiapas Indians, speaking out firmly for the liberation of Tibet, seen at the side of José Bové and fighting against the National Front. He beat his partner until she was unconscious and left her on her bed in a hotel room on the night of July 26 – he just left her there. Both were taken to the hospital in the morning: She was brain dead and was kept alive artificially; he overdosed on medicine mixed with alcohol.

The sad fate of so many women who are victims of household violence suddenly attracted everyone's attention. There was, of course, a discussion about the actual figures. According to one source, at least six women die every month in France as a result of injuries caused out by their male partners. Another source states that about sixty women die every year of partner violence in the city of Paris alone. These are the known facts and figures. One out of ten women in France find her own home to be the most dreadful place to live. In the year 2000 the French ministry for women's rights organized a telephone enquiry through a random sample survey of 6,970 women between 20 and 59 years old in order to research the issue of violence against women. It is very striking to notice that most of the time violence affects the younger generation of women: women from 20 to 24 report that they have to face much more violence, compared to the older women age group. 8.7% of unemployed women say that they have been victims of rough violence in comparison with 4.6% of women who work. All other professional groups have a percentage between 6.8% and 6.0% respectively. We can grasp the complexity of the problem from this research: 18% of the women who have repeatedly suffered physical or verbal violence declared that they were "very much in love" with the partner who inflicted it on them, and 47% said that they were "still in love." This last detail explains perhaps why a large group of women have never reported the violence that their partners inflicted on them. Half of the victims among the respondents of the enquiry in France confirmed that the enquiry was the reason that they admitted to outsiders that they were victims of violence at home. They had not lodged any complaint at all. A possible decision to divorce or to leave the partner does not necessarily mean that all the woman's problems are solved. She has to find a new place to live, often a place that is unknown to her previous partner. Some try to run away from their ex-partners by building up new social networks, unknown to the ex-partners and by looking for another job.[23] This research also clarifies the many subtle aspects of partner violence: physical violence is just one of those, next to psychological, sexual and economic violence. 5.2% said that they have been threatened with death via, for instance, a weapon. In 35% of these cases the partner was the culprit. Alcohol plays a very limited role: in 70% of the situations where partner violence occurred, both were sober. The media attention paid to this subject after the death of Marie Trintignant on August 2 actually helped to break down the barriers: a national alarm number (which had been available for a long time already for women who were victims of partner violence) received more calls than previously.

Statistics lead to very different figures. The World Population Report shows a high percentage of adult women who have lodged a complaint about physical violence caused by male partners: Papua New Guinea: 67%, Bangladesh: 47%, Ethiopia: 45%, India: 40%, Canada: 29%, United States: 22%, Switzerland: 21%.[24] A report of the lobby of the European women states that in the same Switzerland 6% of the women stated that they were victims of physical violence, sexual violence or threat in the year preceding the enquiry. The latest report mentions that partner violence is about 13% in the Netherlands, 12% in the United Kingdom and 10% in France.[25] As an answer to the 1993 declaration of the United Nations against the different forms of abuse of women, the Swedish government commission encouraged the foundation of the National Center for Battered and Raped Women, linked to the Department for Midwifery and Gynecology at the Uni-

---

[23] "La calvaire des femmes battues," in *Le Point* (8 August, 2003), 41-43; "Six femmes meurent chaque mois sous les coups de leurs conjoints," in *Le Monde* (9 August, 2003), 5.

[24] Sadik, *Samen leven in aparte werelden*, 30.

[25] "La calvaire des femmes battues," 42.

versity of Uppsala.[26] This center registered at least about 25 deaths yearly as a result of partner abuse. Every twenty minutes a woman becomes a victim of physical violence in Sweden. This center did not limit itself to the collection of figures into a central databank but developed a policy that was aimed at bringing about changes in mentality. Confronted with the fact that victims, out of their enduring emotional involvement with their partner, tried to minimize or even denied the violence – this was also demonstrated by the French research – Swedish law was changed, with the result that the offenders can be punished even without any complaint from the victim. The establishment of such a center at the Department of Midwifery and Gynecology was not by chance. This can be seen from the special relationship of the midwives and gynecologists with their patients and from the fact that pregnancy is experienced by certain group of men as a threat. Some studies postulate that 30% of all partner violence begins during pregnancy.

Other reasons leading to partner violence seem to be very trivial. The 2000 World Population Report mentions facts such as not obeying the partner, disagreeing with the partner, refusing sexual contact, being late with the preparation of food, how children are taken care of or how the housekeeping is organized, and the fact that the woman does not ask permission to engage in certain activities.[27]

Most often the victims as well as the neighborhood know about the occurrence of partner violence, but they are usually silent about it. Many people see such forms of violence as a private affair that does not require any interference – and certainly not legal interference.

It has been the task of the United Nations to determine the cost of gender-based violence. Gender violence leads not only to the general deterioration of the physical health of women but also to a loss of self-confidence which could possibly end up in depression. Gender violence influences reproductive health: unwanted and/or complicated pregnancies, abortions, STD and HIV, fear of sexuality. The society is also confronted with the consequences of partner violence through some factors such as absenteeism at work, the necessity of having relief centers, medical and psychological guidance, and legal protection.

---

[26] "Geweld tegen vrouwen nog niet in kaart gebracht: Eén op vijf vrouwen wordt mishandeld," in *Campus-krant* (8 May, 2002), 7.

[27] Sadik, *Samen leven in aparte werelden*, 31.

The Family is Holy but not Always Safe: Canadian Church Communities

The Canadian sociologist Nancy Nason-Clark, in cooperation with a multidisciplinary team of academic researchers, social workers and field workers, organized a few large-scale projects in order to encourage cooperation between religious and secular institutions to reduce and eliminate partner violence.[28]

Nason-Clark stated that one out of six women in the USA and Canada had experienced a moment or a period of violence inflicted on them by their partner in the course of the year preceding the enquiry. From this we observe a slow increase in the willingness of women to report such facts even though many victims persistently feel ashamed, guilty and frightened. There has also been an increase in the openness and willingness of social workers and doctors to listen to their stories. In her research, Nason-Clark does not reduce partner violence to a man-woman happening, but looks at the occurrences also from a family context. She looks for answers to questions such as: What happens to children if they are witnesses of violence inflicted by their father on their mother? This seems to be a good question because, in most cases, violence is a learned behavior. More than half of the men who maltreat their partners have themselves been either victims of violence when they were very young or they have been witnesses to the fact that their father reacted aggressively to their mother. Nason-Clark concludes that Canadian women with a violent father-in-law are three times more prone to be victims of partner violence than women with a nonviolent father-in-law.

She also completed qualitative and quantitative research in a few Cana-dian church communities and arrived at a few striking conclusions. One of her conclusions was that informal networks of women

---

[28] N. Nason-Clark, *The Battered Wife: How Christians Confront Family Violence* (Louisville: Westminster John Knox Press, 1997), 9. Her research consisted of a quantitative enquiry among 343 priests of the United Baptist and Wesleyan churches in eastern Canada; 100 interviews with the officeholders in the Canadian Evangelical churches; discussions in focus groups with 247 women from the Evangelical churches in which women who were interviewed were victims and also some who were social workers; 94 follow-up discussions with women from these groups.

are very important among those believers who are strongly involved in the church and who go very regularly to the mass. When women who are victims of violence want to tell their story to another woman, it is mostly to another woman of the same church community whom they can trust enough that they can share their story. These women rarely make use of the secular assistance that is made available by the provincial or municipality. Another striking result can be seen from the research done among more than 300 priests: approximately one out of ten had been confronted regularly with a form of violence in families, be it through the story of a woman who became the victim of the violence of her husband, or through the story of a woman who has been a victim of the violence done by a parent, or through the story of a husband who inflicts violence on his wife or through the story of a couple whose relationship has been upset by violence. It is peculiar to note that only 8% of the 332 priests who were interviewed say that they have been educated to deal adequately with such situations. 37% of them said that they were not really equipped to handle, guide and take care of such situations of violence in families. A big group of those who were interviewed asked for more specific training and education, with the purpose of giving optimum support to the victims of violence in homes through counseling sessions. Nason-Clark observes that this confronts us with the demand concerning the particular contribution that a pastoral counselor can make through discussions with the victims of partner violence. She advises the establishment of strong networks of interdisciplinary and professional social workers who can provide help competently and as a team.[29]

Points of Interest and Pathways to the Future

The Importance of Representation. "Representation" is and has been for a long time one of the key concepts and an element of controversy in women's studies and gender studies. It is important to make sure that women (and minority groups) are present and are represented in sufficient numbers at all levels of policy-making. This will increase considerablythe possibility of bringing certain social issues to the ta-

---

[29] Nason-Clark, *The Battered Wife,* 143-48.

ble for discussion. This applies not only to political and social representation but also in places where negotiations take place about conflict control, post-conflict policy, plans for reconstruction, where decisions should be made about the fight against trafficking of women, and where research and training are developed to combat partner violence. The importance of representation emerges from simple details: when the research is done through polls, we need to keep in mind that the respondents answer differently depending on whether the interviewer is a man or a woman. It surely makes a difference, especially when the poll is done on themes such as incest, maltreatment, prostitution and fertility/infertility. Also, troops of the peace forces who opted to work in post-conflict zones learned the importance of the balanced presence of male and female soldiers: women who were victims of rape did not want to tell their story to the male solider, who reminded them of the rapist. In a very different context, with a comparable reaction, it is understandable that women who were victims of violence at home wanted to tell their storyies only to the women who were present there as social workers, professionals or as volunteers.

Dealing with Research Questions on Gender Consciously. For a long time, very little attention was paid to a gender perspective in analyses about war or conflict (prevention). It is very clear from the above-mentioned information that such a form of gender blindness leads to distorted results. War and conflicts between peoples affect women in a different way than men. We can also speak of gender blindness when analyses speak in general terms of "human trading," because of which the specific problem of "women trafficking" disappears from view. What do the above-mentioned gender considerations about war and conflict, partner violence and human trading have in common? The dichotomy of "private-public" is very important for women's studies and gender studies. The exploitation of women in these three apparently very different contexts has a private nature: women are affected in their corporality and sexuality, in their intimate relationships with their husband and children, in their occupation at home as housekeepers. Due to this private nature that is attributed to it, family members and neighbors remain silent, the police do not take action or they do so only after long insistence, and the feelings of guilt, shame and fear remain with the victims for a long time. This is indeed an important theme that demands further reflection.

Gender-conscious academic research can make use of the gender equality indicators that provide a skillful set of instruments to assimilate the different aspects of a gender approach as part of an analysis. A first indicator is the physical integrity and the absence of force. A second indicator refers to the importance of autonomy in family formation and domestic organization: Do women have the freedom to marry and divorce? Can they make decisions and do they have access to family property? A third indicator is political power: Are women represented at the local level, in trade unions, in Parliament and in government? How many women attain high managerial positions? A fourth indicator, which can also be differentiated, is accessibility to health services and educational possibilities. A fifth indicator refers to the possibility of buying property such as land, house and the possibility of negotiating a loan. The sixth factor is work and income: In what proportion do women participate in the professional job market? How big is the salary difference between men and women? How much unpaid work do they perform? How is the formal and informal work divided between men and women? Time is the seventh indicator: do women have the possibility of sleeping and having free time? A last question investigates the rigidity in the division of labor on the basis of gender, summarized as "gender identity."[30] A GDI (Gender-related Development Index) has been construction on the basis of such factors as an addition to the familiar annual HDI (Human Development Index), which ranks countries, with Norway in first place. Belgium was sixth in the 2004 HDI, following Norway, Sweden, Australia, Canada and the Netherlands.[31]

Management of Study and Visual Materials, in a Gender-Conscious Way. Anyone who considers gender to be an element of relationships and power sees, reads, and hears things that escapes the attention of others. It is a particular way of looking at things that people do not abandon later. As such, it is not difficult to deal with study materials, articles, and visual materials etc. in a gender-conscious manner. People have to keep in mind a few points of special interest when reading texts, listening commentaries, and watching visual material. Is the title of the article relevant or does the title make women invisible? ("People Fleeing from New Violence" is an article that deals with twomen who remained in a village in Bosnia and finally had to flee.)

---

[30] Sadik, *Samen leven in aparte werelden*, 53.

[31] Belgium ranked seventh in the Gender Related Development Index. http://hdr.undp. org/reports/ global/2004.

Even the grammatical structure of a sentence can betray the perspective of the analysis. The actions of men are often described with active verbs while passive verbs are used to describe the actions of women. Take, for example, the sentence: "The Iraqi troops gather together in top speed, while the women and children are brought to safe places." Anthropological research often describes male activities from an independent perspective while the things that women do at the same time are described from a relational context, i.e. as the partner of or as the mother of someone else (a male). Some concepts suggest the association of features, conducts or qualities of one sex. In a fight someone behaves "manly." Does a text write about men as active doers and women as (passive) objects of the actions? Who is presented as the victim and who as the offender? Which theme receives media attention: a somewhat spectacular story about genital mutilation (far away, in an unknown culture) or partner violence in our regions (nearby, in one's own surroundings, and perhaps frightening)?

Gender Analysis: A Standard Analysis or a Surplus Analysis. An organization that pretends to pay attention to the subject of gender must make a fundamental choice about the role ascribed to gender issues in their organizations. Is it meaningful to concentrate on the gender dimension in a separate section of the organization, supported by a (small) group of employees? If people choose this option, then the issue of gender and its various features is guaranteed. Yet it still carries risks such as the reduction of the subject matter of gender to be a concern only for the female employees or its functioning as an alibi so that the rest of the organization does not need to pay much explicit attention to the gender dimension. A few arguments demand the integration of the whole: gender then has the permanent attention of all the employees. The biggest risk with regard to the option for integration is that the subject matter will be overlooked and after some time will disappear from discussions. There is a temptation to assume that the colleagues will remain concerned with gender issues. And what happens if some employees protest against the special attention given to gender and consider the whole "gender dimension" to be pure ideology? The choice has to be made between a gender analysis as a basic part of the organization or as a surplus analysis.

Need for a Profound Ethical Analysis

The main thread running through this entire issue, in spite of the different contexts and realities that have been elaborated in this article, is: human dignity is violated deeply. It is quite clear that this subject requires a profound ethical discussion. This subject should not remain a marginal story: we need to voice the feelings and experiences of many women who suffer under violence throughout the world. Action has to be undertaken to launch research and political action in order to restrict the different forms of violence against women. In this connection we can refer to the necessity of strict judicial rules. An important step in this process was the CEDAW convention, the Convention on the Elimination of All Forms of Discrimination Against Women, in 1979.

The vulnerability of the focus on human rights is criticized regularly from the feminist angle. The legislation that resulted from the human rights charters overlooks the fact that the oppressing practices against women are also violations of human rights. This is because the civil and political rights are valued much more in the hierarchy of human rights legislation rather than the economic, social and cultural rights. Civil and political rights are connected with the public life where the women are excluded in different parts of the world, while the private sphere, the closed sphere of house and family remained to a great extent without much regulation. Although there are conventions like CEDAW and commissions like the Commission on the Status of Women, many still speak of the violation of human rights in general terms. The dichotomy of private-public, which has been receiving a great deal of attention in women's studies and gender studies, confronts us with a hierarchy of values.[32] Is torture during political interrogation a more serious violation of human rights than genital mutilation or forced prostitution? The quest for answers to all these questions leads us again to pay attention to the fundamental factors that do not need to remain unspoken in the whole debate, like poverty and socioeconomic inequality. The old maxim of the feminist movement from the 1970s "the personal is political" has not lost any of its relevance.

---

[32] Handy, *Human Trafficking*, 18-23.

List of Authors

François BOUSQUET (France), 1947, is Professor of Fundamental Theology and Dogmatics at the Faculty of Theology, Institut Catholique de Paris, France (1999-), Director of the Institute for Science and Theology of Religions (2005-); studied philosophy and theology at the universities of Paris-Sorbonne, the Institut Catholique de Paris, Sherbrooke (Québec). He received a doctorate in theology from the Institut Catholique de Paris (1996), a doctorate in the History of Religions and Religious Anthropology fron Paris IV-Sorbonne, 1996. He has published on philosophy, fundamental theology and dogmatics, and is the author of: *L'esprit de Plotin* (1976), *Camus le méditerranéen* (1977), *Philosophie et pluralisme* (1977), *Croire* (1991), *Le Christ de Kierkegaard* (1999), *La Théologie dans l'histoire* (1997, with Joseph Doré), *La Trinité* (2000), *La responsabilité des théologiens* (2002, with Henri-Jérôme Gagey, Geneviève Médevielle and Jean-Louis Souletie), *Les grandes révolutions de la Théologie moderne* (2003), *Dieu et la raison* (2005, with Philippe Capelle).

Veerle DRAULANS (Belgium), 1959, completed her Ph.D. at the Catholic University at Leuven (Belgium). She is Assistant Professor of Moral Theology at Tilburg University and Associate Professor of Gender Studies at the Catholic University of Leuven. She coordinates the interfaculty course "gender studies" at the Catholic University of Leuven. Her research focuses on "values and religion in Europe," "gender and leadership," and "gender and science." She is a member of the research team of the European Values Study Project, a large-scale empirical research project in 32 European countries. Her publications include: *How secular is Europe?*, "Gender and Religious Leadership: Some Critical Observations from a Western European Perspective," *Mapping Contemporary Europe's Moral and Religious Pluralist Landscape: An Analysis based on the Most Recent European Values Study Data.*

Jacques HAERS (Belgium), 1956, studied mathematics and philosophy, and wrote a dissertation in philosophy at Oxford on Origen's understanding of creation. He is a Jesuit and a professor on the Faculty of Theology at the Catholic University of Leuven, and also teaches at the Centre Sèvres, Paris. He is Director of the Master Programme in Conflict and Sustainable Peace as well as for the Centre for Liberation

Theologies. His main interests include theologies of encounter, globalization, and peace studies. His publications include: *Theology and Conversation: Towards a Relational Theology* (2003), *The Myriad Christ: Plurality and the Quest for Unity in Contemporary Christology* (2000).

Norbert HINTERSTEINER (Austria), 1963 is Assistant. Professor of Foundational and Comparative Theology at the Catholic University of America, Washington DC. (2004-), Professor of Intercultural and Comparative Theology at Utrecht University (2005-07). He received his doctorate in systematic theology in 2000 from the Jesuit Philosophisch-Theologische Hochschule in St.Georgen, Frankfurt. He has authored a monograph, *Traditionen überschreiten: Angloamerikanische Beiträge zur interkulturellen Traditionshermeneutik* (Vienna: WUV) (Romanian edtition: *Către o depăşire a tradiţiilor: Contribuţii angloamericane la o hermeneutică interculturală a tradiţiei*, Cluj: Dacia 2003) and is editor of *Naming and Thinking God in Europe Today: Theology in Global Dialogue*, Currents of Encounter 32 (Amsterdam / New York: Ropodi, 2007).

Roger JACOBS (Belgium), 1954, holds degrees in philosophy and human ecology. He has worked for 15 years at the Centre for Basic Education in Hasselt (Belgium). He is co-author of *Het pomphuis van de 21ste eeuw* (2000) and of *Terra Incogita: Globalisering, ecologie en rechtvaardige duurzaamheid* (2006). He has also published numerous articles and books and journals on social ecology and emancipatory education.

Peter Tom JONES (Belgium), 1973, is an environmental engineer and holds a Ph.D. in Applied Sciences (engineering). He is employed as a postdoctoral fellow at the Catholic University of Leuven (Belgium) and is part of the Scientific Council of Attac Flanders. He has published in different journals on topics such as globlization, ecology and social justice, and is co-author of *Ya Basta! Globalisering van onderop* (2002), co-editor of *Esperanza! Praktische theorie voor sociale bewegingen* (2003), and *Terra Incogita: Globalisering, ecologie en rechtvaardige duurzaamheid* (2006).

Jamal KHADER is Palestinian priest from the Latin Patriarchate of Jerusalem. He was ordained in 1988 and, after few years of pastoral work, continued his studies in Rome at the Pontifical Gregorian University where he obtained his Ph.D. in Dogmatic Theology (1999). He is a Professor of Dogmatic Theology at the Latin Patriarchal Seminary, and Chairperson of the Department of Religious Studies at Bethlehem University. His doctoral thesis was published as *Towards Full Communion: Catholics and Orthodox in Dialogue* (in French).

John D'Arcy MAY (Australia), 1942, is Associate Professor of Interfaith Dialogue, ISE, Trinity College (1987-). He received his Licentiate of Sacred Theology from Gregoriana, Rome, 1969, his doctorate in theology (ecumenics) Münster and his doctorate in philosophy (history of religions) from Frankfurt in 1983. He was the Ecumenical Research Officer with Melanesian Council of Churches, Port Moresby, and Research Associate at the Melanesian Institute, Goroka, Papua New Guinea from 1983-87. His publications include *Christus Initiator: Theologie im Pazifik* (Düsseldorf: Patmos, 1990), *After Pluralism: Towards an Interreligious Ethic* (Münster / Hamburg / London: LIT Verlag, 2000); *Transcendence and Violence: The Encounter of Buddhist, Christian and Primal Traditions* (New York / London: Continuum, 2003)

Daniel Franklin PILARIO, CM (Philippines), is on the staff of St. Vincent School of Theology, in Quezon City, Philippines. He received his master's and doctorate in theology from the Catholic University of Leuven in 1998 and 2002 respectively. He is the author of *Back to the Rough Grounds of Praxis: Exploring Theological Method with Pierre Bourdieu* (Peeters, 2005); *Pakiglambigit: A Story of the Basic Ecclesial Communities in an Urban Context* (Paulines, 1998). His fields of research are fundamental theology, inculturation and cultural theories, theological anthropology, methods of theological research and political/social theory.

Gabriela DI RENZO (Argentina) is University Professor at the faculties of law and social sciences (Rosario), at the Argentina Catholic University (UCA) and a clinical psychologist. She is a member of TEOLOGANDA, and of the Argentinean Society of Theology and the International Association of Medical, Psychological and Religious Studies (A.I.E.M.P.R.). Her publications include "Las representaciones de género en la crisis argentina. Lectura interdisciplinaria y desafíos ético religiosos emergentes," *Masculino-Femenino y Hecho religioso*, "El reto de C. Gilligan a la teoría de J. Rawls," "Mujer y maternidad. Una lectura desde el psicoanálisis y el género," en *Las mujeres ante la crisis*.

Hans-Joachim SANDER (Germany), 1959, is Professor of Dogmatic Theology at the University of Salzburg. His recent publications are *Einführung in die Gotteslehre* (Darmstadt: Wissenschaftliche Buchgesellschaft, 2006); "Theologischer Kommentar zur Pastoralkonstitution über die Kirche in der Welt von heute *Gaudium et spes*," in *Herders Theologischer Kommentar zum Zweiten Vatikanischen Konzil*, vol. 4, Freiburg: Herder 2005, 581-886.

Georges De SCHRIJVER, SJ (Belgium) is a doctor of theology and holds a Master's Degree in Philosophy and Literature and is Professor Emeritus of Foundational Theology (1979-2000) in the faculty of theology at the Catholic University of Leuven, In this capacity he was chair of the Center for Liberation Theologies from 1987 till 2000. Since 2000 he has been a professor in Ateneo de Manila University, the Philippines, Dharmaram College, Bangalore, India and St. Joseph's Seminary, Ikot Ekpene, Nigeria. He has published on philosophical theology, political theology, liberation theology, and theology of cultures. He was editor of *Liberation Theologies on Shifting Grounds* (Leuven: University Press / Peeters, 1998) and author of *Recent Theological Debates in Europe: Their Impact on Interreligious Dialogue* (Bangalore: Dharmaram Publications, 2004).

Hendrik M. VROOM (the Netherlands) is Professor of Philosophy of Religion at the Vrije Universiteit Amsterdam. His fields of study are hermeneutics, interreligious relations and dialogue, on which he has published widely. He is co-editor of *Religions View Religions* (2006), on theologies of religion from the perspectives of various traditions, *Wrestling with God and Evil* and co-editor *of Probing the Depths of Evil and God: Multireligious Views and Case Studies* (2007). His latest book is an introduction into the philosophy of religion from a pluralistic perspective, *A Spectrum of Worldviews* (2006). All the above have been published by Rodopi in Currents of Encounter, of which he serves as co-editor.

Siegfried WIEDENHOFER (Austria), 1941, is Professor of Systematic Theology at the J.W. Goethe University, Frankfurt a. M. (1981-). He studied Catholic theology in Graz, Bonn, Münster, Tübingen, Regensburg (where he did his *Habilitation*). His publications include *Das katholische Kirchenverständnis* (Graz 1992); *Kulturelle und religiöse Traditionen* (2005), *Tradition and Theories of Tradition* (2006).

Frans WIJSEN (the Netherlands) is Professor of World Christianity and Interreligious Relations in the Faculty of Religious Studies and Professor of Mission, Intercultural and Interreligious Studies in the Faculty of Theology at the Radboud University Nijmegen, the Netherlands. His areas of specialization are Muslim-Christian Relations in Africa, and African migrants in Europe. He has been a visiting professor in Indonesia and Kenya. His publications include *There is Only One God* (1993), *Geloven bij het leven* (1997), *Seeds of Conflict in a Haven of Peace* (forthcoming), *The Polemical Dialogue* (1997, co-editor), *Mission is a Must* (2002, co-editor), *Pastoral Circle Revisited* (2005, co-editor).